Easter in Kishinev

REAPPRAISALS IN JEWISH SOCIAL
AND INTELLECTUAL HISTORY

GENERAL EDITOR: ROBERT M. SELTZER

Martin Buber's Social and Religious Thought:
Alienation and the Quest for Meaning
LAURENCE J. SILBERSTEIN

The American Judaism of Mordecai M. Kaplan
EDITED BY EMANUEL S. GOLDSMITH, MEL SCULT,
AND ROBERT M. SELTZER

On Socialists and "the Jewish Question" after Marx
JACK JACOBS

Easter in Kishinev: Anatomy of a Pogrom
EDWARD H. JUDGE

EDWARD H. JUDGE

EASTER IN KISHINEV
Anatomy of a Pogrom

NEW YORK UNIVERSITY PRESS
NEW YORK & LONDON

NEW YORK UNIVERSITY PRESS
New York and London

Library of Congress Cataloging-in-Publication Data
Judge, Edward H.
Easter in Kishinev : anatomy of a pogrom / Edward H. Judge.
p.   cm. — (Reappraisals in Jewish social and intellectual
history)
Includes bibliographical references and index.
ISBN 0-8147-4193-2
1. Jews—Moldavian S.S.R.—Kishinev—Persecutions.   2. Massacres—
Moldavian S.S.R.—Kishinev—History—20th century.
3. Antisemitism—Moldavian S.S.R.)—Ethnic relations.   I. Title.
II. Series.
DS135.R93K587   1992
947'.75—dc20   92-16982
CIP

New York University Press books are printed on acid-free paper,
and their binding materials are chosen for strength and durability.

Manufactured in the United States of America

c 10 9 8 7 6 5 4 3 2 1

*This book is dedicated
to the memory of*

**WALTER LIPON
PAT CAMPAGNA
JUDY POWELL.**

Contents

Preface

I am deeply grateful to a number of persons and institutions who have contributed in various ways to the completion of this study. The National Endowment for the Humanities made it possible for me to attend its summer research seminar at Cornell University in 1986, and provided financial support for my research trips to Paris in 1986 and Leningrad in 1990. The Le Moyne College Faculty Research and Development Committee also helped to fund these trips, along with other research excursions to New York, Boston, Champagne-Urbana, Washington, and Dublin. Professor Walter Pintner, and the participants in the NEH summer seminar at Cornell University, provided helpful comments, suggestions, and criticisms when this work was in its formative stages. The librarians and archivists at the University of Illinois Summer Research Institute, the American Jewish Historical Society, the YIVO Institute on Jewish Social Research, the Cornell University Library, the New York Public Library, the Library of Congress, the Archives of the Alliance Israélite Universelle, the Manuscript Department of Trinity College Dublin, and the USSR Academy of Sciences Library provided courteous cooperation and professional help. Mark Kulikowski generously shared with me his wealth of bibliographic knowledge, and made me aware of a number of helpful sources. Raymond Wiley rendered valuable assistance by translating several German texts. John Langdon took the time and trouble to read the manuscript with great care, and to provide a number of useful suggestions and corrections. My colleagues William Bosch, Douglas Egerton, William Telesca, Robyn Muncy, Joseph Curran, Michael Markowski, and James Y. Simms, Jr., supplied various forms of helpful support, commentary, and encouragement. To these, and to all the others who gave me the benefit of their kindness and assistance, I wish to express my sincere appreciation.

I also wish to express my special gratitude to the Histadruth Ivrith of America for permission to use excerpts from the poem "The City of Slaughter" by Hayyim Nahman Bialik, translated by Abraham M. Klein, as published in *Selected Poems of Hayyim Nahman Bialik*, edited by Israel Efros, and to East European Monographs for permission to incorporate excerpts from my article "Urban Growth and Anti-Semitism in Russian Moldavia," as published in *Modernization and Revolution: Dilemmas of Progress in Late Imperial Russia*, edited by me and James Y. Simms, Jr.

Above all, I would like to thank my family. My wife Susan and our sons John, Stephen, Matthew, and Christopher not only put up with my periodic absences and chronic crankiness, but they also helped me to keep things in perspective whenever I got discouraged. Susan in particular has been a collaborator in my endeavors, a companion on our journey, and a guide through many storms. Were it not for her patience, persistence, common sense, enthusiasm, wisdom, faith, and humor, I could scarcely have written this book.

Finally, I should like to mention several conventions which I have adopted in preparing this work. Unless otherwise noted, I have rendered dates according to the "Old Style" Julian Calendar which was used in Russia prior to 1918 and which, in the early twentieth century, was thirteen days behind the "New Style" Gregorian Calendar used throughout the West. And I have employed the Library of Congress system for transliteration of Russian names, except in a few cases (such as Schmidt, Witte, von Raaben, and von Plehve) where the names are of non-Russian origin.

Easter in Kishinev

CHAPTER I

The Jewish Question in Russia

Among the issues facing the Russian Empire at the beginning of the twentieth century, the "Jewish Question" occupied an inordinate place of prominence. The empire's five million Jews, living mostly in the western border provinces, attracted attentions and aroused concerns that were far out of proportion to their numbers, wealth, or influence. The Jews were the targets of fear and suspicion, of legal restrictions and political persecution, of hatred and envy. Their very existence within the tsar's domains, combined with age-old antagonisms and bigotry, seems to have engendered a series of intractable problems that neither the tsar, nor his government, nor the Jews, nor their Christian neighbors were able to resolve. Indeed, most of the policies and programs designed to deal with these problems only seemed to make matters worse.

The Jewish question in Russia involved a complex combination of issues and attitudes relating to the Jews. It included general historical factors: the uniqueness and separateness of the Jewish religion and culture, the tenacity of the Jewish commitment to them, the anti-Jewish hostilities fostered within the Christian religion, the reputed superiority of Jewish intelligence and energy, the prevalent employment of Jews as merchants, bankers, agents, and dealers, and the resulting stereotype of the Jews as exploiters of the common Christian folk. It involved peculiarly Russian circumstances: the xenophobic and ethnocentric tendencies of the Russian church and state, Russia's cultural and technical backwardness, its relatively recent annexation of lands with large Jewish populations, the monolithic and paternalistic pretensions of the Russian government, and the perceived ignorance and vulnerability of the

Russian lower classes. And it was aggravated by the contemporary trends transforming Russian life: the new order created by the abolition of serfdom, the rapid growth of population and peasant "land-hunger," the rise of nationalism and national self-consciousness, the turmoil caused by industrialization and urbanization, and the emergence of a revolutionary movement in which Jews played a prominent role.

The Roots of Russian Anti-Semitism

The Jewish question in Russia was at root a religious question. It was the ancient Judaic religion, with its customs, laws, and traditions, that set the Jews apart and kept them a separate people. And it was the predominant Christian religion, with its inherent rejection of these customs, laws, and traditions, that helped to nourish and maintain an adversarial outlook toward the Jews among its adherents.

Although anti-Semitism in Russia was of relatively recent vintage, it had roots and antecedents stretching back into biblical times. Almost from the beginning the strong national identity of the Jewish people, the uniqueness of the Jewish religion, and the rigors of Jewish law had set the Jews apart. Their diet and their dress, their rituals and their life-style, their general unwillingness to intermarry and assimilate, and their implicit rejection of the gods and values of others all served to emphasize their distinctiveness.[1] Furthermore, although Jewish culture might idealize such devotion, neighboring peoples often found it offensive, hostile, and threatening. Jewish records are full of stories in which Jews were persecuted, or threatened with persecution, for refusing to forsake their God, their laws, their nation, and their ways. Jewish ideas and customs, such as their specifications for food preparation, their ceremonial rites, and their identification as God's chosen people, were easily distorted and misunderstood. Over the centuries, consequently, the Jews frequently found themselves accused of seditious disobedience, arrogant elitism, hatred of all non-Jews, and various criminal activities.[2]

The position of the Jews was further complicated by the predominance of Christianity. The Christian religion was both an offshoot and a rival of Judaism: Christians worshiped the Jewish God and based their faith on Jewish scriptures, but they largely rejected Jewish law, Judaic ritual, and Jewish nationhood. They claimed that Jesus Christ, the "son" of the Jewish God, had instituted a new covenant and a simplified set of standards that superseded the complex Judaic laws and customs. They asserted that Christianity had thus replaced Judaism as the true faith, and implied that Christians rather than Jews were now the "chosen people." The continued existence of the Jewish faith, however, and the refusal of most Jews to accept Christianity, cast some doubt on the validity of these claims, and implicitly challenged Christian credibility.[3]

The two religions had thus emerged as foes, rival claimants to the same inheritance and the same legacy. Early Christian writings tended to portray the Jews as a perfidious people who had rejected God's love, turned their back on God's salvation, and murdered God's son. The destruction of the Jewish state, the dispersion of the Jewish people, and the sufferings and persecutions inflicted upon the Jews were frequently cited as evidence of God's displeasure. In this tradition, the Jews became not just the rivals of Christianity, but the enemies of God himself.[4]

The spread and institutionalization of Christianity, then, had brought with it the enshrinement of anti-Judaic attitudes throughout the Christian world. Jew-hatred was condoned, and sometimes even encouraged, by Church fathers, religious leaders, and political authorities; even some Christian "saints" indulged in crude condemnations and disparagement of the Jews.[5] This did not mean, of course, that Christian hatred of Jews was automatic, or that persecution of Jews was constant and systematic. Indeed, in many places at many times Christians and Jews managed to live together in harmony, and various Christian leaders at times condemned the persecution of Jews. It did mean, however, that there existed in Christianity a certain predisposition against the Jews, and that the normal canons of Christian morality, calling for justice and charity in human relations, were not necessarily applied to relations with the Jews. Instead, Christians were often inclined to justify mistreatment of the Jews, and to attribute Jewish sufferings to some sort of divine curse resulting from the Jews' alleged role in the crucifixion of Christ.[6]

In accepting Christianity from the Byzantine Empire during the tenth century, the Russians bought into this anti-Jewish tradition. According to chronicle accounts, in fact, the adoption of Christianity by the Kievan Russian state was preceded by an explicit and disparaging rejection of Judaism. "How can you teach others," Grand Prince Vladimir is said to have asked the Jews, "when you yourselves are rejected by God and scattered? If God loved you and your law, you would not be dispersed over foreign lands."[7] Although the story is apocryphal, it does bear witness to an anti-Judaic strain among the Christian monks who wrote the Russian chronicles. Further evidence of this attitude can be found in the sermons and activities of eleventh-century Kievan churchmen, and in later law codes and lives of the saints.[8]

This early Russian hostility toward the Jews, it appears, was mainly a religious phenomenon. In Kievan Russia there were relatively few Jews, and these seem to have lived among the Russians without excessive conflict. The city of Kiev itself had a "Jewish gate," and perhaps even a small Jewish community. There is little evidence of the anti-Jewish stereotypes and anti-Jewish violence that were prevalent in the West during this period. But it is also clear that at least some members of the Orthodox Christian hierarchy, struggling to maintain and strengthen the Christian faith against other religious traditions, were especially vehement in their attacks upon the Jews. If anything, they seem to have been seeking to instill an antipathy, rather than reacting to one that already existed. Jew-hatred was thus most likely an import into Russia: it came as part of the package along with Byzantine Christianity.[9]

During medieval times, the disintegration of the Kievan Russian state and the Mongol conquest of the Russian land was followed by the emergence of a new Russian state under the leadership of Moscow. As in the Kievan era, the Russian Orthodox church played a central role, and anti-Jewish attitudes were fostered by various authorities. Certain new circumstances, however, seem to have heightened the hostility toward Jews. Having been dominated by the Mongols and isolated from the West, Muscovite Russia was characterized by an obsessive fear and intense dislike of foreigners, and by a position of relative backwardness in relation to the Western world. The government sought to insulate its subjects against contacts with foreigners, including Jews, who were both despised as religious infidels and feared as a potentially corruptive, hostile influence.[10]

The Muscovite state included very few Jews, and Muscovite authorities sought to keep it that way. Church and state leaders together worked to insulate "Holy Russia" against foreign influence, regarding all outsiders—particularly Jews—with suspicion and distrust. A "Judaizer" movement, blending Christian and Jewish beliefs, did acquire some strength in Novgorod for a time, but it was brutally repressed by both church and state in the early sixteenth century. Following this, the Muscovite government redoubled its efforts to quarantine Russians from the Jewish "contagion," forbidding Jews from moving into Russia on the grounds that they would undermine the health and faith of the Russian people. Over the years, then, despite the fact that there was little real contact between Russians and Jews, hatred and fear of Jews came to be rooted in the Russian consciousness.[11]

Russian antipathy toward the Jews thus had much in common with the general anti-Jewish attitude that pervaded Christian civilization, but it seems to have been aggravated by several peculiarly Russian conditions. One of these was the close identification between the Orthodox church and the Muscovite state, leaving little room for distinction between religious dissenters and political foes. Another was the strong strain of ethnocentrism and xenophobia present in Russia from Muscovite times. A third was the relative backwardness of Russia, its "inferior" cultural status, and the widespread ignorance of the Russian masses. Ironically, what was missing from this picture was the Jewish people themselves: before the eighteenth century, the Russian masses and their leaders had precious little experience in actually dealing with Jews.

The Jews in the Russian Empire

Throughout most of Russian history, the Jewish question remained largely academic: very few Jews lived in Russia, and very few Russians came into contact with Jews. It was not until the eighteenth century, when foreign conquests brought vast new territories under Russian control, that the empire of the tsars acquired a sizable

Jewish population. Expansions to the west and south, at the expense of Poland and Turkey, brought lands with huge non-Russian populations—including hundreds of thousands of Jews—into the tsarist empire. The Russians soon found that they had inherited a vexing and difficult problem, complicated by all sorts of historical antagonisms, religious hostilities, social tensions, and economic conflicts. The Jewish question, it became clear, could no longer be avoided.

Centuries earlier, in an effort to avoid persecution and improve their economic opportunities, thousands of Jews from central Europe had moved to the territories under Polish and Lithuanian control. Here they had found something of a sanctuary: although the Jews in Poland and Lithuania were periodically subjected to indignities and persecutions, they were also protected, at various times and in different ways, by certain of the monarchs and the nobility. They performed valuable services for the crown, the landlords, and the economy—and the Jewish community grew and flourished. By the sixteenth century, the Polish-Lithuanian lands had become the main homeland of European Jewry.[12]

The services that Jews performed for the crown and nobility, however, were hardly designed to make them popular with the Christian masses. In rural areas, many Jews made their living as leaseholders—renting from Polish landlords the right to run farmlands, mills, dairies, orchards, taverns, and various other enterprises—and as tax collectors, financial agents, liquor dealers, and estate managers. In other words, they were used as middlemen by lords and rulers to extract money from, and supervise the affairs of, the Christian peasants, and they thus attracted much of the opprobrium and resentment attached to such activities. In the towns, where the Jews worked as merchants and craftsmen, they were often disliked and feared by their Christian counterparts, who tended to view them as unwelcome outsiders and dangerous, industrious competitors. Such fears and resentments, as often as not, were reinforced by the anti-Judaic sentiments of the Christian church and its clergy. The Jews were widely seen as aliens, parasites, and exploiters, the purveyors of drunkenness, poverty, and immorality among the Christian people.[13]

Likewise, the protection and privileges granted to the Jews by the

Polish crown helped contribute to their unpopularity. The Jews were treated, administratively and legally, as a separate estate. They were permitted, indeed encouraged, to form their own autonomous, self-governing communities or "kahals," based on their own laws, religion, customs, and traditions. On one hand, this helped to provide them with relative freedom in ordering their own affairs; on the other hand, it helped insure that they would remain outsiders. They ate, dressed, and behaved differently from their Polish, Ukrainian, Belorussian, or Lithuanian neighbors, and they often even spoke differently, retaining their Yiddish language. It is little wonder they were frequently regarded with suspicion and concern.[14]

In many areas, the situation of the Jews was complicated by religious hostilities between Catholic and Orthodox Christians, and by national antagonisms between Polish nobles and non-Polish peasants. Poland was a multi-national, multi-lingual, and multi-religious state, encompassing Lithuanians, Belorussians, and Ukrainians as well as Poles and Jews. Especially in Ukraine, Polish Catholic landlords had been given vast landed estates, enserfing the Orthodox peasants who inhabited these lands. The exploitation and oppression of these peasants by absentee Polish lords, combined with periodic attempts to force Orthodox Christians into religious "union" with the Catholic church, helped create a legacy of bitter antagonism. The hatred of the Ukrainian peasants was directed not just at their Polish lords, whom they rarely saw, but also at the many Jewish leaseholders, agents, and retailers who managed the estates, collected taxes, and controlled the local liquor trade. The invisible exploiters were Polish and Catholic, but their visible form, as often as not, was Jewish. Economic oppression, ethnic hostility, and religious rivalry, fed by vicious rumors and distortions of Jewish beliefs, led to hatred, fear, and resentment of the Jews—and sometimes even to violence. Especially notable were the savage persecutions and massacres of Jews which accompanied the anti-Polish, Cossack-led Ukrainian rebellion of 1648 and the brutal wars that followed.[15]

Anti-Semitism in eastern Europe, then, was by no means a Russian creation. Tensions and hostilities between Christians and Jews had existed long before the Russians annexed the lion's share of the

Kingdom of Poland in the course of the eighteenth century. The annexations, however, made these tensions and hostilities a Russian concern, and treatment of the Jews and their neighbors a Russian responsibility. And the Russian government, unlike the Polish crown and nobility, was predisposed to view the Jews as harmful rather than useful.

Not surprisingly, the first impulse of Russian officials in dealing with the Jewish question was to preserve the status quo and, in particular, to insulate the Russian merchants from Jewish competition. A series of decrees and regulations, beginning in 1791, specifically excluded the Jews from residing in Russia proper, limiting Jewish residence to the newly acquired border provinces. This was, in effect, a policy of containment: it sought not so much to solve the Jewish question as to contain it within its current parameters. The lands where the Jews were permitted to live soon came to be known as the Pale of Jewish Settlement. The Pale, which was formalized into law by the Jewish Statutes of 1804 and 1835, encompassed the provinces which made up Lithuania, Belorussia, and Ukraine, along with the formerly Turkish-ruled territories of the southwest.[16] These included eastern Moldavia, also known as Bessarabia, which had been annexed by the Russians in 1812.

The creation of the Pale, which came to be the foremost symbol of anti-Jewish discrimination, was in many respects an attempt to preserve the conditions that had existed prior to the Russian expansion. Jews had previously been excluded from Russia itself; the creation of the Pale simply continued that exclusion. Along with it, however, there came a series of actions, taken by the Russian government in the course of the nineteenth century, which served gradually to diminish the autonomy of the Jewish communities, to undermine the economic situation of the Jews, and to place severe limitations on Jewish rights and privileges within the Pale itself.

Although the Russian treatment of the Jews was by no means consistent, varying between measures of "repression" and "liberalization," it was apparent almost from the beginning that the Russian government was not prepared to accept as permanent either the separate, autonomous nature of the Jewish communities or the position of the Jews as "exploiters" of the rural poor. The former clashed with the monolithic and assimilationist inclinations of the Russians, the latter with the government's paternalistic and protective pretensions toward the peasantry. Polish kings and nobles may have found the Jews' activities useful, but the Russians—who had gotten along without Jews for centuries—saw them as a source of poverty, drunkenness, and discontent among the common folk. Throughout much of the nineteenth century, then, government policy sought to decrease the "separateness" and "harmfulness" of the Jews, while keeping them confined in the Pale as long as they remained "separate" and "harmful."[17]

Government policies thus sought simultaneously to "enlighten" the Jews and protect the Christian peasants from Jewish exploitation. The 1804 "Statute Concerning the Welfare of the Jews," the first serious attempt at a comprehensive Jewish policy, granted Jews the right to attend Russian schools, while declaring that Jewish schools had to conduct their lessons in Russian, Polish, or German —and not in Hebrew or Yiddish. Likewise, although the Jews could retain their separate communities, the kahals, their leaders had to conduct all business in Russian, Polish, or German, and Jews elected to public office had to abandon their traditional Jewish garb. Incentives were provided to Jews who would take up farming in sparsely populated areas; all other Jews living in the countryside (about half of the Jewish population) had to give up their rural occupations and move to the cities or towns. In short, Jews were expected to look and talk more like other Russian subjects, to cease "exploiting" the peasants (as leaseholders, managers, tavern keepers, and retailers), and to either take up farming or move to the cities and towns.[18]

Although all of its features were not fully carried out, the Statute of 1804 helped set the tone of Russian Jewish policy for most of the century. Over the years, a series of steps were taken to reduce the autonomy and distinctiveness of the Jews. Under Tsar Nicholas I (1825–1855), 12–year-old Jewish boys were inducted into the military and forced, as "cantonists," to undergo a brutal reeducation process designed to break down their Jewish identity. An effort was made to replace the traditional Jewish schools with state-operated Russian schools designed to "enlighten" young Jews with secular education, while surreptitiously seeking to make them receptive to

Christian ideals. Jews were prohibited from wearing traditional costumes and hairstyles. And the Jewish kahals, the main symbols of Jewish autonomy, were formally abolished.[19]

Tsar Alexander II (1855–1881), persuaded that repressive and discriminatory measures actually hampered Jewish assimilation, tried a more positive approach. Largely abandoning the methods of coercion, his regime sought instead to reward those Jews who would give up some of their separateness and engage in "useful" work. The onerous policy of juvenile conscription was abolished, and attempts to convert young Jews through mandatory religious education were abandoned. The upper class of Jewish merchants, Jewish artisans, and Jewish graduates of Russian universities were permitted to reside in Russian cities outside the Pale of Settlement. Some of them even became eligible for government service. After serfdom was abolished in 1861, Jews were eventually allowed to buy noble lands that were sold within the Pale. This was by no means a policy of full Jewish emancipation: it mainly encouraged upper-class Jews to "earn" certain privileges by proving their loyalty, morality, and usefulness. The bulk of the Jews, especially those who were unemployed, impoverished, or engaged in "parasitic" and "exploitative" rural occupations, remained confined and oppressed within the Pale of Settlement.[20]

This new approach proved rather successful—in some ways too successful. Attracted by the lures of emancipation and assimilation, Jewish merchants and artisans moved to Russian cities, where they often achieved considerable success. In rural areas, Jews increasingly began to buy and lease lands from the nobility, and to employ local laborers on these lands. Before long, the official mood began to change, as Russians became increasingly concerned about the growing influx of Jews into the empire's economic, educational, professional, and political life. The Jews were assimilating too well: unless they could be held back, it was feared, they might come to dominate the Christians. Publications soon appeared about secret Jewish conspiracies, and anti-Semitic articles showed up in various Russian newspapers. In 1871, in fact, anti-Jewish riots were instigated by Greek merchants in Odessa. By the 1870s, the government had begun taking steps to limit the Jewish advances, and to restrict Jewish access to Russian institutions.[21]

Under Polish rule, although often despised by the lower classes, the Jews to a certain extent had been protected and favored by the crown and nobility. Under Russian rule the situation was reversed: it became increasingly apparent that the government sought, not to protect the Jews, but to protect the peasants and townsfolk from the Jews. The Jews lost their privileged status, their economic situation deteriorated, and they were trapped increasingly in the towns of the Pale between a hostile government and the fearful, suspicious, and potentially volatile townsfolk. The stage had been set for turmoil, and the conditions created for pogroms.

Modernization and Its Impact

By the later years of the nineteenth century, the winds of change were blowing through the Russian Empire, and new developments and conditions were serving to make the situation of the Jews even more precarious. The emancipation of the serfs in 1861, by removing the stratum of landlords between state and peasantry, had made the government more directly responsible for the welfare of the common folk. Before long, anxious to protect the peasants from competition and maintain stability in the villages, imperial officials were busily imposing new restrictions on the Jews. Rapid population growth, combined with inefficient farming methods, was contributing to "land-hunger" among the peasants in the central Ukrainian provinces. This in turn would lead the government to abandon efforts to encourage Jewish agriculture, and instead to force Jews to move away from the villages into the cities and towns.

Meanwhile, the process of industrialization and urbanization was creating massive dislocations, transforming traditional social and economic relationships, and bringing large numbers of uprooted peasants to the cities and factory towns. In the towns and cities of the Pale of Settlement, these frightened and disoriented newcomers frequently found themselves in contact and competition with large numbers of impoverished Jews, contributing further to fears and tensions between the two groups. And, as these towns became the breeding grounds for radical and revolutionary movements, the plight of the Jews became even more complex. On one hand, with their long-established reputation as capitalists and exploiters, the Jews became convenient scapegoats for the sufferings of the new urban workers. On the other hand, as disillusioned young Jews began to play a prominent role in the revolutionary movement, the imperial police came to regard them as dangerous subversives and seditious internal foes.

The spread of nationalism, moreover, was having a strong effect. As the non-Russian peoples of the empire became more conscious of their own national identity and anxious for self-rule, the government began imposing Russian language and laws in an effort to "russify" them. The unfortunate Jews, having no homeland of their own, would find themselves caught in the middle, subject to russification by the imperial authorities and yet often regarded as aliens by the non-Russian peoples amidst whom they lived. And the consequent emergence of Zionism, as nationalistic Jews began to seek their own nation-state, confirmed official suspicions about Jewish disloyalty and subversion.

By the early 1880s, then, these new conditions were beginning to have a significant impact on the Jewish situation. The problem of peasant land-shortage had been aggravated and accentuated by a series of local crop failures in the "black-earth" provinces of Ukraine, the empire's most fertile lands. Russian nationalism, with its strident xenophobia and anti-Semitism, had been strengthened by the recent Russo-Turkish War and the diplomatic events that followed. Industrialization and urbanization had swollen the population of many cities and towns, especially those in the Pale, with dislocated, impoverished, and often rowdy persons seeking employment.[22] And the revolutionary movement had been turning increasingly to violence, achieving its most conspicuous success with the murder of Tsar Alexander II on March 1, 1881.

The assassination of the "Tsar Liberator" sent violent shock waves throughout Russian society. In its wake occurred a series of brutal anti-Jewish riots and massacres in many cities and towns, and even in a number of villages, throughout the southwestern provinces. In town after town, rumors spread that the emperor had been murdered by Jews (one of the assassins had in fact been Jewish) and that a secret imperial decree had been issued calling for attacks on the Jews.[23] Mobs of agitated townsfolk and unemployed laborers, joined by large numbers of itinerant Russians who had gone to the southwest that spring seeking temporary work, invaded the Jewish sectors, vandalized and ransacked Jewish homes and shops, and beat, abused, raped, and murdered a number of Jews. The rioting spread in several waves from town to town, and sometimes from the towns to the local villages. In many places, some of the Christian merchants and artisans seem to have supported, and perhaps even helped to incite, the mob violence. Almost everywhere, the police and local officials were slow to put down the disturbances, and in some places they openly sympathized with the rioters.[24]

The wave of pogroms in 1881 helped persuade the government to focus its attention, once again, on the Jewish question. Despite the obvious irony, many officials tended to place a large share of the blame for the pogroms upon the Jews themselves. Jewish exploitation of the peasantry, they argued, had created a legacy of bitterness and antagonism among the lower classes, which in turn had erupted into violence in a time of economic stress and political upheaval. As a result, the government adopted in May of 1882 a series of "temporary rules" which prohibited the Jews from buying or leasing land, from moving from the towns to the villages, and from doing business on Christian holy days.[25] The Pahlen Commission, which subsequently studied the Jewish question, concluded that these rules were counterproductive: they would increase the Jewish population of the towns, where the pogroms had mostly broken out and, by keeping the Jews off the land, they would prevent Jews from taking up the "productive" and "non-exploitative" occupation of farming. The prevailing opinion in the government, however, was that both peasant welfare and imperial security required that the peasants be protected from the Jews. Consequently, the commission's recommendations, which called for removal of most restrictions, were ignored. The "temporary" rules of May 1882 remained in place until the end of the Russian Empire.[26]

Meanwhile, during the 1880s and 1890s, a whole new series of repressive steps were taken against the Jews. Quotas were established limiting the access of Jews to secondary and higher education, to municipal and local government, and to the legal and medical professions. Many of the Jewish merchants and artisans permitted to live outside the Pale were forced to return and in 1891, after the tsar's anti-Semitic uncle became governor-general of Moscow, the city's entire Jewish community was brutally expelled. A new state liquor monopoly sought, among other things, to supplant the traditional Jewish liquor dealers and tavern owners. The Jews were treated, by and large, as enemies—the historical foes and rivals of the native Christian populace. To protect the natives, and to prevent further violence, they must be restrained and contained.[27]

The implications of these policies were not lost on the Jews. The 1880s and 1890s brought massive Jewish emigration, as thousands decided to seek a new life in the New World. The same years witnessed the growth and spread of Zionism, as many Jews concluded that they could only be truly welcome and truly free if they had their own homeland. The 1890s also saw the renewed growth of the revolutionary movement, as a number of young Jews joined with others who sought radical transformation of the oppressive political order. Treated as foreigners, many Jews decided to leave; treated as enemies, others decided to stay and fight.[28]

The government approach, although shortsighted and unjust, was not entirely irrational. The Jews, after all, were a separate cultural and national group that resisted assimilation. They did, on the whole, tend to be better educated and more industrious than the Christian peasants and townsfolk. Some of them had, indeed, exploited the common people. The antipathy and resentment felt toward the Jews was real and widespread. It mattered little to the authorities that this was not really the fault of the Jews, that they had often been forced into "exploitative" occupations, that these occupations also helped the Russian economy, that oppressive state policies provided the impetus for Jewish radicalism, and that the Jews were the victims—not the perpetrators—of pogroms. Most of these factors were historical realities that were largely beyond state control: they could not be changed easily or quickly. Things such as Jewish residence, Jewish access to education and professions, and Jewish contact with the rural classes, were much more easily controlled. In the long run, perhaps, the liberation of the Jews might make sense; in the short run, however, it could well exacerbate tensions and increase the hostility of the lower classes toward the regime. Trapped by their own fears and biases, and faced with a host of bewildering and threatening problems, state officials opted to seek short-term, repressive control rather than a long-term, equitable solution.[29]

In the short run, at least, the repressive policies, combined with increased efforts to protect, assist, control, and supervise the lower classes, did seem to bring some results. For almost two decades after 1882, revolutionary terrorism was effectively checked, the towns and villages of the Russian Empire remained relatively quiet, and anti-Jewish violence nearly disappeared. For the most part, it seemed, the government had managed to bring things under control.

By the early twentieth century, however, it was becoming evident that government control was temporary and illusory. Behind the facade of apparent calm, dislocation, dissatisfaction, poverty, and unrest had continued to grow, as had population, industrialization, urbanization, and ethnic alienation. Around the turn of the century, a combination of economic depression, crop failure, and radical activism helped bring the problems back to the surface. Strikes and violence among factory workers began to increase steadily and dramatically beginning in 1901. Revolutionary parties started to consolidate, publish, and make impressive inroads among workers and nationality groups. Anti-government terrorism suddenly reappeared, with the assassination of the minister of education in 1901 and the minister of interior in 1902. The specter of peasant revolt also reemerged, with widespread peasant rioting and looting in several Ukrainian provinces in spring of 1902. And, in spring of 1903, anti-Jewish violence erupted once again, this time in Bessarabia province, in the city of Kishinev.

CHAPTER 2

Kishinev

At the beginning of the twentieth century Kishinev—known in Rumanian as Chisinau—was a city of increasing size and growing significance. During the course of the nineteenth century, as the capital of the imperial Russian province of Bessarabia, it had become an important political, administrative, and religious headquarters. It had also developed into a commercial and manufacturing center which handled much of the fruit and grain trade, and the processing of food and food by-products, for a large and fertile region. It had expanded from an obscure Moldavian provincial town with fewer than 7,000 inhabitants into a bustling metropolis with a population of over 100,000. And it had grown in social and ethnic diversity, to such an extent that both Russians and Jews in the city had come to outnumber the native Moldavians. All of this growth and diversity, combined with the potent forces of anti-Semitism, ethnic rivalry, economic competition, and revolutionary agitation, were helping to create an atmosphere of tension and unrest.

Bessarabia and Its Capital

Bessarabia province was located in the extreme southwestern corner of the Russian Empire, along the Rumanian border and the northwestern shore of the Black Sea. It was some 900 miles south of Saint Petersburg and, although linked with the rest of the empire by rail, it was still a few days' travel from the imperial capital. It was a pleasant land whose fertile soil and temperate climate supported farms, orchards, and vineyards, which in turn provided the livelihood for many of its nearly two million inhabitants. By the early twentieth century, however, industrialization and urbanization were beginning to have an impact on the traditionally relaxed and rural atmosphere.

Historically and culturally, the region had been part of the Rumanian principality of Moldavia, and its natives had largely derived their traditions, language, customs, and characteristics from this association. Prior to the nineteenth century, when the area was under Turkish control, the Russian influence was minimal. It was not until 1812, as the result of a victorious war against the Turks, that Russia assumed hegemony. At that point the easternmost part of Moldavia, which the Russians chose to call Bessarabia, became part of the tsarist empire.[1]

In 1812, at the time of the Russian annexation, there were fewer than half a million people living in Bessarabia. There were no cities to speak of: even the largest towns had fewer than 10,000 residents. The bulk of the people were Moldavians, and most of them were peasants. Even then, however, the population was not homogeneous: there were also a number of Ruthenians, Bulgarians, Germans, and Jews who lived among the Moldavians.[2]

In the long run, the Russian annexation was to have enormous consequences for the region. At first, anxious to portray their takeover as a liberation, the Russians treated their new territory as an autonomous entity. Eventually, however, they began to incorporate Bessarabia into the empire's political and economic system. Russian laws, language, currency, and administrative practices were imposed, and migration of peoples from other parts of the empire was encouraged.[3]

During the first half of the nineteenth century, then, substantial numbers of Russians, Ukrainians, Jews, Bulgarians, and Germans moved into the area, some of them encouraged by government policy, others attracted by economic opportunities. Partly due to this influx of outsiders, the region's population not only doubled, it also began to change. The old Moldavian nobility lost much of its influence, and new groups—especially Russians, Ukrainians, and Jews—came to play an increasingly important role. By the late 1850s there were approximately one million persons living in Bessarabia. The majority were still Moldavians, but Russians, Ukrainians, and Jews had come to make up almost a third of the population.

The rest was comprised of Germans, Bulgarians, Gagauzes, Gypsies, Armenians, and a variety of smaller cultural groups.[4]

The second half of the nineteenth century brought further dramatic change. In 1856, as a result of the Crimean War, the Russians lost southern Bessarabia to the Turks, but they got it back in 1878 following another Russo-Turkish War. In 1873, Bessarabia was formally incorporated as a full-fledged Russian province, with its own governor and provincial administration. In the 1880s and 1890s, attempts to "russify" the province were intensified, while urbanization and industrial growth began to make their mark. The villages and rural areas remained predominantly Moldavian, but the region's growing cities became multi-national and multi-cultural enclaves.[5] This was especially true of Kishinev, the capital and largest city.

Kishinev was located in the very center of the province, in the midst of a hilly agricultural region dotted with gardens and vineyards. To the north was an expanse of wooded hills; to the south stretched miles of fertile plains. Some 40 miles to the west was the River Pruth, which ran along the Rumanian border; to the east, a bit closer, was the Dniester River, which separated Bessarabia from Kherson province in the Ukrainian part of the Russian Empire. The city itself sat on the River Byk, a small, marshy stream that flowed into the Dniester.[6]

Kishinev had begun in the fifteenth century as a small Moldavian settlement, and had developed over the years under the control of several noble families and monasteries. When the Russians annexed Bessarabia it was already the area's largest town, but it was still little more than a large village with narrow streets, a few noble estates, several churches, and a major monastery. Its size and location, however, led the Russian administrators and the Orthodox metropolitan to choose it as the site for their headquarters. Their presence immediately brought prominence and prestige; in the long run it also provided incentive for improving the town's appearance, accessibility, architecture, and public works.[7]

During the nineteenth century, then, under Russian rule, the town expanded enormously. At first, it grew haphazardly along the banks of the River Byk, with little thought or planning and few modern comforts or conveniences. Throughout much of the century it remained a dirty and dusty outpost, physically unattractive and remote, lacking adequate water supply and sewage. Despite its relatively mild winters and balmy summers, it was frequently regarded as a hardship post by Russians assigned there. In the early 1820s, in fact, the poet Pushkin had actually been assigned to Kishinev as a form of administrative exile.[8]

By the end of the century, however, things had begun to change. The older part of town, by the riverbank, was still characterized by ramshackle houses and dirty, narrow streets but, to the southwest, a modern city had emerged. Broad avenues and sidewalks, schools and museums, theaters and restaurants had been built, and a large municipal park had been added. The telegraph and the railway, streetcars and coaches, visiting dignitaries and theater companies, and other such amenities had put an end to the sense of isolation and backwardness. Although the summers were still hot and the water supply inadequate, and although urban growth was producing its own brands of misery and blight, the town of Kishinev was clearly taking its place as an important and impressive metropolis.[9]

Its central location, and the fact that it was situated at a juncture between forested hills and arable plains, had also aided its development as a trading and processing center. Throughout the nineteenth century, commerce had been dominated by local products and produce: grains and vegetables, fruits and nuts, wine and tobacco, hides and wool, wax and tallow were either bought and sold in Kishinev or brought there for transport to other places. More recently, especially after Kishinev was linked by rail in 1870 with the port of Odessa, an international dimension had been added to the city's commerce. Meanwhile, as the town expanded, handicrafts, construction materials, and manufactured goods had also come to play an important role. By 1900, a credit and banking industry, and various manufacturing enterprises, had made their appearance. Nevertheless, in the early twentieth century, the industrial development of Kishinev was still at a rudimentary stage: few big factories existed, and only a handful of enterprises employed more than thirty or forty workers. Most goods continued to be produced by individual artisans or small enterprises, and the most prominent industries—wine making, tobacco processing, leather goods, woolens, candle making, and food processing—were still those linked with farming or animal husbandry.[10]

As trade and industry had grown, so had the number of towns-folk. During the early and middle years of the nineteenth century, the population had increased at an especially rapid rate, doubling every ten or fifteen years. Although the rate of growth had slowed toward the end of the century, the actual number of residents continued to expand. By 1865, after a half-century of Russian rule, the town had grown from under 7,000 to approximately 90,000 inhabitants; three decades later, in 1897, official census figures registered 108,483 residents. The increase appears to have resulted from migration rather than natural growth since, throughout much of the nineteenth century, the city's death rate was equal to or greater than its birth rate. Large numbers of people, it seems, had moved to the city to take advantage of its economic, cultural, and administrative opportunities.[11]

This influx of people from other places greatly increased the city's social, cultural, and ethnic diversity. By the early twentieth century, in fact, Kishinev was divided into several different communities, each with its own unique character, and each with its own distinctive flavor. South of the River Byk, but north of Aleksandrov Street, the town's main thoroughfare, was the older or "lower" section of town. It was composed of narrow, winding, unpaved streets, aimlessly arranged, rising gradually from the river bed along the sloping hillside. The streets were crowded with wooden and earthen shanties, and various multi-family dwellings, that served as shops, homes, and workplaces for the city's poor. This part of town tended to be muddy in the spring and dusty in the summer, with few trees, limited vegetation, and minimal open space. Here lived a variety of ethnic groups, each in its own neighborhood, often destitute or nearly so. Along Aleksandrov Street, and stretching to the south and west atop the city heights was "upper Kishi-nev," the newer part of town. Here the streets were broad and straight, many were paved and tree-lined, and they were laid out in a typical grid that gave witness to more careful planning. Along them were stone buildings that included administrative offices and residences of the well-to-do, together with schools, theaters, churches, and stores. Here resided government officials and professionals, merchants and industrialists, military officers and members of the nobility.[12]

Within these larger social and economic divisions were smaller communities, usually divided along ethnic lines. The city encompassed a polyglot conglomeration of nationalities, cultures, and languages. Ukrainians, Greeks, Armenians, Poles, Germans, Serbs, Bulgarians, Gypsies and others were represented among the various minority cultures. The largest and most important nationalities, however, were the Russians, the Moldavians, and the Jews. Together these groups made up over 90 percent of the city's population. More importantly, perhaps, it was their interactions and antagonisms that dominated city life, and helped set the stage for tension and unrest.[13]

The Russians and Moldavians

According to the imperial census of 1897, there were approximately 29,000 Russians and 19,000 Moldavians then living in Kishinev. These figures might not be entirely accurate: critics later claimed that the census-takers tended to underestimate the number of Moldavians throughout Bessarabia. Nevertheless, it is likely that Russians and Moldavians together accounted for something like 45 percent of the Kishinev population, with their combined numbers being roughly equal to the number of Jews in the city.[14]

The Russians in Kishinev fell into several distinct categories. The most influential among them were the several thousand administrators, civil servants, and military officers who made up something of a governing class in Bessarabia. Russians dominated the provincial administration, the police establishment, and the military garrison, all of which were headquartered in or near Kishinev. They often tended to be somewhat contemptuous of other city residents—condescending to the Moldavians and hostile toward the Jews.[15]

But not all the Russians living in or near Kishinev were government officials or soldiers. During the earlier part of the nineteenth century, when serfdom was still in force in most of the empire, many peasants from Russia and Ukraine had fled to Bessarabia. The tsarist government, anxious to increase the size and diversity of the region's population, had refrained from imposing serfdom there so as not to inhibit migration. Meanwhile, throughout the century, others had been attracted to growing cities like Kishinev for the economic opportunities they seemed to offer. Dislocated and disoriented, uneducated and unskilled, they often served merely to swell the ranks of menial laborers—and thus increase unemployment—in a strange city filled with alien peoples of different language and background. They provided a receptive audience for revolutionary ideas: by 1900 Kishinev, with its distance from the capital and its proximity to the Rumanian border, was becoming an important center of anti-government activity. These new arrivals also provided fertile ground for anti-Semitic agitation, bringing their traditional fears and hatreds to a city teeming with Jews.[16]

The Moldavian people, despite the fact that they were native to the region, had little political or economic clout. They were, for the most part, peasants and former peasants from the surrounding countryside who tended to be employed mainly as farmers, gardeners, manual laborers, and servants. Although they made up almost two-thirds of the population in the surrounding area, they accounted for less than 18 percent of the people in Kishinev itself. Their male literacy rate (about 18 percent) was much lower than that of the city's Russians (42 percent) and Jews (51 percent). Politically and militarily, they were under the control of the Russians, who dominated the higher ranks of the civil and armed services. Economically, they were also dependent on "outsiders," especially the Jews, who dominated the city's commerce.[17]

To some observers, the subservient status of the Moldavians seemed quite consistent with their character. By stereotype they were a kindly and simple folk: good-natured and courteous, uneducated and carefree, and even a bit lazy. In political affairs they were regarded as unsophisticated, unambitious, and obedient—although they sometimes displayed an impulsive violent streak. In financial matters they were reputedly naive, uncompetitive, and easily swindled, with a tendency to mismanage their affairs, live beyond their means, and get themselves in debt. They were engaged mainly as primary producers, supposedly content to sell their commodities for whatever they could get and to leave the complex businesses of government and law, commerce and finance, to others.[18]

There is evidence, however, that some Moldavians were becoming increasingly unhappy with their lot in life. By the early twentieth century, revolutionary socialism, Rumanian nationalism, and strident anti-Semitism—sometimes interrelated, other times at odds—had all begun to have an impact on the Moldavian consciousness.

Revolutionary socialism, although a recent phenomenon in Bessarabia, was becoming a force to be reckoned with in Kishinev. Beginning in the 1880s and 1890s, Russian and Ukrainian radicals had managed to make some inroads among the city's impoverished workers and idealistic youth. Radical ideas had been spread, socialist circles had been formed, and by 1902 the city's social democrats were printing underground newspapers and organizing illegal strikes. Their growing strength was attested to by the imperial police, who formed a special "security section," patterned after those already operative in other major cities, to combat "sedition" in Kishinev. Although the socialist movement, like so much else in the city, was dominated by Russians and Jews, a growing number of Moldavians were beginning to get involved.[19]

Meanwhile, Rumanian nationalism was also becoming a force. With the emergence of an independent Rumania in the 1860s and 1870s, and with Russian reconquest of southern Bessarabia in 1878, the region had become something of an *irredentum*. By nationalist logic, based on historical and ethnic affinities, it should rightfully be part of Rumania, not Russia. From the 1870s through the 1890s, tsarist attempts to russify the region, and thus undermine its Rumanian heritage, had further served to heighten nationalist tensions. By the early 1900s, clandestine Rumanian nationalist groups were beginning to form in Bessarabia province. As yet, only small numbers of persons were involved, and most Moldavian aspirations were expressed in cultural, not political, terms. Still, it is apparent that nationalist sentiments were beginning to make an impact even before the emergence of a genuine separatist movement during the Russian Revolution of 1905.[20]

Anti-Semitism, too, was a prominent factor among the Moldavians. Over the centuries, even before the Russian annexation of Bessarabia, Moldavia had witnessed periodic episodes of intolerance, persecution, libels, and atrocities directed against the Jews. Although the Moldavians had generally managed to lived in peace with other nationalities, in times of economic or political stress it had not been uncommon for authorities and people to turn against the Jews. This tendency had continued even under Russian rule. Like other cities in south Russia, for instance, Kishinev had experienced anti-Jewish disturbances in 1881 in the wake of the assassination of Tsar Alexander II. The disorders were not serious, but they did show that the Moldavians harbored anti-Semitic attitudes which could lead to violence during situations of stress.[21]

On top of this, by the late nineteenth century, the traditional fears and prejudices in Bessarabia were being compounded by the rapid increase in the size of the Jewish community. The economic influence of prominent Jews aroused concerns about Jewish domination while, ironically, the growth in numbers of impoverished Jews led to fears that there would be lower wages and fewer jobs for working class Moldavians. And Rumanian nationalist sentiment, which had emerged earlier in the nineteenth century, also incorporated a strong anti-Jewish strain. Nationalist leaders, seeking to unite the Rumanian people, had found it useful to appeal to their xenophobic prejudices. This had led, among other things, to the systematic repression of Jews in the new Rumanian state, a development which was favorably chronicled in the leading Kishinev newspaper.[22]

Anti-Semitism, for the Moldavians, was a relatively safe pursuit. It was dangerous for them to be socialists or nationalists: these were illegal and seditious activities that involved risky defiance of the Russian authorities. Jew-hatred, however, was fairly respectable, encouraged by the Russian officials and condoned by the Orthodox clergy. This was one sentiment that Moldavians could share with Russians, and prominent persons could share with the lower classes. For Russians and Moldavians alike, anti-Semitism could be patriotic, politically acceptable, religiously tolerable, and—for those who felt the strain of financial competition—perhaps even economically useful.

The Jews of Kishinev

The targets and victims of this anti-Semitism came from a rather different background than their Russian and Moldavian neighbors.

Although there had been a small Jewish community in Kishinev even before the Russian takeover, the nineteenth century had witnessed a vast influx of Jews into the Bessarabian capital. They had come from other provinces in the Russian Pale of Settlement, from neighboring Rumania, and from elsewhere in Bessarabia itself.

The Jews constituted one of the fastest-growing and most influential groups in all of Bessarabia. In 1812, at the time of the Russian annexation, there had been no more than 20,000 Jews in the region, and they accounted for less than 5 percent of its population. Some of them were Sephardic Jews, merchants who had come from other parts of the Turkish Empire and settled in eastern Moldavia during the sixteenth and seventeenth centuries. Others were Ashkenazim who had come more recently, mostly from Poland and Ukraine. The latter migration continued and expanded throughout much of the nineteenth century, in part because Bessarabia seemed to offer greater opportunity—and less repression—than other provinces of the Pale. The favorable climate, the expanding economy, the increasing production of fruit and grain, the growing size and commerce of the cities and towns, and the relatively mild enforcement of anti-Jewish restrictions all served to make Bessarabia an attractive destination. In the countryside, in various places, Jewish agricultural colonies were established, while in the cities Jewish communities grew and flourished. By the late 1850s, there were about 80,000 Jews in Bessarabia, and they comprised over 8 percent of the region's population.[23]

Even in the latter half of the century, despite increases in anti-Semitic activities and anti-Jewish regulations, the Jewish population had kept on growing at a very rapid rate. Continued resettlement, combined with a relatively low rate of infant mortality, had more than offset the trickle of Jewish emigrants leaving Bessarabia for the West. By 1900 the province was home to some 230,000 Jews, who made up nearly 12 percent of its inhabitants.[24]

Partly as a result of government regulations that sought to keep them away from the peasants, most of the Jews settled in cities and towns. This was especially true after the promulgation of the May Laws of 1882, which drove many Jews out of the countryside and resulted in the liquidation of 11 of the 17 Jewish agricultural settlements formed earlier in the century. By 1900, only about 7 percent of the Jews in Bessarabia were actively engaged in farming, and the

Jews themselves made up less than 4 percent of the agrarian population. Instead, they were concentrated in the urban areas, where
they worked primarily as merchants and artisans. According to the
1897 census, about three-fourths of the Jews in Bessarabia lived in
the cities and small towns, and more than two-thirds of them derived their living from commerce, crafts, and industry. More importantly, perhaps, they tended to dominate these areas: over 80 percent of the merchants in Bessarabia were Jews, and the crucial grain
trade was almost entirely in Jewish hands. This circumstance not
only increased Jewish influence and visibility; it also added to the
concerns of those who feared that the province's economy, especially in the cities, was coming increasingly under Jewish control.[25]

Nowhere was this more evident than in the provincial capital. In
the 1860s, according to various estimates, Kishinev's 18,000 Jews
made up about 20 percent of the city's 90,000 residents. By 1897,
based on the census data, their numbers had risen to almost 50,000,
and they now comprised over 45 percent of the populace. If these
figures are at all credible, they chart a remarkable phenomenon: in
the last third of the nineteenth century, Kishinev's Jewish community had nearly tripled in size, while the city's non-Jewish population had actually declined. Most of the change seems to have come
from immigration: in 1897, nearly 30 percent of all Kishinev residents had been born outside of Bessarabia, mostly in other provinces
within the Pale of Jewish Settlement. Some Jews apparently were
attracted to Kishinev because of the favorable climate and expanding economy, while others were forced to move to the city by the
May Laws of 1882 and further restrictions on Jewish rural residence.[26]

In economic terms, the Jews were even more influential than
their numbers would indicate. The majority of Kishinev's commercial, financial and industrial enterprises, including three-fourths of
the city's factories, were in Jewish hands. Jewish-owned businesses
included flour mills, wineries, tobacco processing plants, credit and
loan agencies, trading companies, and the like. The skilled trades,
especially sewing, tailoring, shoemaking, and cabinetmaking, were
likewise dominated by Jews. By general reputation, Jewish businesses were better organized than others, their prices were more
competitive, and their merchandise was often superior. Karl Schmidt,

the city's longtime mayor, was candid enough to admit that the city owed its prosperity largely to the Jews.[27]

This economic strength, however, had brought neither prosperity nor peace to the Jewish community. For one thing, it seemed to confirm the stereotype of Jews as opportunists and exploiters, thus giving the government a convenient justification for continued repression of them. For another thing, it tended to increase the resentments of non-Jewish townsfolk, and to exacerbate the ethnic, religious, and social tensions that already existed. These factors, in turn, reinforced one another, with popular anti-Semitism serving as a rationale for government policies, and government policies contributing to the growth of popular anti-Semitism.

In economic terms, then, Kishinev's Jews were in an anomalous situation. Although some Jews controlled the economy and many others lived comfortably, the majority were quite poor. The large number of artisans had created a fierce competition which kept prices and profits low, despite the existence of guilds. Poorer still were the unskilled Jewish laborers, since industrial wages afforded only enough for bare survival. Even worse off were the unemployed, who lived off the charity of their fellows: by 1900 there were over 2,000 Jewish families seeking such aid, and their numbers were growing steadily.[28]

In cultural and religious terms, meanwhile, the Jews of Kishinev were further set apart from their neighbors. They were, for the most part, a traditional lot who tended to dress in distinctive garb, discourage intermarriage with non-Jews, and keep their social and cultural life within their own community. The majority were quite orthodox in their religious practice, strictly observing the laws regulating food preparation, diet, and Sabbath activity. They ran their own schools, which provided Jewish youth with instruction in Yiddish and Hebrew and gave them a basic familiarity with Torah, Talmud, and other aspects of their faith. They even had their own welfare institutions, including an orphanage, a dispensary, a hospital, a dining hall, and various agencies to distribute food, fuel and supplies among the poor. As a result of these activities, in spite of Jewish poverty there generally seems to have been a much higher level of education and sanitation, a lower death rate, and a much lower level of drunkenness and anti-social behavior, within the

Jewish community. Unfortunately, these factors tended to strengthen the specter of Jewish domination, and to reinforce the resentments, fears, and jealousies of those who disliked the Jews.[29]

Kishinev's Jews, therefore, had serious political problems. Their large numbers, cultural achievements, and economic accomplishments made them a potential threat, and increased the determination of tsarist officials to limit Jewish influence. Anti-Jewish laws were thus strictly enforced: Jews were forbidden to vote in city elections, they could only serve on the city council if appointed by the authorities, and even then they could comprise no more than 10 percent of the council. Certain restrictions were carried to extremes: since Jews were forbidden to move to rural areas, for example, Kishinev officials would not let them work at the stone quarries seven miles out of town. To make matters worse, Russian administrators tended to sympathize with those who mistreated Jews, to ignore Jewish grievances, to look the other way when Jews were harassed or abused, and to condone the anti-Semitic activities of the local press. It is little wonder, then, that a number of Jewish intellectuals and youths—deprived of an outlet for their political energies and oppressed by various laws and deprivations—had begun joining revolutionary groups. Nor is it surprising that this would further alarm the Russian authorities, confirming their fears about the Jewish "menace," and reinforcing their view of the Jews as dangerous, unreliable, and undesirable aliens.[30]

At the beginning of the twentieth century, then, Kishinev was a city of conflicts and contrasts. Its growing wealth and influence contrasted sharply with the increasing poverty and destitution within its older sections. Its modern conveniences and amenities clashed with the backwardness and ignorance of the local peasants and native townsfolk. Its expanding revolutionary movement conflicted with the autocratic Russian authorities and their political police. The awakening national stirrings contrasted with the outward success of the government's russification policies. And its various nationalities, especially its Russians, Moldavians, and Jews, clashed with each other's religious, cultural, economic, and political aspirations.

The situation was further complicated, in the first few years of the new century, by economic hard times. The years 1900 through 1903 brought a general decline in the Russian industrial economy, and this decline was felt in Bessarabia. A number of businesses were forced to close, and many workers and artisans were left unemployed. This circumstance helped to spur the growth of revolutionary activism among the working classes, and to heighten the levels of anxiety and tension within the population.[31]

This is not to say that Kishinev was irrevocably headed toward turmoil. Indeed, its various groups and cultures had many interests in common and their differences, in most cases, were by no means irreconcilable. Kishinev's problems were not necessarily any more severe than those of a number of other cities which had been growing and changing rapidly in recent years. The fact is, however, that the ingredients for violent conflict were present and, given the proper conditions and catalysts, things could well explode. Patient, sensitive, and non-inflammatory leadership might well have been able to lower the tension level. Unfortunately, by 1903 patience and sensitivity were in rather short supply, and a number of prominent persons were actively pursuing a most inflammatory course.

CHAPTER 3

Agitation and Provocation

If national, cultural, economic, and social tensions supplied the fuel for the Kishinev pogrom, agitation and provocation served as the kindling material. Using a variety of means, local anti-Semites, aided and abetted by government officials, consciously sought to create a climate of fear and hostility toward the Jews among the Christian populace. A mysterious homicide in a nearby town, widely reported as an incident of Jewish ritual murder, provided an effective catalyst. By spring of 1903, when a series of incidents and rumors threatened to spark a conflagration, the city had become a tinderbox ready to ignite.

The Agitators and the Authorities

In the early years of the twentieth century, a number of prominent persons helped to foster an atmosphere of hatred and distrust toward the Jews in Kishinev. Some, like publisher Krushevan and contractor Pronin, actively worked to inflame passions and hostilities among the Christian populace. Others, such as Vice-Governor Ustrugov and various police officials, gave the impression that the government itself tolerated and encouraged anti-Jewish activities. Still others, including Governor von Raaben and Orthodox Bishop Iakov, contributed by their inaction, failing to take the necessary steps to calm tensions and forestall disorders.

Pavolachi Krushevan, a native Moldavian, was one of the most influential persons in Kishinev, and perhaps in all of Bessarabia. His newspaper, the *Bessarabets (Bessarabian)*, was the city's only daily, and thus served as the major source of information for most of its inhabitants. His printing press, furthermore, produced many of the books and pamphlets that helped define how Bessarabians looked at themselves and the outside world. A strong supporter of the Russian autocracy, he had powerful connections among tsarist officials, both in Kishinev and in Saint Petersburg.[1]

Born in 1860, Krushevan had witnessed during his career two important developments: the tsarist government's efforts to russify and assimilate Bessarabia, and the rapid growth in numbers and influence of the Jews in Kishinev. Both had a profound impact on him. The former had originally caused him some concern, but he had eventually become an outspoken and effective advocate for Russian influence and authority. The latter, on the other hand, had caused him great anxiety, and he had become an ever more vociferous alarmist about the Jewish "threat."

Krushevan's thinking and writing were influenced both by his love for his native land and by his own ambitions. He published guidebooks and descriptive works about Kishinev and Bessarabia, and he himself wrote glowingly of the province and its people. In his younger days, he may have been something of a liberal, and a champion of Moldavian culture. As he grew older, however, he apparently decided that the best interests of the Moldavians—or at least the best interests of his own career—lay in the full assimilation of Bessarabia into the Russian state and culture. This was especially true after 1897, when he founded and began publishing the *Bessarabets*. He may have been motivated in part by the fact that the local news had been dominated by two fairly liberal Odessa newspapers; at any rate, he opted to counter these by adopting a staunchly conservative editorial policy. As time went on, and as the rivalry with the other papers intensified, the *Bessarabets* became increasingly reactionary and anti-Semitic in tone.[2]

Krushevan's strident editorial policy evidently served him well. His advocacy of Russian policies and Russian ways won the approval of the imperial authorities, who in turn gave him political, juridical, and at times even financial support. Russian officials, no doubt pleased at having such an effective Moldavian spokesman, provided Krushevan and his paper with relative freedom in publishing stories and opinions. There was, it seems, a certain amount favoritism shown to Krushevan by the imperial censorship. Its directors, both in Saint Petersburg and in Kishinev, apparently felt that government interests were best served by avoiding action against *Bessarabets* and thus keeping it in print. Toward the end of 1902, in fact, Krushevan was allowed to begin publishing a new newspaper, called the *Znamia (Banner)*, in the city of Saint Petersburg.[3]

To Krushevan, the Jews were far more than simply a talented and industrious people with an alien cultural and religious heritage. They represented rather an evil force in the world, a well-organized, conspiratorial group seeking to subjugate the Christian masses. In his desperate struggle to prevent this calamity, it seems that no tactic was too base, and no slander too vile, for Krushevan to employ. His writings and publications came to be imbued with incredible accusations that went far beyond any real or imagined danger the Jews could possibly have posed. Diatribes against the Jews became standard fare in *Bessarabets*, and apocryphal stories of Jewish crimes and conspiracies appeared regularly in its pages.[4] Krushevan, in fact, would become one of the main originators and publicizers of the mythical Jewish plan for world conquest that came to be known as the "Protocols of the Elders of Zion." Whether or not Krushevan himself actually believed these slanders, he found them to be useful weapons in his campaign to rouse the people for a violent crusade against the Jewish "menace."[5]

Krushevan's sometime collaborator and associate, Georgii Alekseevich Pronin, had a rather different background. He was a Russian townsperson, a small businessman from the city of Orel in the central provinces, some 500 miles northwest of Kishinev. A man of humble origins, he had come to the southeastern provinces to seek his fortune as a paving and construction contractor. In Odessa he had achieved wealth and prominence, but in so doing he had gained a reputation as a corrupt egotist and a brutal exploiter of his workers. According to one account, he had also run afoul of the city's mayor, who reportedly had threatened to beat him up.[6]

In Kishinev, subsequently, he had achieved even greater success, partly through his own shrewdness and readiness to take advantage of the native Moldavians, and partly through his ability to obtain government contracts. The latter he seems to have achieved largely by currying favor with the Russian authorities: he liked to portray himself as a true Russian patriot with influential connections in

Saint Petersburg. He was not above using bribery and intimidation to advance his interests or to gain appointment to prestigious positions, such as the title of Persian consul and the directorship of the Kishinev Prison Committee. By 1903 he had become a wealthy man with considerable capital and landed property in the vicinity of Kishinev.[7]

As a businessman, however, Pronin had found himself in serious competition with a number of Jewish contractors. Although the latter lacked his connections, they were often able to win contracts by underbidding him, providing their clients with better service and more favorable terms. This infuriated Pronin, decreased his profits, and increased his animosity toward the Jews in general. As time went on, he started to cut back on his business interests and get more and more involved in anti-Semitic pursuits. Unable to better the Jews in open competition, he tried a different tack: he began using his wealth and influence to undermine the Jewish community through political intrigue and public slander. He joined prominent committees and made friends with local police officials and others charged with enforcing anti-Jewish restrictions. He loaned substantial sums to the newspaper *Bessarabets*, which was in financial difficulty, thus ingratiating himself with Pavolachi Krushevan. Krushevan, in turn, had little choice but to publish Pronin's articles and poems, which were largely in tune with the paper's "patriotic" and anti-Jewish tenor.[8]

Like Krushevan, Pronin sought to portray himself as a sort of "savior," determined to warn and protect the simple Christian folk against the machinations of the Jews. His self-serving anti-Semitism was wrapped in a cloak of humanitarian concern for the lower classes, especially the Christian workers and artisans. He donated considerable amounts of time and money toward efforts to improve their lot and to win their favor. Although his own wealth was based in part on exploitation of the working people, he insisted that he was their true friend and that the Jews, whom he accused of all sorts of exploitative and criminal practices, were their mortal enemies. The Christians of Kishinev, according to Pronin, were dominated and abused by the Jews, and thus they had no choice but to fight back. And he saw it as his duty to support them in this struggle.[9]

Krushevan and Pronin, it was generally recognized, played the most prominent role in agitating the lower classes toward anti-Semitic violence. Their activities, however, could scarcely have been successful had they not been countenanced, and even encouraged, by the local authorities. Prominent officials, from the governor on down, not only failed to pull the reins on these men; they actually increased their credibility by showing them favor, thus fostering the impression that anti-Jewish activity was viewed by the government as both permissible and patriotic.

Governor Rudolf Samoilovich von Raaben, the highest official in the province, was generally recognized as a man of goodwill, completely lacking in viciousness or animosity. He had been governor of Bessarabia since 1899 and, on the whole, his relations with the inhabitants—including the Jews—had actually been quite good. Although he came from a military background, he was by no means an authoritarian; indeed, he enjoyed a certain popularity as a result of his amiable nature and relaxed attitude toward affairs. He participated broadly in the city's cultural and social life, regularly visiting the various clubs—including the Jewish university club, where he was a welcome guest. His sincere desire to be on good terms with everyone seemed to fit well the mood of the province and to make him an unlikely contributor to anti-Semitic violence.[10]

Yet the governor, in his own way, helped set the stage for violence by failing to assert any control over affairs and events. A former professional soldier and highly decorated general, he tended to look upon the governorship as a sinecure, a fitting reward for a long career of faithful service. He delegated almost all his responsibilities to subordinates, paid little attention to administrative affairs, and failed even to learn much about laws and customs relevant to his position. Instead he lived a life of ease and entertainment, enjoying the perquisites of his status, the hospitality of his subordinates, and the pleasures of life in Bessarabia. He apparently saw himself as a dashing bon vivant: his life in Kishinev was dominated by card playing and gambling, dinner parties and social events, and various amorous adventures—he even had a semi-official mistress who accompanied him to certain events. These attitudes and activities, unfortunately, left him with little understanding of, or influence over, events in the province and its capital. By preference and personality, he was poorly prepared either to foresee and forestall troubles, or to deal with them effectively once they occurred.[11]

Thanks to von Raaben's disinterest, the actual day-to-day administration of Bessarabia fell upon the shoulders of Vice-Governor V. G. Ustrugov, a man of totally different stamp. Lacking neither talent nor ambition, Ustrugov gladly assumed the responsibilities delegated to him, performing his duties with efficiency and dispatch. Anxious to advance his career, and no doubt aware of the anti-Semitic attitudes of the tsar and his advisers, he enforced with extreme rigidity the various restrictions against the Jews. He saw them as a "plague" infesting the province and the bane of his own existence: to him they represented a troublesome tribe of energetic and talented lawbreakers who systematically sought to circumvent or evade the legal limitations that had been placed upon them. Indeed it is true that some Jews, deprived of their right to lease lands or reside in the rural villages, got around these restrictions by employing various subterfuges and bribing the local police. But the initiative here came as often as not from the police, who tended to use their discretionary powers in applying the laws to extort money from the Jews.[12]

Nevertheless, in Ustrugov's view, the Jews were largely to blame for the corruption of the police and, in general, for the tensions and resentments that existed in Kishinev. Their economic predominance and circumvention of the law, combined with the high level of unemployment and discontent among the city's lower classes, was to him a recipe for trouble. The vice-governor's self-appointed mission thus seems to have been to keep the Jews in their place by an excessive and merciless enforcement of the anti-Jewish regulations, often going beyond the actual letter of the law. He saw to it, for example, that rural Jews who left their villages for military service or business were prevented from moving back home, on the grounds that the May Laws of 1882 forbade Jews from taking up residence anywhere but in designated cities and towns. At the same time, Ustrugov went out of his way to protect persons accused of abusing or mistreating the Jews, and to prevent the Jews from obtaining legal redress for their grievances. Even when many of his decisions in these matters were appealed and overturned, he continued his legal persecution of the Jews, ignoring or misinterpreting the rulings of the imperial Senate.[13]

The impact of Ustrugov's attitude, moreover, went far beyond the range of his personal activity. As the province's de facto chief administrator, he set the tone and established priorities for the whole governing apparatus. Under his direction, harassment of Jews became a primary focus of policy, and the impression was left that anti-Semitic actions were welcomed and condoned. Officials, soldiers, and police often took it upon themselves to mistreat the Jews, acting with impunity, secure in the knowledge that they were unlikely to be taken to task for this. Tax collectors and police who used their positions illegally to wrest money from Jews could count on official favoritism should charges be brought against them. Persons who wrote and published false and provocative anti-Semitic articles could be assured of a lenient attitude from the local censorship bureau, which was under the purview of the vice-governor. Among the common people, all this merely served to reinforce the perception that the authorities themselves favored persecution of the Jews, and that those who engaged in anti-Jewish activities were more likely to be rewarded than punished.[14]

Other prominent officials seemed to take their cue from the vice-governor. The chief of police, Aleksandr Konstantinovich Khanzhenkov, was a former soldier, now in his early forties, who had retired from the military as a sergeant-major. Popularly known as "the Beard" because of his impressive chin whiskers, he had little use for the Jews. He regarded them as troublemakers who caused many of their own problems by their insolence and contempt toward the Christian lower classes.[15] The head of the local gendarmes, Colonel I. G. Charnoluskii, was preoccupied mainly with the struggle against anti-government activities. He saw the Jews as the predominant source of such activities since, according to his estimation, about 90 percent of the local revolutionaries were Jews. He was also a supporter and defender of Krushevan, and he tended to view both *Bessarabets* and *Znamia* as bastions of truth and counterweights against the lies and machinations of the Jews.[16]

Andrei Ivanovich Stepanov, the elected head of the Kishinev artisans' council, nurtured a bitter hostility toward the Jews. A collaborator of Pronin's, he cherished a reputation as a spokesman for the Christian workingmen in their alleged struggle against Jewish competition and exploitation. Despite the fact that he was a rather crude individual with little education or erudition, Stepanov managed to publish a number of anti-Jewish articles in Krushevan's Saint Petersburg newspaper.[17]

The Christian religious leadership was scarcely more enlightened. Bishop Iakov, the Orthodox metropolitan, was the most prominent clergyman in town. As such, he no doubt could have done much to ease tensions and improve relations by denouncing the vicious anti-Semitic rumors and assuring his flock that there was no truth in them. But the bishop was largely ignorant of the Judaic faith, and he seems to have believed some of the stories that spread concerning the rituals of various Jewish sects. At any rate, he took no action either to spike the rumors or to urge his followers to be tolerant and charitable toward their Jewish neighbors. His silence and passivity thus lent credibility to the notions that the Jews were the enemies of Christians, and that some Jews used Christian blood for ritual purposes.[18]

Of all the officials in Kishinev, the most mysterious was Baron Levendal, the chief of the secret police. Unlike the others, his connections with Kishinev were tenuous and brief. He showed up toward the end of 1902, and was transferred away less than ten months later. He did not have time either to become deeply acquainted with local issues and events, or to establish a reputation like those of Krushevan, Pronin, and Ustrugov. Furthermore, unlike the others, he operated quietly and secretly behind the scenes, rather than openly and provocatively.

Outwardly, at least, Levendal's mission in Kishinev was clear: he had been sent to combat and destroy the town's growing revolutionary movement. Originally, he had been an officer in the Separate Corps of Gendarmes, the main government agency designed to investigate political crimes and combat seditious activity. He did not come to Kishinev as the head of the local gendarmes, however; that was Colonel Charnoluskii's position. Instead, Levendal came as a representative of the Special Section of the Department of Police of the Ministry of Interior.

For several decades, the Department of Police had operated "security sections" *(okhranniia otdeleniia)*, designed to combat the revolutionary movement, in Saint Petersburg, Moscow, and Warsaw. Unlike the gendarmes, these "Okhranas" were secretive, covert operations that made use of conspiratorial, and sometimes extra-legal, devices such as spies, informers, and *agents provocateurs*. In 1898 the Special Section had been established to supervise and coordinate Okhrana activities, and in 1902 the legendary Moscow Okhrana chief Sergei Zubatov had been appointed as its head. Before long, an "all-Russian Okhrana" had been formed, with new security sections established in places like Odessa, Kiev, and Kishinev. At the head of these new sections were placed vigorous young gendarme officers who, in Zubatov's opinion, had not yet lost their creativity and flexibility. Among these were A. I. Spiridovich, the dedicated and effective officer who took charge of the Kiev Okhrana, and of course Baron Levendal, who was assigned to the Kishinev Okhrana.[19]

Levendal arrived in Kishinev at a time when the growth of the local social-democratic movement was beginning to pose a serious threat. For several years, young Marxists had been agitating and distributing illegal newspapers and pamphlets among the city's workers, students, and soldiers. Not surprisingly, given the anti-Semitic attitudes of local officials and the size of the city's Jewish population, some of the most prominent young revolutionaries were Jews.[20]

At any rate, the new Okhrana chief came to town in December of 1902, took up residence in a house on Aleksandrov Street owned by S. Landau, and began his duties. According to his eventual successor, he was young, good-natured, and deeply interested in his work. But his behavior also aroused suspicion within the Jewish community. Over the space of several months, his landlords noted a number of regular visitors coming to talk with him, including the contractor Pronin. What actually took place at these meetings was unknown, but the very fact that they occurred added to the impression that Pronin enjoyed government favor. This, combined with the increase in anti-Semitic agitation following Levendal's arrival, eventually gave rise to conjecture that the Okhrana chief was actually directing these activities from behind the scenes. Some even went so far as to speculate that he was doing this on imperial authority, on a secret mission from the tsar.[21]

Not all Kishinev officials, of course, were inveterate Jew-haters. V. N. Goremykin, the local prosecuting attorney, was a talented and tolerant official who, although he was by no means pro-Jewish, sought to maintain an attitude of impartiality and professionalism in his work. Lieutenant General V. A. Bekman, the senior commander of the Kishinev garrison, likewise made an effort to be businesslike and tactful in his dealings with one and all. Unfortunately, however, his subordinates were not always so inclined. His second-in-command was a rabid anti-Semite, as were many of his officers and soldiers. The garrison, as a result, tended to be a hotbed of anti-Jewish hostility.[22]

The mayor, Karl Aleksandrovich Schmidt, was deeply committed to the maintenance of good relations in his city. For over 25 years he had been in office, repeatedly chosen by the city council, which was itself elected by the more prominent citizens and property owners. Especially after 1892, when the empire's new municipal law had disfranchised the Jews and restricted their presence on the council, he had become a hero to the Jewish community. Since the Jews, who boycotted the restructured council, had no representation of their own, they had relied increasingly on the good offices of the mayor to meet their needs. And he had continued to do so, in a thorough and conscientious manner, despite the council's subsequent trend toward reaction and anti-Semitism. Schmidt himself was deeply disturbed by the growth in anti-Jewish agitation but—lacking any authority over the police or military, and faced with an irresponsible governor and an anti-Semitic vice-governor—he was powerless to stem the tide.[23]

Blood Libel

Prior to the beginning of 1903, anti-Jewish agitation in Kishinev appeared to be more annoying than ominous. Tensions existed, to be sure, but these seemed no more dangerous than tensions in other cities of the Pale. Periodic instances of Jew-baiting occurred, but most often these were the actions of isolated individuals. In the first several months of the new year, however, there spread through Kishinev and the surrounding environs a series of rumors and reports that served to focus attention on the Jews and intensify the fears and hostilities felt toward them.

Not surprisingly, the vehicle for many of these canards was Krushevan's newspaper. The Jews, according to the *Bessarabets*, had invented a new process for producing wine without using grapes; with this they threatened to undercut and undermine the entire local grape-growing and wine-making industry. Jewish doctors, a later issue reported, had formed a secret syndicate to swindle and defraud their unsuspecting patients through charlatanism and quackery. Most Jews, another edition implied, belonged to some form of secret society: they thus should not be trusted in any form of public service. Almost daily, the paper's "City Chronicle" section carried accounts of Jewish misdemeanors, Jewish misbehavior, and Jewish attacks against Christians. Such items, repeated regularly in the pages of the city's only daily, could not help but have an impact, not just on its readers, but on the semi-literate masses who heard these slanders by word of mouth.[24]

The most provocative stories, however, concerned the events surrounding the death of a Christian boy in the nearby town of Dubossary. Dubossary was located in Kherson Province, along the Dniester River just across from Bessarabia, about 25 miles northeast of Kishinev. Like Kishinev, it had a substantial Jewish community, comprising nearly half of its 12,000 inhabitants, and a large number of Moldavian and Ukrainian townsfolk. On Thursday, February 13, 1903, a visiting peasant from Bessarabia, having stopped to relieve himself in a garden along the Dniester, discovered the corpse of a teenage boy. This turned out to be the remains of Mikhail Rybachenko, a 14–year-old youth who had disappeared the previous Sunday after going to church with his grandparents. The multiple bruises and stab wounds left no doubt that the lad had been murdered.[25]

Even before the boy's body was discovered, a bizarre rumor had begun to spread among the coarse and superstitious folk who passed their time in gossip at the town's two marketplaces. The Jews, according to this legend, needed the blood of a Christian youth in order to prepare their matzah, the unleavened bread eaten by them during Passover. Indeed, a Christian girl who worked for Jews had supposedly heard them discussing this need prior to Mikhail's disappearance. The boy himself, according to a young comrade, had last been seen going into the shop of a local Jew to purchase some tobacco. When his corpse was found, it was allegedly so thin and pale, and so carefully pierced near all the main arteries, that it seemed clear that the blood had been drained from it. The medical examiner, Leib Polinkovskii, refuted these claims, but—since he was a Jew—many townsfolk refused to believe him. Instead, influenced by rumors, fortune-tellers, and the dream visions of Mikhail's friends, they concluded that young Rybachenko had been murdered by the Jews so his blood could be used for ritual purposes. The boy's grandparents, having enlisted the help of a literate acquaintance, even went so far as to write the minister of justice requesting an investigation.[26]

The townsfolk of Dubossary were by no means original in concocting and crediting the tale of ritual murder. Such "blood libels," in fact, seem to have had their origins in ancient times, rooted in primitive superstitions concerning the powers of blood, as well as in misunderstanding and resentment of the laws and customs of the monotheistic Jews. Even before the time of Christ, the Jews had been accused of fattening, slaughtering, and eating the flesh of kidnapped Greeks. Early Christians, ironically, were persecuted by the Romans under similar charges, derived apparently from the Christian practice of consuming the "body and blood" of Jesus in sacramental form. In the Middle Ages, after Christianity had come to dominate the Western world, the libel was transposed to the Jews, the most visible "aliens" within the Christian world and the alleged "murderers" of Christ. In the eleventh through fifteenth centuries, Jews in various places were accused—and at times even slaughtered—for "crimes" ranging from desecration of communion hosts to the torture and murder of young Christian "martyrs" in conscious reenactment of the passion of Jesus. Despite the lack of evidence to support these legends, and in spite of their condemnation by various emperors and popes, the myth proved quite tenacious, finding its way even into literature such as Chaucer's "Prioress' Tale."[27]

Eventually, the legend had spread to eastern Europe, and had become increasingly identified with Jewish "sorcery" and the alleged use of Christian blood in preparing the Passover matzah. Although there was an apparent link with the crucifixion story, since Jesus was reportedly executed at Passover time and pierced so as to lose all his blood, there was no clear connection with any actual Jewish practice. Indeed, it flew in the face of the fact that Jewish law strictly forbade blood sacrifice and even the consumption of animal blood. Nevertheless, the myth became a standard feature of anti-Semitic rhetoric in the Russian Pale of Settlement, resurfacing on occasion throughout the nineteenth century in charges brought against Jews in various places. The Russian government, it seems clear, did not originate this legend, but neither did it act consistently to combat the libel or to discredit those who fostered it.[28]

At any rate, in investigating the death of Mikhail Rybachenko, the authorities did make an effort to discredit the rumors of Jewish ritual murder. According to the procurator of the Odessa Circuit Court, who reported on this matter to the minister of justice, 30 different witnesses were interrogated, and no evidence whatever was found to implicate the Jews. The Christian girl who had supposedly heard her Jewish employers plotting the murder admitted that she had heard no such thing, and conceded that she could not even understand the language spoken by Jews. From Mikhail's friends, it became clear that he had not gone to the Jewish shop to buy tobacco, but had instead gone ice skating on the frozen River Dniester, remaining there after all the others had left. Suspicion came to focus, not on the Jews, but on the victim's cousin and uncle, who stood to gain the inheritance of the boy's wealthy grandfather once Mikhail was out of the way. On March 2, scarcely two weeks after the corpse was discovered, a Christian medical examiner was brought in from Tiraspol', the district capital, to perform a second autopsy. This he did on the grounds of the cemetery, in the presence of a priest from the local cathedral and a large number of other persons. His findings, on the whole, corroborated those of the Jewish examiner Polinkovskii, ruling out any likelihood of ritual murder. The crowd of onlookers seemed satisfied and, although it would be some time until the boy's uncle was identified as the murderer, and although many townsfolk continued to believe the rumors of Jewish treachery, it looked as if the issue of blood sacrifice had largely been laid to rest.[29]

Unfortunately, this was not to be the case. By this time, the legend of the ritual murder had spread beyond Dubossary and, in several places, had taken on the aura of fact. On March 3, the day after the second autopsy, anti-Jewish riots broke out in the market-place of the nearby town of Tumanovo; they were apparently triggered by a visiting peasant who spread the word that the Jews in Dubossary had slaughtered a Christian boy. A crowd of about 200 rioters, shouting "beat the Jews," did substantial damage to Jewish shops and property. No lives, however, were lost: most of the Jews reportedly fled, and the crowd itself dispersed after about an hour or two. The local authorities did not actually stop the pogrom, but they did soon arrest and charge about a dozen of the leading agitators. At about this same time there was reported anti-Jewish ferment, apparently inspired by similar rumors about the Dubossary murder, in the Bender district of Bessarabia province.[30]

That same week, in Kishinev, Krushevan's *Bessarabets* began publishing reports on the Dubossary murder. The first story, repeating the false report that the victim had last visited a Jewish tobacco shop, went on to announce that many rumors and speculations, including suspicions of ritual murder, were circulating among the people of Dubossary.[31] Later reports were full of inaccuracies and provocative insinuations which tended to implicate the Jews. They repeated a story, allegedly told by a Jewish woman, about the kidnapping of the boy by the Jewish shopkeepers. They claimed that the body of young Rybachenko had been found without any wounds or bruises, excepting puncture marks on the veins of its arms and legs, and that its eyes, ears, and mouth had been sewn shut. They indicated that all the blood had been drained out, that one eye had been torn from its socket, and that the arms were covered with rope marks. They speculated that the boy had been crucified by Jews, and that his blood had been prepared by them for use in some sort of ceremony. And they intimated that one of Mikhail's murderers, a Jew, had already been discovered and had revealed many details about the crime.[32] The reports were totally false, but they had a widespread impact, especially when they were picked up by other papers like *Novoe vremia*, the main Saint Petersburg daily.[33]

These accounts, it turned out, were based largely on unverified stories told by Dubossary townsfolk. One correspondent, whose articles were published in both *Bessarabets* and *Novoe vremia*, had actually traveled to Dubossary. There, it seems, he discussed the murder with such "authorities" as the man who maintained the postal station and Mikhail Rybachenko's grandfather. He reportedly even paid the latter to recount in detail the story of the boy's disappearance. Then, without having talked to either the police officials or the judicial authorities, he filed his reports.[34] *Bessarabets*, which was always anxious to expose the Jewish "menace," apparently had no hesitation about publishing such an inflammatory and unsubstantiated account. Besides, the newspaper itself was in dire financial straits, and was in the process of being sued by a man who claimed that he had actually bought the business from Krushevan but never received control.[35] In these circumstances, a sensational story involving Jewish ritual murder may well have seemed attractive.

The Storm Clouds Gather

In any event, the reports from Dubossary did create a sensation in Kishinev, among both Gentiles and Jews. They broke during the month before Passover, at a time when the Jewish people traditionally would prepare the various types of food—including matzah—to be consumed at their Seder meals. Among the uneducated Christian masses, who were already predisposed against the Jews by agitation, provocation, prejudice, and superstition, they created new anxieties. They aroused not only anger at the reported Jewish treachery, but also fear that a similar ritual murder might well occur in Kishinev.[36]

Alarmed by these conditions, the procurator of the Odessa Chamber of Justice wrote to Governor von Raaben, exposing the falsity of the reports and urging the governor to take steps to prevent the circulation of such stories. An official refutation was in fact published in *Bessarabets* on Wednesday, March 19, 1903. It admitted that many of the details published earlier were completely without foundation. The autopsy established that Mikhail Rybachenko had died as a result of multiple stab wounds, not ritual murder. The boy's mouth and ears and other apertures had not been sewn shut, and his body bore no evidence of prick-holes from which blood could have been drained. Contrary to what had been printed in previous reports, the article went on, there were no Jewish persons who had come forward with details of an alleged kidnapping and murder, and there were no earlier cases where ritual murder was suspected. This retraction helped to set the record straight, but it came too late to undo the damage, and was dismissed by many townsfolk as a coverup issued under pressure from the Jews.[37]

The province's official newspaper, *Bessarabskiia gubernskiia vedomosti (Bessarabian Provincial Record)*, made an even more determined effort to counteract the effects of the sensational reports coming out of Dubossary. On Thursday, March 20, it published on its front page an official refutation very similar to that printed by *Bessarabets* on the preceding day. On its second page, in addition, it ran a long, detailed article giving the history of the Dubossary affair, explaining how "evil-intentioned" persons had spread stories about Jewish ritual murder and far-fetched tales that eventually found their way into newspapers like *Bessarabets*. In its next issue, on Saturday, March 22, it printed another long article, this one focusing on the "harmful legend" of Jewish ritual murder. It featured an interview with a certain Father Petrov, an expert on religious sects, who pointed out that the consumption of blood of any sort was in direct contradiction to Talmudic teachings and Judaic religious dogma.[38] Even these efforts, however, failed to put to rest the fears and resentments aroused by the original Dubossary reports.

Meanwhile, a sinister but persistent rumor had begun to circulate among the lower classes in Kishinev. According to this tale, the tsar himself had issued a secret decree granting them the right to beat and plunder the Jews, without interference by the authorities, for a three day period beginning on Easter Sunday. Strange rumors were not uncommon among the crude and simple folk who frequented the taverns and bazaars, and many were still wont to view the tsar as a friend and "little father" who would side with them against their oppressors. This particular story, however, seems to have gained unusually wide credibility when printed proclamations—apparently issued by Pronin—showed up in taverns and meeting places during the week before Easter. These proclamations, repeating the ritual murder slanders and other anti-Semitic accusations, called upon loyal Christians to take action against the Jews in the name of the tsar. The legal restrictions on the Jews, the government's tendency to treat them as undesirable aliens, and the evident anti-Semitism of many local officials and officers also lent credence to the legend. It was widely believed among the Christian masses that the authorities would permit them, at Easter time, to enrich themselves at the expense of the Jews. This, along with the rumors of ritual murder and the ongoing social and economic tensions, helped create an inflammatory atmosphere in the city of Kishinev.[39]

As the rumors and libels continued to spread, the city's Jewish community became increasingly alarmed. Talk of a possible pogrom, most likely to take place over Easter, had begun to reach Jewish ears. So had stories about groups of "dark people," including some outsiders, who were assembling in local taverns to discuss patriotic and anti-Semitic exploits. Later accounts claimed that a number of foreigners —described variously as Albanians, Turks, or Rumanians—had begun to appear in town during the several weeks before Easter. Some of these people reportedly spent time agitating the local Christians and preaching to them about the need to fight back against the growing power of the Jews. Anti-Semitic leaflets, calling upon the local Christian population to "beat the Jews" over the Easter holidays, were distributed and circulated in various working-class establishments.[40]

Alarmed, the leaders of the Jewish community began to look for ways to defend their people against a possible attack. Delegations of prominent Jews were formed to seek protection and help from the authorities. On several occasions, they managed to speak with Governor von Raaben himself, who seemed to be listening with sympathy and concern. The governor reportedly sought to calm the Jews, reassuring them that there would be no violence. He even ordered some modest measures to increase the presence of police and soldiers in the city during the Easter holidays. But he apparently took no extraordinary measures to squelch the rumors or to head off violence.[41]

Another delegation approached Bishop Iakov, the Orthodox metropolitan of Kishinev, with a request that he take a public stand against the legend of ritual murder and urge his clergy to do likewise. The Christian clergy, it was hoped, could do much to refute the dangerous slanders, calm their agitated flocks, and instill a sense of decency and humaneness in the popular attitude toward Jews. The churchman, however, was evasive and non-committal. He seemed to have little knowledge of Jewish religious practices or dietary laws, and his listeners got the impression that he himself actually believed in the ritual murder legend. This impression was confirmed several days later when the bishop told an acquaintance that it was "useless to deny" that some Jews use Christian blood for ritual purposes. Not all Jews, he was quick to add, were guilty of this crime: it was only the so-called "Khuzid" sect that actually consumed Christian blood, concealing their actions from the rest of their Jewish brethren.[42] Little help, it was obvious, could be expected from the Orthodox hierarchy.

Meanwhile, another rumor began to spread, further fueling the passions already existing in Kishinev. A Russian girl who worked as a housemaid for Dr. Kohan, a Jewish physician, apparently took her life. She was taken to the Jewish hospital where, according to later reports, an examination of her corpse and bodily emissions revealed that she had poisoned herself. But the popular version that circulated among the common folk was that she had actually been murdered by Jews, who were intent on using her blood, and that her corpse had been marked by wounds on the heels and other suspicious places. This tale was not reported in the newspapers, so it did not have as much impact as the Dubossary reports. Still, it served to further heighten tensions, and it provided another sign of approaching trouble for the Jews of Kishinev.[43]

As Passover and Easter of 1903 approached, then, the situation in Kishinev became increasingly tense. *Bessarabets*, although it refrained from printing any more ritual murder stories, continued to publish derogatory articles about Jews.[44] An atmosphere of foreboding enveloped the city's Jewish community, and many other residents came to expect that the Easter holidays would be marred by some sort of incident.[45] Okhrana chief Levendal, aware of these expectations, reported to his superiors in Saint Petersburg that trouble was brewing in Kishinev.[46]

Local police officials also knew of the danger but, in view of the prevailing anti-Semitism of the authorities, hesitated to take any action that would seem to support the Jews. In anticipation of possible problems, it is true, some actions were taken by the chief of police and the commander of the local military garrison. Police were dispatched to the public gathering areas and, in order to augment the police, soldiers were stationed at various points throughout the city for the first three days of Easter. Little was done, however, to counteract and discredit the rumors and fears that continued to spread among the working-class Christians and Jews. Many community leaders, including the mayor and prominent Jews, refused to believe that a massive pogrom could occur in the twentieth century in a city like Kishinev: the Jewish community was too large, there were numerous police and gendarmes in town, and there were 10,000 soldiers in the vicinity.[47] Events, unhappily, would prove them very wrong.

CHAPTER 4

Pogrom!

The Kishinev pogrom began on Easter Sunday and lasted two full days. Numerous bands of Christian rioters, moving throughout the Jewish sectors of the city, wreaked havoc and destruction upon Jewish shops and homes. At first their attacks were directed mostly against property but, as time went on, they became emboldened by the inactivity of the local police and began making brutal and murderous attacks against the Jewish people themselves. Not until late afternoon of the second day did the authorities take effective measures to quell the disorders, using soldiers from the local garrison. By that time, an appalling amount of damage and bloodshed had occurred.

The Rioting Begins

Sunday, April 6, 1903, was a major holiday in Kishinev. It was Easter, the holiest of holy days on the Orthodox Church calendar, and it also marked the last day of the Jewish Passover. Spring was just beginning in Bessarabia and, for Christians, the long Lenten fast was over. The weather this Easter, unlike that of the previous year, was excellent. It was a good day to be outdoors, a day of rest and celebration, and the people were in a festive mood. But there was also a sense of tension and anxiety, owing to the anti-Jewish rumors and libels that had spread among the Christians during the past several months.[1]

In the early afternoon, as was their custom, some of the townsfolk began to stroll along the broad boulevards of upper Kishinev, enjoying the nice day, while others started to congregate in various places about town. One particularly popular spot was Chuflinskii Square, a large open area in the southeastern part of town, not far from the city's New Marketplace. In the square there stood a merry-go-round, a number of booths, and various forms of amusement. By mid-afternoon, a crowd of about 600 persons had assembled, most of them simple folk from among the area's unskilled workers and lower classes. Many of them were youngsters, who amused them-selves by playing a variety of children's games. Several among the adults were already drunk. Sometime around one o'clock the chief of police stopped by the square, observed the carousing crowd, and advised some of them to disperse. A few objected, arguing that "even on a holiday like this there is no law against being outdoors."[2]

According to several witnesses, the young people in the holiday crowd eventually found other, more troublesome ways to amuse themselves. Some of them gathered around individual Jews who happened to be present in the square and began shouting, as if it were a joke, "Beat the Yids!" They hounded their unfortunate vic-tims, and chased them from the square. This spectacle continued for some time, and the Christian adults, gathered in the square and strolling along the adjoining streets, apparently did nothing to stop it.[3]

By late afternoon, things were beginning to get out of hand. The size of the crowd was growing, drunkenness was increasing, and adults were beginning to get into the act. Gradually, smaller groups began to separate from the crowd and move out from Chuflinskii Square along the adjoining streets. One crowd gathered on Kirov, a small residential street that ran north from the square. Another assembled along Aleksandrov Street, which formed the square's northern boundary. They began to throw rocks at nearby Jewish residences, breaking a window in the home of Ruvin Feldman, which sat on the corner of Kirov and Aleksandrov.[4]

Before long a number of small groups, each composed of 10 or 15 rioters, had begun to fan out from the square. According to one account there were 24 such groups, each acting similarly and simul-taneously. The young hooligans took the lead, whistling, shouting, throwing rocks, and breaking the windows of Jewish homes and shops. Behind them came more rioters, mostly men armed with canes and crowbars, who engaged mainly in vandalism. In their wake, finally, came the looters and scavengers. These included both men and women, bystanders who smelled plunder and decided to help themselves. Often, it was reported, the rioters were accompanied by people who urged them on and who pointed out to them which establishments were Jewish.[5]

There does not appear to have been any single incident which touched off the rioting. Later, the official report would claim that the disorders began in response to a dispute involving the merry-go-round and its owner. According to this account, the trouble began when the "Jewish" carousel owner clashed with a Christian woman and knocked her child from her arms.[6] This, however, could not have been the case. For one thing, the owner of the merry-go-round was not Jewish; for another thing, the carousel itself was not operating that Easter Sunday. The previous year, in an effort to preserve internal calm, the Ministry of Interior had sent out a letter ordering that these sorts of amusements be kept closed on such holidays.[7]

Indeed, the evidence suggests that the outburst was not entirely spontaneous. The very fact that the rioters divided themselves up into small groups, and fanned out in various directions, seems to indicate at least some degree of planning. So does the fact that they all engaged in similar activities: rock throwing, window breaking, and looting. Had the disturbances been merely an unplanned response to some provocative incident, it seems quite likely that the rioters would have stayed together, acting as a mob, and would have been much more varied in their vandalism.

Furthermore, the places that they attacked were almost exclusively Jewish. Many local Christians, anxious to protect their shops and homes from violence, had chalked large crosses on their doors or displayed holy icons prominently in their windows. The crowds, in general, refrained from attacking these premises. But in several cases where Jews, hoping to deceive the rioters, displayed crosses or icons, the vandals were undeterred. The crowds may have been drunk and disorderly, but they clearly knew their targets. They did not, for the most part, engage in the sort of indiscriminate violence that would have been typical of a spontaneous, unplanned outburst.[8]

At any rate, if the rioters were prepared, the police most definitely were not. Despite the fact that rumors had circulated for several weeks about impending Easter violence, and despite the fact that Jewish leaders had more than once appealed to the authorities for protection, relatively little had been done to anticipate trouble. Beefed up police patrols had been stationed at those areas where crowds were most likely to gather, and several military patrols from the local garrison had been placed at the disposal of the police.[9] These measures, however, were by no means exceptional, and they soon proved to be far from adequate.

The lack of an effective police response, in fact, seems to have contributed greatly to the spread of the disorders. The police largely were conspicuous by their absence that Sunday afternoon, and those few who were present took little action. Several officers did try to detain some young lawbreakers, according to later reports, but the hooligans easily eluded them by scattering in various directions amidst the holiday crowds. Other than this, no concerted effort was made to disperse or arrest the rioters, lending credence to the rumors that the anti-Jewish violence was officially condoned, and emboldening those who might otherwise have been hesitant to take part.[10]

The Orthodox bishop, too, may have contributed to the impression that the vandalism was authorized and approved. While riding to the home of a local nobleman to partake in Easter supper, Metropolitan Iakov traveled through the streets where the vandalizing crowds already were at work. True to his usual custom, he apparently gave the bystanders his blessing as he passed by in his carriage. Whether or not he was fully aware of what was taking place, his actions could only have encouraged and legitimized the rioters.[11]

By early evening, unhindered by serious resistance, the disorders had become widespread. From Chuflinskii Square the riotous groups had gone off in various directions, throwing rocks and breaking windows as they went. Some moved along Aleksandrov Street to the New Marketplace, where they overturned some wooden bins and tried to make off with the goods inside. Other bands, led mostly by juveniles, moved along adjoining streets, shouting, breaking windows, and occasionally carrying off some loot. Along Gostinnii Street, a major thoroughfare running parallel to Aleksandrov, they fell upon a tobacco store and a shoemaker shop, both owned by Jews. In the vandalism that ensued, each building was seriously

damaged, and the property inside was either carried off or destroyed. For about four hours, from roughly six to ten o'clock in the
evening, the small crowds ran rampant. After nightfall, however,
the rioting gradually ceased, although some of the hooligans continued to break windows as they moved homeward along the roads to
the working class suburbs. By eleven o'clock the city was quiet.[12]

The violence wrought by the rioters that Sunday was extensive,
but it was limited in scope and restricted largely to property damage. The participants were mostly men and boys of lower-class
background. Some sought to enrich themselves at Jewish expense,
but most were content simply to engage in wanton vandalism.
Their targets, apparently, were mainly Jewish shops. Windows were
broken, stores looted, products and possessions destroyed. The damage was confined mostly to the easternmost part of town, in the
general vicinity of the square where the riots began. And, while
Jewish businesses bore the brunt of the attack, Jewish homes and
apartments were pretty much left unscathed.[13]

On Sunday evening, therefore, it looked as if the disturbance had
been relatively mild. According to the official indictment, only 60
persons were arrested for taking part in that day's disorders, and
physical violence was minimal. At least one prominent Jew even
began to wonder whether his earlier fears had been exaggerated. To
others, however, the situation was more alarming. Dr. Sitsinskii,
the head physician at the city hospital, would later testify that 22
injured persons were admitted on the first day of the pogrom and
four dead bodies—two Christians and two Jews—were also brought
in that day. His testimony, however, seems more consistent with
what happened the following day, when violence and bloodshed
enveloped the entire city.[14]

The Easter Monday Massacres

Monday, April 7, the day after Easter, turned out to be the bloodiest
and most eventful day of the Kishinev pogrom. During the course of
that day, the riot came to encompass much of the city and several
of its working-class suburbs. During that day, the crowds moved
from commercial into residential districts, attacking the homes,
apartments, and residences of local Jews. And during that day the

attacks against property turned into atrocities against persons, manifesting themselves in beatings, bludgeonings, and murders. Meanwhile, at least until late afternoon, local authorities did little to contain the violence or stop the terrible carnage.

The first signs of trouble appeared early on Monday morning. Small groups of Christians began to assemble in various places throughout the city and in the surrounding area, apparently determined to renew the attacks upon the Jews. Meanwhile, a number of Jewish merchants, dismayed by the lack of police protection they had thus far received, decided to take steps to defend themselves. Around 6:00 A.M., it was later reported, over 100 Jewish men assembled in the city's New Marketplace, determined to prevent a repetition of the previous day's vandalism. According to official accounts, most were armed with stakes and canes, and a few may have even had firearms. Likewise, several smaller groups of Jews gathered elsewhere that morning for mutual protection and defense.[15]

The Jewish efforts at self-defense, however, were of little use. The merchants assembled at the New Marketplace easily drove away a small group of potential rioters, but their actions also attracted the attention of the authorities. Before long, the police arrived and confronted the Jewish crowd. Its leaders explained that, since the authorities seemed unable or unwilling to give them protection, they had decided to provide it themselves. In spite of their protests, however, the police dispersed the group, arresting several Jews in the process. The Russian authorities, so slow and ineffective in responding to Christian rioters, showed themselves quite capable of moving decisively when it came to restraining the Jews![16]

This incident, along with several other attempts by Jews to organize an effective resistance, gave rise to all sorts of wild rumors that circulated among the Christians. The word spread that the Jews were on the attack, that they were beating up Christians, and that several had already been hurt. Before long the stories were embellished and distorted beyond recognition. According to one rumor, which probably originated when a group of Jews sought protection from an Orthodox cleric, the Jews had allegedly plundered a cathedral, defiled its holy objects, and murdered its priest.[17]

The rumors spread quickly, by word of mouth, throughout the city's Christian population, which was already inflamed by the pamphlets, posters, and tales which had circulated before Easter. The anti-Semitic articles which had been printed in *Bessarabets* lent credence to even the most absurd charges. The actions of the police and soldiers, which seemed to condone the violence, made plausible the notion of an officially sponsored, three-day period of Jew-beating. And the widespread reports that Jews were attacking Christians, however inaccurate, stirred up emotions of fear and anger among the rioters. As a result, what had started out as an limited exercise in holiday violence, expressing itself in vandalism and looting at the expense of the local Jews, now turned into something much more bloody and grisly.[18]

It was in the vicinity of the New Marketplace, not far from Chuflinskii Square, that the violence resumed on Monday. Several groups of rioters seem to have entered the city by mid-morning from various points in the working-class suburbs. Many of them congregated first around Chuflinskii Square, and then moved in groups to the New Marketplace. From there they fanned out in smaller groups along streets and lanes, attacking homes and apartments as well as shops and stores. In the process, a number of spectators joined in, swelling the size of the crowds. They fell upon one building after another, breaking in the windows and doors, smashing the furniture, tearing things into shreds, and littering the floors and streets with their handiwork.[19]

In the beginning, the disorders on Monday followed much the same pattern as they had the previous day. Small groups of 15 or 20 rioters, composed mostly of youths and unskilled workers, spread out over the city wreaking havoc and destruction. As on Sunday, they were often led by teenage boys, shouting and breaking windows as they went. As on Sunday, they encountered no real resistance from the police. As time went on, however, the crowds grew in number, reinforced by onlookers who were urged to join in by the rioters and emboldened by the lack of resistance. Some joined the rampaging mobs, others broke off and formed their own groups, and still others simply followed behind the rioters, observing the spectacle and occasionally helping themselves to some loot. All this was done in plain view of the general public, which was still enjoying the Easter holidays. Although the participants themselves were mostly lower-class males, their actions were observed—and sometimes even encouraged—by a number of middle-class townsfolk, and even some officials, notables, and nobles.[20]

As the disorders progressed on Monday, they became much more extensive than they had been before. On Sunday, the rioting had been confined to a limited area and, according to one estimate, fewer than 500 people had taken part. On Monday, disorders occurred throughout the entire city, and large numbers of people got into the act. The exact number of participants is unknown, but it is known that upwards of 800 people were eventually arrested or detained. Many more, no doubt, managed to avoid detection, and were thus never brought to account. It seems probable, then, that at the height of the pogrom on Monday as many as several thousand people may have been involved.[21]

Those who made up the rioting crowds fell into several distinct categories. First came the young men and teenage boys, often at the forefront of the crowds, who engaged mainly in window-breakage and vandalism. Some of these appear to have been youthful hoodlums and hooligans, who joined in for the sport, but many were also respectable students from the local schools and seminaries. A second group of rioters were the "dark people"—illiterate and semi-literate artisans, unskilled workers, and vagabonds. Some of these were outsiders who had come to the city for the holidays, while others were local Moldavians, Ukrainians, and Russians from the working class suburbs on the outskirts of the city. Most of them were adult males. These people, often armed with clubs and crowbars, carried out much of the wholesale destruction, and many of the beatings and murders. A third group, which included both men and women, was composed mainly of townsfolk who witnessed the riots and decided to get in on the act. Some of these actually took part in the violence; others simply looted and plundered.[22]

By Monday afternoon the whole town was enveloped, especially the Jewish sectors. The ruffians broke into shops and stores, destroying everything they came across. Some of the articles they tore up or smashed to smithereens; others they simply threw out into the street to be picked up by looters or destroyed by other rioters. At the dress shops and apparel stores, the clothing that was not torn to shreds was often picked up and tried on by looters, who then went on their way dressed in the stolen apparel. At the wine shops and liquor stores, the bottles were broken indiscriminately, and their contents were either poured out on the ground or consumed on the premises by the rioters.[23]

It was in the residential neighborhoods, however, that the most serious crimes took place. Breaking into the homes and apartments of working-class Jews, the rioters took out their fury on both property and persons. Pieces of furniture—tables, beds, sofas, and cabinets—were smashed to pieces or thrown out on the street. China and glassware were broken, clothing and bedding torn apart, and cooking utensils destroyed. Feather beds and feather pillows, possessed by even the poorest Jewish families, were torn to shreds, creating an eerie scene in the Jewish neighborhoods. The air was filled with the small white feathers which were bandied about by the breeze and then settled, almost like snow, over the scenes of violence and mayhem.[24] Some of the Jews, fearing for their lives, tried to run away; others sought to hide or barricade themselves in their homes. Many, however, were caught and beaten by the mobs. Most often they were battered about the head, with the attackers using clubs, canes, crowbars, and other such blunt instruments.[25]

For administrative purposes, Kishinev was divided up into four police precincts, with a fifth incorporating a number of the suburbs. Disorders occurred in all of these areas, but some were hit harder than others.[26]

The first precinct, which encompassed the "better" sections in the central and southwest parts of town, was the one least affected by the violence. This was where the city's wealthiest citizens lived, in stately stone buildings along broad, tree-lined boulevards. Not surprisingly, this is where police protection seems to have been strongest. Relatively few Jews lived in this area, although it did include a number of Jewish shops and stores. A few groups of rioters did venture into this precinct on Monday afternoon, but they limited themselves to attacks against property rather than persons. Several Jewish stores on Pushkin Street and Nikolaevskii Boulevard were damaged, as were a number of commercial establishments and private apartments along Politseiskii Lane. Grocery stores, wine shops, and other small businesses also were vandalized, and even some private homes had their windows broken. For the most part, however, the crowds did not attack people, and there were no murders reported in this part of town.[27]

The situation was quite different in the second precinct, located in southeastern Kishinev. This was a commercial and residential area with a predominantly Jewish population consisting mainly of merchants and artisans. Its people lived mostly in middle-class neighborhoods; they were not as prosperous as those in the first precinct, but neither were they impoverished. It was in this sector, at Chuflinskii Square, that the riots had begun on Sunday. It was in this sector, at the New Marketplace, that the Jewish merchants had tried to defend themselves early on Monday morning. It was in this sector, that same morning, that the disorders had resumed. Not surprisingly, then, it was this area that experienced the most widespread damage, as well as the greatest numbers of murders and beatings. The rioting bands attacked homes and shops along every street and lane in this precinct, focusing almost exclusively on Jewish properties and avoiding those owned by Christians.[28]

The most extensive bloodshed in the second precinct occurred along Gostinnii Street, where much of the Sunday violence had also taken place. At least four men and one woman were killed in the household at address number 33, where some sixteen families lived. When the rioters approached, many of the residents concealed themselves in the loft, but they were soon discovered and beaten. One young Jew, Benjamin Baranovich, had hidden in a closet; the crowd broke in through the ceiling and, despite his own pleas and those of his father, mercilessly beat him to death. Rose Katsap, an elderly woman, was bludgeoned to death in the yard while her grandson looked on from hiding. A baker named David Drachman, a cattle dealer named Ben-Zion Galantor, and a joiner named Joseph Kantor were also killed by the mob. Up the street, at address number 66, the mayhem was just as bad. Here, according to the official indictment, a Christian boy named Gregory Ostapov was mortally wounded by a gunshot as the crowd attacked the house. Enraged, the rioters murdered a cabdriver named Joseph Greenberg, who allegedly had refused to take the boy to the hospital. In the courtyard of the home they also killed Aaron Brachman and his son-in-law Isaac Rosenfeld, while seriously wounding Aaron's wife.

By early evening, when the rioting finally ceased, at least eighteen Jews had lost their lives in the second precinct alone, while scores of others had been injured by the rampaging mobs.[29]

The fourth precinct, in the northeastern sector of town, also suffered extensive damage. This area was located just north of the second precinct, where the riots had begun. It was a poor Jewish area, part of "lower Kishinev," the older and less prosperous part of town. Smaller homes, often housing a number of families, crowded the narrow, dusty streets and the tiny, stone-walled courtyards. Once the disorders had resumed on Monday, it did not take long for the violence to spread to this district.[30]

Around ten o'clock in the morning, according to later accounts, a policeman arrived along Asia Street with news that trouble was brewing in the upper part of town. He apparently advised the Jews to lock themselves in their homes and be silent; aside from this he took no action. Within an hour or so the crowds arrived, coming from the vicinity of the railway station and Chuflinskii Square, armed with clubs and crowbars, and wreaking havoc everywhere they went. Businesses and shops—including the New Bessarabia hotel, several groceries, bakeries, wine shops, a jewelry store, and even a brothel—were ransacked and destroyed, with pieces of furniture and merchandise left strewn about the streets. One Jew, a certain Chaim-Leib Goldis, was beaten to death; another Jew named Elik Rosenberg reportedly shot at the crowd in a futile effort to save his home.[31]

By the time they reached Asia Street, a few blocks from the River Byk, the marauders had tasted blood, and any sense of restraint or moderation had long since disappeared. Attacking the building at 13 Asia Street, which housed eight Jewish families and a grocery store, they went into a furious rage, breaking the windows and doors, tearing up bibles and bedding, littering the area with paper scraps and feathers, and hunting for the unfortunate residents. One Jew, a glazier named Mottel Greenspoon, was found hiding in an outdoor shed; he was stabbed to death by several Moldavian rioters, at least one of whom he had known. The landlord, Moses Makhlin, along with a certain Hosea Berlatsky and his daughter, tried to hide in the attic. When the mob approached, they then broke through to the roof, but the ruffians followed them, beat them, and pushed them down onto the street, where they were killed with crowbars by the crowd below. Chaim Nissenson, who had hidden in the cellar, was chased to the street, beaten with clubs, and left lying in a huge puddle; he died from his wounds the following day. This scene, later described by novelist V. G. Korolenko in "House Number 13," was repeated elsewhere on a smaller scale. At least seven Jews were murdered in the fourth precinct, in the midst of appalling damage and bloodshed.[32]

The third precinct, in the northwestern part of town, did not suffer as severely. It, too, was a working-class area which encompassed part of "lower Kishinev." It, too, was home to many poor Jews, along with poor people of other nationalities. In this sector was the Old Marketplace, as well as numerous small shops and homes. Extensive damage was wrought in this area but, perhaps because it was furthest from the origin of the disorders, the bloodshed was less extensive. At least one Jew, however, a certain Isaac Belitskii, did lose his life in this precinct.[33]

Aside from the four precincts of the city proper, the violence extended even into the suburbs. These areas were populated largely by working-class Moldavians, interspersed with some Russians, Jews, and others. Many of the rioters, in fact, seem to have come from the suburbs. Some went into the city to take part in the riots; others took out their aggression against the Jews in their own neighborhoods. As a result, the disorders in the suburbs bore a somewhat more personal character: the rioters were not "outsiders," as in the city, but local residents. On the whole, they were a slightly more prosperous group than those who went into the city, and they were more likely to be acquainted with their victims. These factors, however, did not mitigate the violence: the Jews in the suburbs did suffer greatly, and the disorders there continued for some time after they had ceased in the city itself.[34]

The violence in the suburbs began late in the morning on Monday, the second day of the pogrom, and got increasingly brutal as the day went on. The regions hardest hit were the areas known as Skulianskii Turnpike and Muncheshtskii Road, to the east of the city. A carpenter's shed on Skulianskii, used for repairing carriages, was the scene of several grisly killings, including the reported assault and murder of an adolescent girl. Along Muncheshtskii, in a stretch between the railway station and the Nobel company's kerosene storehouse, six persons were murdered, one house was gutted by fire, and 44 Jewish homes, shops, and workshops were badly damaged by crowds. Elsewhere there were similar atrocities, including an incident in which a certain Meyer Weissman, already sightless in one eye, was blinded completely by a young Christian boy. At least 12 Jews lost their lives in the suburbs, and numerous others were wounded.[35]

The rioting in the outskirts of the city extended late into Monday evening, and in some spots even resumed and continued on Tuesday, April 8. As in the city, properties owned by prominent Jews were attacked and ransacked, with furniture destroyed, glass broken, and books and papers scattered about.[36] In Kishinev itself, however, the pogrom ended on Monday evening, when the authorities finally took decisive measures to halt the wanton violence.

The Actions of the Authorities

The response of the authorities to the Kishinev pogrom was at best confused and inadequate, and at worst perhaps even criminal. The governor, the police chief, and other key officials should not have been caught unawares: they had received ample warning of impending violence even as Easter approached. Still, they failed to take any exceptional steps to prepare for possible violence. They did make an effort to increase police patrols, and to augment the police with soldiers in the areas where trouble was considered most likely. But, once the pogrom actually broke out, they were unable—and in some cases unwilling—to coordinate activities and respond effectively for over 24 hours. This delay not only allowed the riots to continue, it actually helped make them worse. The rioters, seeing the inaction of the police and soldiers, became increasingly convinced that their plunder and pillage was authorized from above.[37]

The city's mayor, Karl Schmidt, first became aware of the rioting late Sunday afternoon. He was enjoying dinner at a friend's home, between five and six o'clock, when his meal was interrupted as a group of young vandals passed by breaking windows. He took this as a sign that the Easter riots, about which he had heard rumors, had actually begun. Although he himself was a Lutheran, Schmidt was known to be sympathetic to the Jews, so he feared for the safety of his family. Arriving home, he came upon several groups of rioters, one of whom was about to throw rocks at his windows. In the nick of time, however, one of the leaders shouted that this was the mayor's house, and pointed instead to the home of a local Jew named Grossman. Badly frightened, Schmidt holed up in his home with his family. Despite his reputation, he did nothing to stop the disorders or help the victimized Jews. He does not even seem to have contacted the police or the governor, nor did he take any action of his own until the governor called him, the following day, after the worst of the rioting was over.[38]

Meanwhile, the law enforcement authorities were beginning to respond. According to his own later testimony, Police Chief Khanzhenkov made several routine stops at Chuflinskii Square on Easter Sunday. The first time, around one o'clock, he noted some unruly behavior among the 600–odd persons who were there celebrating the holiday. The second time, between four and five o'clock, he learned that groups of vandals had begun throwing rocks through windows. He tried to persuade the rabble-rousers to go home, but he was only partially successful: many of them left the square, but only to resume their unruly behavior elsewhere.[39]

Khanzhenkov's first instinct, after the early efforts to disperse the crowds had failed, was to ask for military support. By his own account, he had received several anonymous warnings about the impending disorders, but he had not given them much credence. Now, faced with the growing disorders on Easter afternoon, he found his police forces badly undermanned and unprepared. To patrol the entire city, according to his own estimate, he had at his disposal scarcely more than 200 policemen. So he paid a visit to Governor von Raaben and asked him for reinforcements from among the local troops. The governor, who was already aware of the problem, directed Khanzhenkov to the commander of the local garrison, Lieutenant General Bekman. According to one account, von Raaben acted with little sense of urgency and, as was his custom, spent the evening playing cards at a local club. Precious time was lost, then, as Khanzhenkov left the governor's residence and went to visit the garrison commander. Arriving between eight and nine o'clock that evening, he proceeded to explain the situation to Bekman and to ask him, in the governor's name, to increase the number of troops on guard in the city.[40]

Not surprisingly, Governor von Raaben had a different recollection of the way things developed. He recalled that he first learned of the troubles around five o'clock on Easter Sunday, when a phone call informed him that anti-Jewish riots had broken out near Chuflinskii Square. He immediately phoned the police, only to learn that the chief was already on the scene, and that all available policemen had been called out on street duty. This was followed by a long series of phone calls, as information began to pour in about the various acts of violence. Knowing that police strength was inadequate, von Raaben then decided to call out the troops, but ran into delays because so many soldiers were off duty on the holiday. Those who were called up, the governor later insisted, were given clear instructions to take forceful measures, and even to use firearms if necessary to stop the devastation. While all this was going on the police chief appeared and, as darkness was setting in, reported that the rioting had ceased.[41]

By this time, the local officials in Kishinev were also taking pains to inform the central government of what was going on. The minister of interior, who had accompanied the emperor to Moscow for the Easter holidays, was one of the first high officials to learn about the pogrom. According to his chancellor, he received a late-evening wire from Governor von Raaben explaining that disturbances had broken out, and that soldiers would have to be called in to restore order. That same night, the minister of justice learned from the Kishinev prosecutor, V. N. Goremykin, that there had been an attack upon Jewish shops and homes. Goremykin's telegram went on to report that the governor had asked for troops, that 60 arrests had been made, that firearms had not been used, and that the disorders had apparently ceased.[42]

Meanwhile, on the outskirts of Kishinev, the commander of the local garrison was beginning to take action. Responding to the requests of the governor and police chief, according to his later testimony, General Vladimir Aleksandrovich Bekman ordered three infantry companies and two cavalry squadrons to take up positions in the city.[43]

General Bekman, a man of some wealth and distinction, was 54 years old, a career military officer, and a Lutheran. He was described by a Jewish acquaintance as an honorable man, professional and correct, with no trace of anti-Semitism.[44] And, in theory, his actions that evening seemed quite appropriate to deal with the situation: when the additional troops joined the police and soldiers already on duty in Kishinev, substantial forces would be available to combat potential disorders. But in practice they were neither timely nor effective: the new soldiers did not move in until Monday morning, and no clear orders were given them as to what their duties would be. General Bekman apparently thought he was placing them at the disposal of the governor, whose duty it was to direct the military unless and until a direct order to use weapons was given. Von Raaben, perhaps unaware of this, seems to have assumed that he had done his duty merely by calling out the troops and instructing them to use their discretion.[45]

On Monday morning, then, as the rioting resumed, the Jews began to press the authorities for more effective protection. At first, when a group of Jewish leaders stopped by the governor's residence to ask for help, they were told that von Raaben was still asleep. Despite their entreaties, the officer in charge refused to disturb his superior. The Jews then visited Mayor Schmidt, who reportedly burst into tears and told them he could do nothing. After this they approached the vice-governor, Ustrugov, who likewise pleaded impotence and informed them that only the governor had the power to act. Finally, joined by a prominent Jewish doctor, lawyer, and rabbi, they went back to the governor's residence and actually met with von Raaben.[46]

The governor at this point seemed genuinely concerned, and spoke as if he were determined to head off further trouble. He talked about making a personal tour of the city, to see what he could do, and at one point he apparently had the horses hitched to his carriage. However, after a conversation with Okhrana chief Levendal, he changed his mind and decided that he had to stay by the telephone so he could receive information, issue orders, and coordinate activities. What Levendal said is unknown, but the circumstances of his visit gave rise to suspicions that he had purposely dissuaded von Raaben from taking decisive action.[47]

The governor himself, however, would later defend vigorously his decision to stay put. In a situation where numerous small riots were breaking out simultaneously, he claimed, it would have been futile for him to try to direct the troops in person. Since he could not possibly be present everywhere at once, he decided to remain in his residence, following developments and issuing directives by phone. From this central location, he would have a better grasp of the overall situation, and more complete information on which to base his decisions. From his office, as from nowhere else, he would have ready access by phone to the police and civil authorities, as well as to the banks, jails, factories, hospitals, and railway stations. As it turned out, in fact, he was able to coordinate and initiate a number of activities without ever leaving his home. From his perspective, then, the decision not to travel about the city was justified by the unique circumstances of the actual pogrom.[48]

It does appear, however, that the governor's lack of visibility contributed greatly to the inaction of the soldiers, and to the overall impression of administrative indifference. As a result of it, there was no one present to issue orders to the troops once the violence began to get out of hand. Assuming they had no authority to use force except in self-defense, many patrols remained inactive for hours while awaiting further instructions. The chief of police would later complain that the troops acted independently of the police, largely ignoring instructions and refusing to make arrests. Some limited themselves to dispersing the crowds, which then reassembled elsewhere. Others merely asked the troublemakers to go away, or looked on passively while the looting and vandalism occurred. Some soldiers, it was later alleged, actively urged on the rioters, and a few even joined in the looting. On several occasions, military units actually marched down the middle of a street, ignoring the plundering and pillaging occurring on either side.[49]

Unfortunately, therefore, the augmentation of the police by military forces had little impact in preventing further violence. If anything, it seems to have had the opposite effect. Even when they did witness serious crimes and outrages, the soldiers often did nothing to stop them. Lacking clear instructions, and sympathizing in some instances with the anti-Jewish crowds, they made only sporadic and ineffective efforts to restore order. The impression was left, on many Jews and Christians alike, that the soldiers were there mainly to protect the property of prominent Christians, and that both military and civilian "peacekeeping" forces were actually supporting the rioters.[50]

Despite the impression his actions may have created, the governor later insisted that he had been neither indifferent nor inactive. At nine o'clock on Monday, even before the rioting resumed, he had met with the police chief and instructed him to be on the watch for signs of further trouble. By 9:30, as a preliminary step, he had sent a message to General Bekman asking that all troops be placed on alert. At 10:00, when he learned by phone that the troubles were starting anew, he began taking calls and receiving concerned visitors, including the Jewish delegation and the chief of the local Okhrana. At 11:30, as the disorders spread throughout the entire city, he met with the garrison commander and other military leaders to plan an effective response. They agreed to divide the town into sectors, to place an officer in charge of each sector, and to call in the remaining troops from their barracks. When the military officers pointed out that they could not use firearms without a direct order from the governor, von Raaben later testified, he gave them written authorization to use weapons as needed. Remaining in his office, he then sent the vice-governor out in his place, instructing him to visit the scenes of disorder, urge the soldiers to act energetically, and invoke the governor's authority to end the disorders. From his central location, then, he proceeded to issue directives dispatching troops to various locations, protecting banks and industrial establishments, closing down wine shops, and arranging for medical help. In response to a phone call from the Jewish hospital, he sent over a detachment of soldiers to guard that facility; when the doctors ran short of bandaging material, he arranged to have a supply provided. Later, when it became apparent that there were insufficient jail spaces to house all the arrested rioters, he phoned the mayor and enlisted his help in arranging appropriate facilities. With the mayor's assistance, he also took steps to protect the city's food and water supply.[51]

The governor's actions, however energetic, appear to have been more concerned with protecting the city than they were with defending the Jews. Rather than taking strong measures to end the disturbances, he instead sought to limit their damage. Above all, it seems, he was anxious to prevent the riots from taking on an anti-government character, as he had reason to believe that a political demonstration might in fact occur. But this only detracted from the overall effort to restore order. At one point, for example, a number of soldiers were sent to hide near the city gardens, where a large political gathering was expected. But the information supplied by the Okhrana soon proved to be inaccurate, and the troops waited in vain for a meeting that never took place.[52]

As a result of all this, the riots continued, and the actions of the authorities did little to stem the violence. Vice-Governor Ustrugov, with his anti-Semitic reputation, was a poor substitute for the governor, and he appears to have done little to bring things under control. It was later alleged, in fact, that he actually encouraged the rioters.[53] Police Chief Khanzhenkov, although he did make several efforts to disperse the crowds, was hardly a model of responsible law enforcement. According to some accounts he insulted Jews, drove around smoking cigarettes, and made visits to friends in upper Kishinev.[54] Another police official was said to have led a crowd of rioters, while a third was accused of using his apartment to store loot which had been plundered from the Jews.[55]

General Bekman, meanwhile, spent the early afternoon traveling about the city and communicating instructions to the various military units. His efforts, however, were frustrated by the lack of coordination between the military and civil authorities, and by the governor's attempts to handle things over the phone. The troops were ordered about, he would later complain, without organization or system. When reports of trouble came in, individual units were dispatched to the scene, but they often arrived after the damage had been done and the crowds had moved on.[56] Throughout much of the day, it is apparent, confusion and disorganization reigned supreme.

By mid-afternoon, it was clear to the authorities that things had gotten totally out of control. Governor von Raaben, in a long, coded telegram to the minister of interior, painted a very bleak picture. The rioters, he reported, appeared to be following a prearranged plan: they were often led by intelligentsia, armed with crowbars, and were striking simultaneously in numerous places. The police had proven inadequate, the riots were becoming more acute, and there was growing fear of anti-government demonstrations. The troops had been called out, but order had not been restored. As governor, he was prepared to do everything necessary to bring the disorders to an end, and would not hesitate to order the use of firearms. A bit later, prosecutor Goremykin also reported to his superiors in Saint Petersburg that the situation was getting worse, and that people were being injured and killed.[57]

That same day, according to several reports, the minister of interior sent von Raaben a strongly worded telegram urging him to take decisive measures to restore order at once. Later on, the minister would formally place the city in a state of "strengthened security," similar to martial law. This conferred extraordinary powers on the governor to forbid assemblies, make mass arrests, and do whatever was necessary to bring the disturbances to an end.[58]

By this time, however, the governor had finally decided to take exceptional measures of his own. At 3:30 P.M., he issued a written order to General Bekman calling for the use of full-scale military force, including firearms, in putting down the riots. According to Bekman, this order finally gave him the authority he needed: it effectively turned over full control of the troops to the military authorities. The general immediately had the order published, and began making the rounds of the various units, scattered throughout the city, to give them new instructions and move them to new locations. By five o'clock, the orders had been communicated and the soldiers were on the move. By six o'clock they had begun clearing the streets, making massive arrests, and taking energetic steps to bring the violence to an end.[59]

Within several hours, once the troops got moving, order had been restored. An energetic and systematic show of force proved to be sufficient to end the violence in a relatively short period of time. For the most part, in fact, the soldiers had little need to use force or resort to firearms. Once the rioters realized that the authorities were serious, and that people were being arrested for their outrages, they began to disperse on their own. Finally, by eight o'clock, the city itself was quiet.[60]

Sporadic violence, however, continued into the evening in the outskirts of the city, where no troops had yet been sent. It was not until the next morning, when reports came in about continued disorders, that soldiers were finally dispatched to the suburbs. By noon on Tuesday, even these riots had ceased, and calm had descended over most of the area. At long last, the authorities had done their job: the Kishinev pogrom was over.[61]

The Rioters and Their Victims

The end of the pogrom, of course, did not put an end to the suffering. Hundreds of persons, most of them Christians, had taken part in the violence, either as rioters or as looters. Hundreds of others, most of them Jews, had been injured, maimed, widowed, orphaned, or dispossessed. In the days that followed the rioting, the city's prisons and hospitals were filled to overflowing with those who had been involved and those who had been victimized. These people, the rioters and their victims, were the ones who experienced most directly the force and impact of the pogrom.

During the course of the disorders and the day or two that followed, over 800 persons were arrested for taking part in the pogrom. The numbers were so great that there was not nearly enough room in the city's jail to accommodate them, and officials had to find vacant buildings to use as detention sites. The logistics of feeding, identifying, questioning, and charging such a large throng strained the resources of the local police and the detention system. Many of the prisoners, for example, were brought in by military patrols, without a formal report as to where and under what circumstances they had been detained. Some had not themselves been involved in the violence, but merely were onlookers arrested for disobeying the police. At the same time, it was inevitable that many of those who were actively involved would manage to avoid arrest.[62]

Of the several thousand persons who took part in the riots, the vast majority had engaged mainly in looting and vandalism, so the bulk of the arrests reflected this fact. Most of the 800 persons arrested, in fact, were charged only with minor crimes and misdemeanors. Still, more than 100 persons were eventually placed on trial for more serious crimes, including robbery and murder.[63]

By all accounts, the rioting crowds were made up primarily of people from the lower classes, workers and peasants from Kishinev and the surrounding region. Among those whose social status was published when they were brought to trial, slightly more than half (51 percent) were identified as townsfolk of the city of Kishinev, and almost one in five (19 percent) were listed as local peasants. The remainder consisted mostly of reserve soldiers, townsfolk, and villagers from other places. Several foreign subjects, from Persia and Rumania, were also included in the mix. Only one of those who stood trial, a young man named Ivan Grigorzhevskii, identified himself as a nobleman.[64]

This is not to say, of course, that there was no one from the upper and middle classes involved in the disorders. The persons brought to trial, after all, represented only a portion of those who actually took part, and they were not necessarily a representative sample. A number of prominent people—including a notary named Pisarzhevskii, a wealthy man named Sinadino, the sons of a Circuit Court member and a justice of the peace, a landowner, an engineer, and several students—were mentioned in various sources as having taken part.[65] And, of course, there were other notable persons who helped set the stage for the pogrom but did not actually join the crowds. On the whole, however, it seems quite clear that the majority of rioters were working-class Kishinev townsfolk and peasants from nearby villages. And, although a number of women may have taken part in the looting, the rioters themselves—to judge from those brought to trial—were almost exclusively men.[66]

According to several reports, the riots were started mainly by youths, and young people played a prominent role throughout the two days of disorders.[67] Be that as it may, however, the group that was later placed on trial was not remarkable for its youth. The average age among those whose age was published was almost 33, and their median age was 31. Since the average age of non-Jewish Kishinev residents, 15 years of age and older, was approximately 35, these defendants were only slightly younger than the city's general populace. They ranged in age from 17 to 60, with the majority being in their twenties and thirties. Fewer than 10 percent, in fact, were in their teens; a similar small percentage were 50 years of age and older. Although this group, once again, represented a rather small portion of those who took part in the pogrom, there is no reason to suspect that the average age of the rest of the rioters would have been substantially higher or lower.[68]

The ethnic composition of the rioting crowds, although it cannot be precisely determined, also seems to have been more or less representative of the city's non-Jewish residents. Judging from the names of those who were brought to trial, it appears that the majority of the defendants were of Russian or Ukrainian heritage, with the rest being mostly Moldavians. This is hardly surprising, given the make-up of Kishinev's non-Jewish population. According to the 1897 census, of the city's 58,000 non-Jews about half (29,000) were Russians, about a third (19,000) were Moldavians, and about 6 percent (3,400) Ukrainians.[69]

On the whole, then, the people who took part in the pogrom, judging by those who later stood trial, seem to have represented a broad cross section of Kishinev's Christian population. They were, it appears, slightly younger than average, and they were drawn almost entirely from the lower classes. But there is no evidence that the rioters were dominated by any particular age or ethnic group. Nor, for that matter, does it appear that they were dominated by outsiders: most of the defendants, at least, hailed from Kishinev and its environs.[70]

Meanwhile, as the rioters were being arrested and charged, their victims were being cared for by the members of their own community. The Jewish hospital, to which most of the injured were taken, was forced to cope with an unprecedented disaster. As early as Monday morning, the wounded had begun to arrive, along with some who were suffering psychological trauma and others who were just seeking shelter. Those with serious injuries were taken into surgery for emergency operations; those with lesser wounds were treated on the spot. By evening, the hospital and its courtyard were overflowing with dead and wounded victims. The dead were laid on the floor of a wooden barracks, surrounded with candles and mourners, while the hospital staff worked all through the night to treat those who were still alive. On Tuesday, once the pogrom itself was over, the remaining victims were rounded up from all over town and brought in. These included disfigured corpses with broken skulls, spilled-out brains, distorted faces, and twisted jaws, as well as injured persons whose gaping wounds were caked with dirt, mud, and

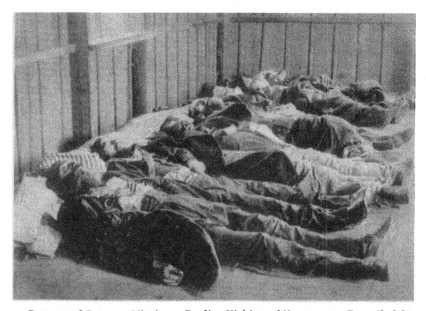

1. Corpses of Pogrom Victims. Credit: *Kishinevskii pogrom*. Compiled by the editors of *Osvobozhdenie*. Stuttgart: Verlag und Druck von J. H. W. Dietz, 1903.

feathers. Before long, friends and families showed up, and soon the hysterical sobs of the mourners competed with the anguished cries of the victims.[71]

The Kishinev pogrom, it became apparent, had taken a frightful toll. By the time the violence ended, a total of 43 persons had lost their lives. Almost all of the dead were Jews, the main victims and targets of the massacre. The only Christians to die were Gregory Ostapov, the boy who was shot in front of house number 66 on Gostinnii Street, and a man name Solov'ev, who was apparently killed by his comrades in a drunken scuffle. Eight more persons, all of them Jews, eventually died from injuries they had received during the riots. In the end, then, a total of 51 people perished as a result of the pogrom, and 49 of the dead were Jews. Of these, 38 were men and boys, and 11 were women and girls.[72]

The dead, of course, were not the only victims. By official count, according to the figures later released by the Ministry of Interior, some 424 persons were wounded, 74 of them seriously. The actual

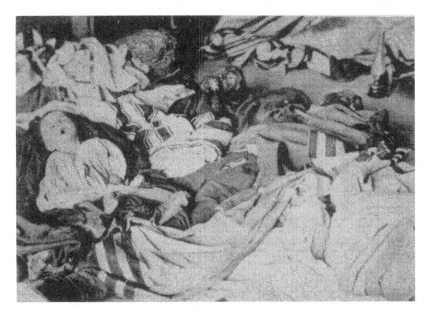

2. Battered Bodies of Pogrom Victims. Credit: *Kishinevskii pogrom*. Compiled by the editors of *Osvobozhdenie*. Stuttgart: Verlag und Druck von J. H. W. Dietz, 1903.

number of injured, however, was substantially higher than this. The bill of indictment, published in fall of 1903, set the number at 456, but even this is probably too low. Dr. M. B. Slutskii, the senior surgeon at Kishinev's Jewish hospital, would later assert that his hospital alone treated 495 persons. Ninety-five of these, he added, were seriously injured, including the eight who eventually died. The bulk of the injuries were to the victims' heads and faces, sustained as they were beaten with clubs, canes, and crowbars.[73]

Alongside the dead and wounded, there were many others who suffered terribly as a result of the pogrom. These included not only those who were widowed and orphaned, but also all of those who lost their homes and livelihoods as a result of the violence. The extent of the wreckage, according to those who toured the city in the wake of the pogrom, was appalling. On many streets, house after house and shop after shop lay in ruins, with broken glass, pieces of furniture, down feathers, and vandalized merchandise scattered everywhere. Approximately 700 homes, and about 600

3. Wounded Victims of the Kishinev Pogrom. Credit: *Kishinevskii pogrom.* Compiled by the editors of *Osvobozhdenie.* Stuttgart: Verlag und Druck von J. H. W. Dietz, 1903.

shops and stores, were victimized by the violence. Property damage, which included furniture and merchandise as well as buildings, was estimated at up to two million rubles. The most extensive destruction, of course, occurred in the city's second and fourth precincts, where the worst of the riots had taken place. In the second precinct alone, more than half of the buildings suffered, including some 600 houses, stores, and shops. According to one detailed survey, 1,350 of the 4,149 buildings in Kishinev, and 130 more structures in the suburbs, were subjected to harm by the rioters. In the city itself, then, almost one-third of all the buildings were damaged or destroyed![74]

Significantly, the areas that suffered the most were the less wealthy sections of upper Kishinev, and the impoverished neighborhoods of lower Kishinev. As a result, the bulk of the pogrom victims were working-class Jews and poor Jews, mostly artisans, shopkeepers, and their families. The dead, for example, included an apartment owner, a poultry dealer, a cattle dealer, a baker, a bread dealer, a glazier, a joiner, a blacksmith, a former bookkeeper, a bootmaker, a carpenter, a student, a wine shop proprietor, and several other shopkeepers, as well as a number of wives and mothers, and even a few children. They represented, in short, a cross section of Kishinev's Jewish community, unfortunate people who happened to be in the path of the rioters and were unable to escape their violence. Despite all the talk about Jewish exploitation, there appears to have been little pattern to the murder and destruction. The violence was directed against Jews in general, and not against specific individuals who may have been seen as exploiters.[75]

The Easter riots, then, were a major disaster for the Kishinev Jewish community. The Jews were the ones who had been vandalized, plundered, beaten, and murdered; they were the ones who had borne the brunt of the attack and experienced most of the suffering. Before long, however, it became apparent that the Jews were by no means the only victims of the massacre. As time went on, in fact, the Kishinev pogrom was to have an impact that was felt by many outside the Jewish community, and repercussions and reverberations that reached far beyond the outskirts of the city on the Byk.

CHAPTER 5

Repercussions and Reverberations

The Easter pogrom inflicted enormous destruction upon the city of Kishinev. Some of it was physical: 51 of its citizens were killed, about 500 more were injured, nearly one building in three was damaged, and hundreds of people were left homeless and jobless. Much of the damage, however, was psychological: the social and economic bonds that held the city together had been ruptured by the riots. Fears, angers, and resentments gripped the town residents. The fact that one part of the population had turned upon another part with savage fury could not be swept aside, nor could things return to normal unless painful questions were faced. Why had this happened? How could it be prevented from happening again? And, most disturbingly, who was to blame for what had taken place?

The early reports coming out of Kishinev, and the first official accounts, tended to portray the pogrom as a spontaneous outburst fueled mainly by deep-seated hostilities between the Christians and Jews. As time went on, however, and as apparent evidence of prior planning and official complicity began to surface, more and more questions were raised. Accounts in the foreign press tended to place the blame on government officials, both in Kishinev and Saint Petersburg, creating widespread indignation in many parts of the world. The Russian government, its image badly tarnished by a storm of worldwide protest, finally took steps to stabilize the situation in Kishinev, counteract the negative publicity, and repair its battered reputation.

Early Reports and Reactions

The immediate concern in Kishinev, once the violence had ceased, was to make sure the pogrom was over. For several days after calm had been restored in the city, reports of sporadic disorders continued to come in from the surrounding region. As late as Thursday, April 10, three days after the pogrom, a visiting official found that the situation was still extremely tense. By Friday, however, this same visitor was able to report that all was quiet and that, with the military in charge, things seemed to be under control.[1]

By this time, a variety of government officials had begun to descend on Kishinev, looking for clues and comments as to what had taken place. As soon as the disturbances ended, in fact, a formal investigation was initiated by the Kishinev prosecutor, V. N. Goremykin, with the aid of the local gendarmes. Within a few days A. I. Pollan, the procurator of the Odessa Chamber of Justice, arrived in town to assess the situation. His preliminary conclusions focused on the inactivity of the police and soldiers, and placed a major share of the blame on the governor and local officials.[2] "If appropriate measures had been taken on the first day of Easter," he asserted, "there would have been no disorders at all, or if they did arise somewhere they would have been stopped at once."[3]

Meanwhile the regional military commander, Count Musin-Pushkin, had likewise come to Kishinev to learn what had occurred. He met with General Bekman and other officials, then toured the Jewish hospital and spoke with patients and staff. Like Pollan, he blamed the governor for neither taking sufficient measures to end the pogrom nor authorizing the military to do so. A few days later, in response to the anxieties expressed by a Jewish delegation, he arranged to have the troops remain in Kishinev to prevent a recurrence of the disorders.[4]

The early reports from local observers soon triggered a response from the central government. On Saturday, April 12, only five days after the pogrom, the director of the Ministry of Interior's Department of Police arrived from Saint Petersburg to conduct his own investigation. It was to be a quick and rather cursory inquest: he spent less than two days in Kishinev, and concerned himself mainly with interviewing and listening to those who had been involved.[5]

Aleksei Aleksandrovich Lopukhin had been head of the imperial police for less than a year when the Kishinev pogrom occurred. He was reputed to be an open-minded man, and even something of a liberal. But he was also an ambitious young official who served under people with anti-Semitic reputations. Lopukhin's conduct in Kishinev, and the government report that followed, suggest that he and his ministry were more concerned with calming the situation, and deflecting blame from the government, than with conducting a thorough examination of what had happened and why.[6]

When Lopukhin arrived he was greeted in the city by large crowds of Jews. According to one newspaper account, they lined the sidewalks along Aleksandrov Street, and did not leave until after his carriage had passed. The next morning, a crowd of Jews "literally besieged" the hotel where the police director was staying, dispersing only when their representatives were summoned inside to talk.[7]

On Sunday, April 13, then, Lopukhin met with a delegation of about 40 Jewish leaders, including jurist E. S. Koenigshats and senior surgeon M. B. Slutskii. The Jews presented him with a long and detailed petition, couched in respectful, subservient language. It rejected the notion that the pogrom was a reaction against Jewish exploitation, asserting that there had hitherto been little conflict between Christians and Jews in Bessarabia. It instead pointed to the inflammatory articles in *Bessarabets*, the anti-Semitic attitudes of local officials, the libelous tale of "ritual murder" in Dubossary, and the vicious handbills proclaiming in the name of the tsar a three-day period of Jew-beating at Eastertide. More disturbingly, it indicated that the governor and police officials had ignored warnings of a possible pogrom, that the police and soldiers had taken no effective action until the end of the second day, that many of them had watched passively while atrocities were committed, and that some had actually urged on the rioters.[8]

According to Dr. Slutskii, Lopukhin remained passive and unmoved throughout the entire Jewish presentation. He skimmed through the petition, but he did not read it carefully. He listened to the delegates without betraying any response: he neither objected to their stories nor tried to defend the police. He instead maintained an "Olympian silence" which left them bewildered and confused.[9]

Before leaving town, the police director also held discussions

4. Imperial Police Director A. A. Lopukhin. Credit: Obninskii, Viktor Petrovich. *Posliednii samoderzhets: Ocherki zhizni i tsarstvovanie imperatora Rossii Nikolaia II-go*. Berlin: Eberhard Frowein, [1912].

with other officials and community leaders. According to one account, he even interviewed a local policeman, who claimed to have received orders not to defend the Jews. Lopukhin himself allegedly blamed the pogrom on the inaction of the local authorities, and indicated a need to strengthen the local police and gendarmes. But on Monday, April 14, he left Kishinev without having committed himself as to what his conclusions were. As he returned to Saint Petersburg to make his report, the local leaders—Jews and Christians alike—anxiously awaited the results.[10]

The formal government response came two weeks later, toward the end of April, in the form of a circular letter from the minister of interior to the governors, town supervisors, and police chiefs throughout the Russian Empire. Although it was based largely on Lopukhin's report, it was issued in the name of the minister of interior, and it may not have fully incorporated all of the police director's conclusions. At any rate, it became the official government version of what had happened in Kishinev on Easter Sunday and Monday.[11]

The minister's circular painted a rather different picture from the one supplied by the Jews of Kishinev. Ignoring their claims that Jews and Christians had lived together in relative harmony, it instead asserted that "these disorders arose as a result of the aggravated relationship existing in Bessarabia province between Christians and Jews." The situation was so acute, it went on, that "any absurd rumor about the Jews," such as the reports of ritual murder in Dubossary, "could serve as a pretext for an explosion of popular passion." Although the letter did refer to "handwritten leaflets" which called for the slaughter of Jews, no mention was made of the provocative articles in *Bessarabets*, or of the anti-Semitic activities of people like Georgii Pronin.[12]

Likewise, in contrast to the Jewish account, the official version of events scarcely mentioned the inactivity of the police and soldiers, and entirely omitted any reference to their incitement of the rioters. Instead, it almost seemed to exonerate them. The police were "disorganized," it claimed, because they did not have proper leadership. The streets, therefore, became clogged with rioters and "crowds of curious people." As a result of this, the soldiers called in were unable to get through to put down the disorders. Only after the troops had been systematically distributed throughout the city, on the evening of the second day, were the disorders brought to an end.[13]

Most troubling, perhaps, was the letter's implication that the Jews themselves were partly at fault for what had taken place. The pogrom began, it asserted, following the alleged incident in which a Jewish carousel operator struck a Christian woman, causing her to drop her baby. This story, which Lopukhin apparently picked up from Odessa procurator Pollan, was later shown to be false, and the government account of the start of the riots was to some extent discredited.[14] Similarly, the minister's circular stated that the riots resumed on the second day in response to attacks made by Jewish merchants on Christian peasants at the New Marketplace. It failed to point out that the Jews had assembled, not to attack the Christians, but merely to defend their property in the face of renewed violence.[15]

At any rate, the letter did conclude with instructions to the local officials on how to prevent future troubles. On the emperor's authority, it emphasized that, "under their own personal accountability," they must do everything possible to "prevent violence and calm the population." If disorders did occur, and military forces were called out, they must "be personally present on the spot, and direct the united activities of the troops and police toward a skillful and energetic quelling of the riot."[16]

Implicit in all this was a thinly veiled criticism of the Bessarabian governor, who had neither been present on the spot nor directed the troops, and the Kishinev chief of police. Within a week after the publication of the circular, in fact, both officials had been removed. In early May, the governor received a letter from the minister requesting the dismissal of Police Chief Khanzhenkov for "failing to make an effective use of the power he was invested with as an official responsible for the security of the town inhabitants."[17] Shortly thereafter, Governor von Raaben himself was formally relieved of his duties. His failures to leave his office and lead the troops were cited as clear derelictions of duty.[18]

These stern words and actions, however, came as small comfort to the Jews. Although the minister's circular did call for firmer steps to preserve order, it also informed officials that they must not tolerate Jewish self-defense organizations. *Bessarabets*, which welcomed the circular as a vindication, went on to publish its own version of "The Truth about the Kishinev Pogrom," accusing the Jews of having started the violence by shooting a number of Christians. And Vice-Governor Ustrugov, the bane of Jewish existence, took over as acting governor in the wake of von Raaben's dismissal.[19]

The government's response, then, did little to relieve the anxieties created by the pogrom, or to restore the confidence needed for the resumption of normal life. A month after the pogrom, the city and its commerce were still paralyzed by the fear of new disorders which, it was widely assumed, might break out at any time. Many Jewish businesses remained closed, partly due to damage and partly due to fear, and some of the wealthier Jews actually left town. Even those establishments that did reopen were hesitant to employ Christian workers, who in turn became resentful of the Jews for depriving them of their livelihood. Military troops remained on duty in the city, which had effectively been placed under martial law by the Ministry of Interior.[20]

In this atmosphere, rumors about new attacks on the Jews circulated freely, and not all were without foundation. According to information gathered by government agents, a number of persons already suspected for their role in the Easter riots were actively planning new violence. These disorders, it was reported, were scheduled to take place either on May 14 and 15 or on May 25 and 26, corresponding with the Christian religious feasts of the Ascension and the Holy Trinity. Acting upon a prearranged signal, small groups of Christians were planning to attack the Jews simultaneously in all parts of the city for a period of no more than 20 minutes. Then, before the troops could be called out to make arrests, the rioters would quietly and quickly disperse.[21]

This time, however, the authorities acted quickly. On May 6, Okhrana chief Levendal reported to Police Director Lopukhin, by memo, that new disorders were being planned. On May 12 Acting Governor Ustrugov held a special meeting with police and military leaders, and plans were made to occupy the entire city within twenty minutes in the event that new riots broke out. Under the conditions of martial law, he also published an "obligatory resolution" prohibiting meetings and gatherings.[22] On May 14, then, Ustrugov sent a telegram to the minister of interior informing him of the steps that had been taken. The minister responded immediately by wiring Ustrugov that "disorders must not be permitted" and that the acting governor had "personal responsibility for preventing them."[23]

Meanwhile Konstantin Pobedonostsev, the procurator of the Holy Synod in Saint Petersburg, was also taking steps to head off trouble. On May 8, in response to an earlier communication, he informed the minister of interior that the Kishinev bishop had been asked to assemble his clergy and give them specific instructions. They were to tell their flocks that violence against Jews was not permitted, and that relations with the Jews must be guided by the commandment that Christians should love their neighbors.[24]

These precautions apparently had an impact: Ascension Thursday and Trinity Sunday passed without serious incident. There were, it was reported, several minor attempts to initiate disorders on May 14 and 15, but these were quickly put down by the police. Likewise, on May 14, soldiers on the outskirts of the city allegedly turned back a crowd of Moldavians who were heading quickly toward Kishinev with boots slung over their shoulders. They were going, they said, because they had heard that there were "not enough people to beat the Jews." No one was arrested, but Okhrana chief Levendal did report on the incident to the police director in Saint Petersburg. A week later, Levendal further informed his superiors that, according to the information he had received, the disorders planned for May 25 had been postponed indefinitely. The would-be organizers apparently had decided not to strike while military forces were still stationed in the city.[25]

Anxieties in the city nonetheless remained quite high. The fears and concerns of working class Christians were magnified by the ongoing investigations and economic hardships engendered by the pogrom. On June 1, police confiscated from local workers a petition they were trying to deliver to Bishop Iakov; it called on the Church to protect them against the false accusations of the Jews. A number of anti-Jewish diatribes, some of them issued by prominent Christians, surfaced around this time. Contractor Pronin and artisan leader Stepanov, meanwhile, took the lead in setting up a relief fund for the families of arrested rioters.[26]

The Jewish community, for its part, continued to live in terror. The Kishinev Jews had hoped that the visit of Police Director Lopukhin would result in "effective, energetic, and decisive measures" to protect their "personal security and property." Instead, they found themselves blamed for their own misfortunes and prohibited from organizing a defense. It soon became apparent that, rather than resolving tensions and conflicts, the imperial authorities had simply managed to cast suspicion upon their own activities and attitudes.[27]

The Indignation of the Outside World

Meanwhile, as the Russian government was formulating its response, the outside world was beginning to learn about the Kishinev tragedy. Within a few days of the riots, rumors and reports had begun to circulate, and newspapers had begun to print preliminary accounts of what had taken place. Before long the name of Kishinev, hitherto unknown to most people outside of Bessarabia, had become a household word in many parts of the world.

The first articles about the massacre were published in *Bessarabets*, the Kishinev daily, on Thursday, April 10. They made no mention of instigation by local agitators or inaction on the part of the police. Instead, they asserted that the disorders were perpetrated by "huge crowds of drunken rioters" who fled at "the appearance of troops and police." And they played down the anti-Jewish nature of the violence: although the rioters "struggled primarily against the Jews," damage was also done to the apartments of local police, the homes of tax officials, social clubs, military halls, and even the *Bessarabets* press. The riots were portrayed as spontaneous and indiscriminate, with Christians as well as Jews numbered among the victims.[28]

By the following day, the news was being reported in the main Saint Petersburg daily. On Friday, April 11, *Novoe vremia* informed its readers that the Kishinev Jews had been "subjected to an attack by a crowd of workers" on April 6 and 7. "Despite the efforts of the police and military units called in to help," it went on, "the disorders took on an ominous character."[29] The story gave no hint that there had been prior agitation, or that the response of the local authorities had been anything less than adequate.

On that same day, the first reports about the pogrom were published in the West. The Reuters agency provided a short announcement, published in the London *Times*, that the "workmen in Kishineff" had made "an attack on the Jews," that 25 people had been killed, and that the Russian Ministry of Interior had ordered "special measures to be taken to preserve order." The *New York Times* ran a nearly identical report. No particular prominence was given the story, and only the sketchiest of details were provided.[30]

Initially, although these reports caused consternation, they did not have a great deal of impact on the European and American public. The earliest impulse in the Jewish communities, naturally, was to provide relief to the victims. A "committee to render assistance to Jews who suffered from the disorders" was set up in Kishinev itself, and organizations such as the Paris-based Alliance Israélite Universelle, and the Hilfsverein der Deutschen Juden in Berlin, began collecting donations.[31] In New York, a "Kishinev Relief Committee" was formed to solicit American contributions, and various meetings were held to organize relief efforts. A benefit play called "The Rioting in Kishinev," written in three days by a Jewish professor, was performed for large crowds which included the New York mayor. As time went on, more plays were written, more benefits were held, and other organizations—including the Hearst newspapers—got involved in the fund-raising. These efforts not only raised large sums of money, they also helped keep the Kishinev massacre before the public eye.[32]

Meanwhile, as more information surfaced, the Kishinev story began to grow in magnitude. On April 14 and 15, several Russian newspapers published accounts of varied atrocities which had allegedly occurred during the riots.[33] A few days later, an account supposedly smuggled out of Russia was published in New York: it declared that the number of dead and wounded was much higher than previously reported, and it described the rumors of ritual murder and tsarist support for a slaughter of Jews that had circulated prior to the riots. In London, a report from a "correspondent" in Kiev filled in some of the details about the Dubossary murder, the inflammatory articles in *Bessarabets*, the "extraordinary dilatoriness" of the governor and police, and the "savage and wanton cruelty" of the rioting mobs.[34]

Shortly thereafter, other stories began to appear that focused increasingly on prior organization and official culpability. The massacre, according to an account in the London *Times*, was not "an outburst of fanaticism on the part of the masses," but rather was "accomplished by small bands of 20 to 50 in number." More importantly, the story went on, it "appears to have been prepared beforehand with considerable organizing skill." Even worse, it concluded, the authorities "appear to have played the part of disinterested spectators while scenes of pillage and outrage were taking place around them . . ."[35]

Then, about a month after the pogrom, the focus of attention was shifted dramatically to Saint Petersburg. On Monday, May 5— May 18 on the Western calendar—the *Times* printed "what purports to be the text of a confidential despatch addressed by the Russian Minister of the Interior to the Governor of Bessarabia shortly before the anti-Semitic riots broke out in Kishineff . . ." It was dated March 25, 1903—twelve days before the pogrom—and it was captioned "Perfectly Secret." It conveyed the following message:

It has come to my knowledge that in the region entrusted to you wide disturbances are being prepared against the Jews, who chiefly exploit the local population. In view of the general disquietude in the disposition of the town populations seeking a vent for itself, and also in view of the unquestionable undesirability of instilling, by too severe measures, anti-Governmental feelings into the population which is not yet affected by (revolutionary) propaganda, your Excellency will not fail to contribute to the immediate stopping of disorders which may arise, by means of admonitions, without at all having recourse, however, to the use of arms.[36]

Here indeed, as the *Times* editorialized in the same issue, was a document which "fully explains the conduct of the authorities at Kishineff, if it be authentic." The minister himself had "tied the hands of the local authorities," and they "had done nothing but comply with his express and recent orders." The real villain, it now seemed clear, was the Russian government itself![37]

Concurrently, the *Times* also ran a letter from two prominent London Jews that added an element of the macabre to the descriptions of the pogrom. "In some cases," they asserted, "children were flung from the upper storeys of houses on to the pavement below," while elsewhere "women were outraged" and "men had their brains battered out." According to this uncorroborated report, unspeakable crimes were also committed against the dead: "One man had his tongue torn out, another had nails driven into his head, several were disembowelled, and one woman had her abdomen opened in the form of a cross and then stuffed with feathers."[38]

These stories, and others like them, released a torrent of criticism and abuse directed against the Russian government. Almost daily there appeared new revelations of atrocities, and new accusations made against the imperial authorities. Protest meetings were held, appeals were made, and speeches were delivered. New York City, with its large Jewish population, became the focal point of much of this activity, but anti-Russian demonstrations were also held in various other cities throughout Europe and North America. What had started out as a localized tragedy was now developing into a major international incident.

By this time other Western newspapers, sensing that a major story was developing, had begun to publish articles about the Kishinev pogrom. Among the most imaginative were two New York newspapers, the *Journal* and the *American*, both owned by William Randolph Hearst. Even before the "Kishinev dispatch" was published in the London *Times*, they had hired an Irish nationalist named Michael Davitt to travel to Kishinev, conduct an on-the-spot investigation, and report what he found out.[39]

Michael Davitt, although he had written and traveled extensively, was not a career journalist. Rather he was something of a celebrity: an active and eloquent Irish politician who had been deeply involved in the struggle for Irish home rule. He was also a heroic figure who had lost an arm in a childhood industrial accident, been a member the Fenian movement, spent years in and out of British jails, founded the Irish Land League, and even served for a while in Parliament. More recently, having grown disillusioned with politics, he had earned a living as a traveling journalist, making a variety of trips to Europe, Asia, Africa, Australia, and North America.[40] A "striking figure with a black beard, armless sleeve, and trilby hat," he was also known as a champion of the oppressed,[41] and he brought an air of righteous indignation to the pursuit of the Kishinev story.

Davitt arrived in Kishinev on May 8, a few days after the *Times* had published the alleged ministerial dispatch. He spent eight days in the city, meeting with Jewish leaders, rabbis, doctors, the town mayor, pogrom victims, and anyone else who would talk to him. He toured the Jewish hospital, the cemetery, and the scenes of the riots, taking copious notes, and compiling all sorts of impressions and information. Then, once he had left and was safely beyond the reach of the Russian censors, he sent detailed letters, complete with photographs, back to the New York newspapers.[42]

On the whole, Davitt's accounts tended to confirm the sensational rumors and reports which had been circulating for weeks. They refuted the official Russian version of the events, and they told how groundwork had been laid for the riots by Krushevan's *Bessarabets*. They described the apparent indifference of the officials and the active participation of some policemen and soldiers. In gruesome detail, they recounted the victims' stories, telling of brutal beatings, multiple rapes, dismemberment of corpses, senseless slaughter, painful suffering, and unbearable grief. Davitt's photographs, including pictures taken at the Jewish hospital and cemetery, served to corroborate his stories and heighten their impact.[43]

The reports of Michael Davitt were printed first in the New York *Journal* and *American*, then recounted in other publications in Europe and America. As the independent testimony of an observer who was neither Jewish nor anti-Russian, they carried a great deal of credibility and made an enormous impression. Davitt's recommendations, including a suggestion that a prominent American be chosen to seek an audience with the tsar on anti-Semitism, were given broad publicity. Reference was made to his reports in a variety of editorials, speeches, and meetings. By early June, widespread indignation was being expressed in many places, and the Russian government found itself on the defensive almost everywhere.[44]

In Russia itself, despite the pressures of censorship, several protest meetings were held, and a few liberal newspapers managed to print articles implicitly critical of the authorities for their handling of the pogrom.[45] A variety of prominent Russians also weighed in with expressions of outrage and shame. Leo Tolstoy, in a letter widely reprinted throughout the Western world, wrote that the pogrom was "a direct consequence of the propaganda of lies and violence that the Russian government pursues with such energy."[46] Maxim Gorky, in an article censored in Russia but published abroad, placed greater blame on "cultivated society" in Russia than he did on the mob itself.[47] And Vladimir Korolenko, who actually traveled to Kishinev, produced a short story called "House Number 13" which recounted in detail some of the worst atrocities and blamed Christian Russia as a whole for the pogrom.[48]

In Western Europe, beyond the reach of the Russian censor, the protests were much more direct. Russian revolutionary groups and emigré publications, as might be expected, were quick to denounce the tsarist government and hold it accountable for the slaughter.[49] The revolutionary journal *Liberation*, based in Stuttgart, was especially vehement in this regard, and it provided its readers with extensive coverage of the entire Kishinev story.[50] But it was not just the revolutionaries who condemned the imperial regime: in the wake of the *Times* "dispatch" and the Davitt reports, newspaper after newspaper denounced the Russian authorities. Prominent Jewish publicists, such as Lucien Wolf in England and Alexander Braudo in France, played a leading role in criticizing the imperial government's behavior. In Paris, several protest meetings were held, one of which attracted over 5,000 persons. Similar demonstrations were staged in Brussels, London, Vienna, various German and Italian cities, and even Melbourne, Australia.[51]

It was in the United States of America, however, that public indignation reached its height.[52] Throughout the months of May and June, protest activities occurred almost daily. Editorial articles appeared in numerous newspapers across the country, many of them denouncing the Russian authorities as well as the riots themselves. Protest meetings were held in dozens of cities, large and small, ranging from Boston and San Francisco to places like Sioux City, Iowa, and Fort Smith, Arkansas. Prominent among those who addressed the various meetings were Clarence Darrow, Jane Addams, and former president Grover Cleveland. At least seven separate meetings were held in New York City alone. On top of this there were countless speeches made, resolutions passed, and sermons delivered—all relating, in some fashion, to the Kishinev tragedy. The bulk of the protests were organized by Jews, but many were staged independently by supportive American Christians.[53]

In the United States, almost from the very beginning, there was strong public pressure for a diplomatic initiative on the part of the American government. Within a few weeks of the pogrom, in fact, at the behest of prominent Jews, the State Department had asked its ambassador in Saint Petersburg to secure "reliable information about these outrages," and to inquire about the possibility of relief aid to the victims. This initiative, however, met with a cold response from Russian officials, who denied both the existence of any suffering and the need for any aid.[54] For the next month, then, the U.S. government refused to get involved, since the Secretary of State could see no possible advantage to be gained from officially interfering in a matter of domestic Russian concern. So cautious was this approach that President Theodore Roosevelt was advised not even to make a private contribution to the Kishinev Relief Fund.[55]

By June, however, public outrage had become so intense that U.S. officials felt compelled to change their policy. Although still unwilling to lodge an official protest, the president and the secretary of state did meet with the executive committee of B'nai B'rith, one of the country's most prominent Jewish organizations. Both men gave cautious, non-committal speeches which praised the Jews in general and deplored the Kishinev tragedy, but avoided direct criticism of Russia. President Roosevelt even asserted that "the government of Russia shares the feelings of horror and indignation" expressed by the American people. At the same time, however, he did agree to consider supporting a B'nai B'rith petition addressed to the Russian emperor.[56]

The petition, couched in respectful language, called upon the tsar to prevent future pogroms and proclaim religious liberty for all his subjects. It was circulated throughout the United States and signed by over 12,000 people, including senators and congressmen, justices and judges, governors and mayors, bishops and clergy, educators and lawyers, and many other persons of prominence. In July, then, at the president's request, it was forwarded through diplomatic channels to Saint Petersburg. The Russian government, however, refused to accept it, and the initiative came to an end. The petition itself was later bound and placed in the archives of the U.S. State Department.[57]

Within a few months after the riots, then, the Kishinev pogrom had become a subject of widespread international concern. The Russian government, as time went on, found that it could not just ignore the issue and hope it would go away. Saint Petersburg officials had little choice but to defend themselves in the face of the worldwide opprobrium.

The Imperial Russian Response

At first, the Russian government seems to have been caught unawares by the fire storm of bad publicity. Perhaps, unused to having to deal at length with hostile public opinion, imperial officials were slow to grasp the significance of what was taking place. At any rate, they tended to respond slowly and clumsily to the charges made against them, thus making the charges more credible. As the Kishinev story continued to grow, however, and as it became apparent that serious damage was being done to Russia's international standing, they made a concerted effort to restore their credibility and perhaps even win some sympathy.

The earliest Russian efforts to deal with the problem tended to be repressive. A few weeks after the riots, for example, the Ministry of Interior announced that several Russian newspapers were being censured for "pernicious attitudes" expressed in their stories about the pogrom. The minister of justice called in Vladimir B. Nabokov, who had dared to criticize the local authorities in his article on "The Kishinev Bloodbath," and delivered a verbal reprimand. And the minister of interior instructed the editor of *Novosti* not to publish any more articles by E. P. Semenoff, a Paris-based correspondent who wrote critical accounts of the pogrom in several French periodicals. However, rather than squelching the negative publicity, these actions merely left the impression that the authorities were trying to intimidate those who ventured to write the truth.[58]

Meanwhile, in the United States, the Russian ambassador made a clumsy effort to deflect the criticism being leveled at his government. In a statement to the Associated Press, Count Arthur Cassini contrived to place the responsibility for the riots largely on the Jews themselves. The Jews, he asserted, "prefer to be money lenders," and in this capacity they "take advantage of the Russian peasant," causing widespread resentment, hostility, and occasional attacks. In spite of these attacks, however, "the Jews continue to do the very things which have been responsible for the troubles that involve them." [59] Needless to say, this attempt to blame the victims won little sympathy for Cassini or his government: it was seen as one more example of Russian anti-Semitism. Since his words were never officially disavowed, they came to be accepted in America as the official Russian position. [60]

Even more disastrous was the Ministry of Interior's response to the London *Times*' publication of the alleged "Kishinev dispatch." The danger of this document should have been readily apparent: it seemed to show that the minister had known the pogrom was coming, but had instructed the governor not to use force in trying to prevent or contain it. Still, it took a whole week before the ministry made any public response. According to one official, the minister himself did not know of the "dispatch" until several days after it was published in the *Times*, when he first read about it in an emigré revolutionary journal. Assuming it to be genuine, he reportedly called in the police director for consultation, only to be told that no such "dispatch" had ever been sent to the Bessarabian governor. At any rate, it was not until May 13, eight days after the report first appeared, that the government finally got around to denying its authenticity. The denial itself is plausible, since the existence of the "dispatch" is indeed rather dubious (see chapter 6). Still, due to the long Russian silence, much of the world came to accept it as genuine and authentic. [61]

Viacheslav K. von Plehve, the Russian minister of interior, had already acquired a reputation as a repressive authoritarian and inveterate anti-Semite even before reports linked him to the Kishinev pogrom. [62] Now, once he realized the seriousness of the situation, he began to devote his considerable talents and energies to repairing the damage that had been done. On the one hand, he took several steps to improve the position of Russian Jews and to normalize the state of affairs in Kishinev. On the other hand, he mounted an energetic public relations campaign designed to counteract the bad publicity he and his ministry had been receiving.

5. Minister of Interior V. K. von Plehve. Credit: Russia. Gosudarstvennaia kantseliarii. *Gosudarstvennaia kantseliarii, 1810–1910*. Saint Petersburg: Gosudarstvennaia tipografiia, 1910.

The ministry's efforts to better the lot of the Jews involved several important adjustments in the rules governing Jewish residency. Early in May, the tsar approved a new series of regulations which had been proposed by von Plehve even before the Kishinev riots. These rules, although they increased restrictions on Jewish land ownership outside the Pale of Settlement, opened up for Jewish residence within the Pale 101 new settlements which had lost their "rural character." The Russian authorities, it appeared, were finally taking steps to relieve the overcrowded conditions of Jews living in large urban centers. From a public relations standpoint, these changes could not have come at a better time, for they seemed to show that the Russian government was not insensitive to the needs of its Jewish subjects.[63]

Later that month, the ministry took a significant step toward stabilizing the situation in Kishinev. On Friday, May 30, it was announced that the vice-governor of Tambov province, Prince Sergei Dmitrovich Urusov, would be the new Bessarabian governor. A talented young official with no hint of anti-Semitism, Urusov would eventually win high praise for his fair and honest handling of the Kishinev situation. Von Plehve himself, despite his reservations about Urusov's "philo-Semitism," would later cite this appointment as evidence of his own goodwill.[64]

The appointment was, in some respects, an odd one: Urusov had never been to Bessarabia, and he knew almost nothing about Kishinev. Similarly, he had precious little experience in dealing with either Jewish people or the Jewish question. The few Jews he had met had left a favorable impression, it is true, but like many Russians he harbored a "certain indefinite racial antagonism and distrust" toward the Jews in general. In many ways, however, his ignorance worked to his advantage, for he approached his duties unencumbered by strong preconceptions about the character of the Jews or the situation in Kishinev.[65]

It took Urusov the better part of a month to assume his new duties. He first had to travel to Saint Petersburg to meet with the minister of interior and have an audience with the tsar. While there, he also took the opportunity to read the police reports on the pogrom and to acquaint himself, as thoroughly as possible, with the situation in Kishinev. Finally, after brief stops in Moscow and Kaluga, he headed south. Arriving in Bessarabia on June 23, he was greeted by Vice-Governor Ustrugov, who accompanied him on the last leg of his journey to Kishinev.[66]

The first impressions made by the new governor were not entirely favorable. During the course of their joint train ride, Ustrugov had managed to impress on him the seriousness of the situation and the difficulty of dealing with Jews. Urusov was told by the vice-governor that new riots were about to break out at any time, that the Christians in general disliked and resented their Judaic neighbors, and that the Jews themselves were a "plague." Thus, despite his triumphal reception with crowds lining Aleksandrov Street and shouting "hurrah" as his carriage passed by, the prince began his duties on a sour note. When he received a deputation of Jewish leaders, a few days after his arrival, he lectured them on their need to "comply faithfully with the limitations of their personal and property rights imposed by the law." He also enjoined them to avoid exploiting the local population, and to put aside all resentments and hostilities that were left over from the pogrom. He seemed almost to be blaming them for the tensions in Kishinev, or at least to be asserting that it was their responsibility to restore peace and calm. The Jews left his office with heavy hearts, convinced that the anti-Semites had "already managed to influence" the new head of the province.[67]

Their fears, however, soon proved to be unwarranted. Convinced that normal relations could not resume while the city remained under martial law, Prince Urusov proceeded to take some risks. First, reversing the earlier decision to keep the troops on duty in Kishinev, he informed the garrison commander that the soldiers were no longer needed. This caused great consternation among both the Jews and the local police, but Urusov stuck to his decision, giving his personal guarantee that order would be maintained. Secondly, in response to a request from local rabbis, he allowed the Jews to hold a formal burial ceremony for the scrolls of the Torah, which had been desecrated by rioters during the Easter pogrom. Despite the misgivings of the police, who feared that the large crowd attending the burial would reignite local passions, the ceremony took place without incident.[68]

These gambles, it would seem, paid off. The military authorities,

6. Torah Scrolls Desecrated by the Rioters. Credit: *Kishinevskii pogrom.* Compiled by the editors of *Osvobozhdenie.* Stuttgart: Verlag und Druck von J. H. W. Dietz, 1903.

the soldiers, and the Jews were all pleased, and the city became more stable. Tensions and anxieties remained, to be sure, but as time went on the city's social and commercial life began to gradually revive.[69]

This did not mean, of course, that cordiality and tranquillity reigned in Kishinev. The pogrom was over, but the residue of fear and resentment continued to exist. Anti-Semitic attitudes remained, poverty and deprivation continued, and hundreds of Jews left Kishinev in search of a safer life.[70] The threat of repeated violence never fully disappeared. Emotions cooled somewhat, but they did not go away: any new incident could easily arouse the dormant fears and inflame the smoldering passions.

Even before the new governor had settled into his job, in fact, several events occurred that showed how volatile the situation was. On June 4, in the streets of Saint Petersburg, a young Jew named Pinkus Dashevskii attacked *Bessarabets* editor Krushevan with a knife. The attack, which was intended as an act of vengeance against the man who had laid the groundwork for the Kishinev pogrom, proved to be unsuccessful: Krushevan escaped with only minor neck wounds and lived to continue his anti-Jewish crusade. Dashevskii, in turn, was sentenced eventually to five years at hard labor, even though his victim called publicly for the death sentence.[71] In Kishinev that same month the young notary Pisarzhevskii, who was widely accused of having led a group of rioters during the pogrom, shot himself to death. A few weeks later Pronin, who had reason to fear indictment for helping to instigate the pogrom, published an inflammatory poem in *Bessarabets* calling for Christian solidarity in the struggle against the Jews.[72]

As the summer wore on, however, thanks to some more judicious appointments by the Ministry of Interior, things began to improve. Vice-Governor Ustrugov, whose anti-Semitic reputation made him an obstacle to the easing of tensions, was transferred to Georgia in July. His replacement, I. L. Blok, was an honest and hard-working bureaucrat who soon helped put an end to many of the abuses fostered by his predecessor. That same month a new Okhrana chief named P. P. Zavarzin arrived in Kishinev to replace the suspect Levendal; the latter maintained a low profile until his own reassignment to Khotin in October. In August Colonel Paul Reichardt, a capable and experienced administrator, was appointed chief of police in place of the discredited Khanzhenkov. By the end of the summer, thanks largely to these appointments and the efforts of the new governor, calm had been restored to Kishinev, and the city's cultural and commercial life was beginning to revive.[73]

The Public Relations Campaign

Meanwhile, the imperial government had also been moving to implement its public relations strategy. One tactic used was for the minister of interior himself to meet directly with Jewish leaders, knowing that whatever was said would eventually be published abroad. V. K. von Plehve could be cordial, charming, and articulate: he was often at his best in personal encounters and in small group situations. He knew how to make a favorable impression on almost any person or group. A second approach was to arrange for articles to be published in the foreign press which defended the

Russian position. This was done in several ways: interviews were granted to foreign correspondents, articles were submitted indirectly through Russian friends abroad, and stories were planted directly by Russian agents in various countries.

On Sunday, May 11, less than a week after the publication of the alleged "Kishinev dispatch," the minister of interior met personally with a group of Kishinev Jews to discuss the impact of the riots. The delegates, according to one account, were impressed by von Plehve's "amiability" and by the "attention with which he listened" to their complaints. When he was asked to demonstrate "in some unmistakable way his disapproval of the recent outrages," he pointed out that he had already dismissed the governor and police chief for their ineffective response to the pogrom. When the delegates asked for greater restrictions on the anti-Semitic press, he also responded positively: it was announced the next day that retail sales of *Znamia*, Krushevan's anti-Semitic Saint Petersburg newspaper, had been suspended. The meeting and its results were portrayed quite favorably in the foreign press.[74]

Whatever goodwill may have been created by these measures, however, was soon undone by the ministry's ugly public battle with the London *Times*. The dispute began in May with the *Times*' publication of the alleged "Kishinev dispatch." The Russian government, caught by surprise, made no immediate response. In the meantime, the British writer Sir Arnold White wrote a letter to von Plehve offering to help prevent "the artificial creation" of anti-Russian sentiment "based upon inaccurate information, probably furnished by Russian Jews." He was confident that he could do this privately through the press, "in such a way as to turn the current of public opinion." Taking him up on his offer, Police Director Lopukhin wrote back that the letter published by the *Times* was an "obvious concoction," and that "no letter containing such statements was ever sent." Articles containing this message soon were published in Russia and abroad.[75]

The ministry then followed up with a clumsy attack on the *Times* of London itself. On Friday, May 16, it was announced that Dudley Disraeli Braham, the chief Saint Petersburg correspondent for the *Times*, was being expelled from Russia. The expulsion came as a surprise: Braham himself was not linked directly with the publication of the "dispatch," and he had just published a favorable report on the minister's meeting with the Kishinev Jews. He was told, however, that the Russian government objected to the "hostile tone" of his articles, and of the *Times* in general. His banishment, according to the official announcement, was evidence of the "Russian desire to have good relations with England."[76]

It had, in fact, the opposite effect. The expulsion of Braham created a minor sensation in the journalistic world, and led to widespread criticism of the Russian government. Rather than appearing as the aggrieved party, defamed by the irresponsible publication of a spurious dispatch, the Russian government now came across as a heavy-handed bully bent on "going to war" against a foreign newspaper.[77]

Undeterred, the Ministry of Interior continued its efforts to influence the foreign press. Later in May, about a week after the Braham expulsion, Lopukhin sent a letter to the *Christian Herald* providing an official Russian version of the Kishinev events. The underlying cause, according to this letter, was the "constant antagonism" between Jews and peasants, due to the "material advantages and widely developed commercial instincts of the Jews." These had been exacerbated by the rumors of ritual murder in Dubossary, and then violence had been triggered on Easter by the alleged attack of a Jewish carousel owner on a Christian woman. The riots had spread due to the inactivity of the local police and governor, and had ceased only when the military took control. Once it learned of the disorders, according to Lopukhin, the ministry had responded firmly, declaring martial law in Kishinev and dismissing the governor and chief of police. The Russian government, he concluded, deplored such violence, but it could not "give the Jews new rights of citizenship," since this would be "sure to drive the Russian population into new excesses against the Jews."[78]

Lopukhin's letter, most likely written in collaboration with von Plehve himself, summarized well the Russian government's position. The blame for the riots was placed on Jewish exploitation, peasant superstition, and irresponsible local authorities. The central government, far from being at fault, had done its best to end the disorders and punish those responsible. And the restrictions placed on Jews were actually helpful in protecting them from peasant violence. This artful attempt to portray the government as a sort of peacekeeping force between peasants and Jews, who were naturally and historically antagonistic, was a common theme consistent with prevailing perceptions within the state bureaucracy. It was repeated and reinforced in a nearly identical letter, published in the London *Times* the following week through the intermediacy of Arnold White.[79]

A few weeks later, in an effort to prevent further damage to the Russian reputation, the ministry again made use of Arnold White to publish its views in the London *Times*. By this time, in mid-June, a story had been published asserting that three times during the pogrom Bessarabia governor von Raaben had telegraphed the minister asking for permission to use force against the rioters. In order to squelch this rumor, von Plehve authorized a carefully worded statement denying that von Raaben had ever requested such permission, and listing "all communications" sent by the ministry to the governor. According to this statement, these were limited to a telegram ordering von Raaben to crush the riots, another one placing Kishinev under martial law, and two later communications dismissing the police chief and the governor from their posts.[80]

These attempts to influence the foreign press, however, were at best only minimally successful. The ministry had no control over the Western newspapers, no way to insure that its stories would be given favorable review, and no means of preventing hostile editorials and articles. Von Plehve's agent in Paris, Ivan Manasevich-Manuilov, did achieve some success in manipulating the French press through bribery: this made it possible for Russian releases to be published without contradiction in some Parisian papers.[81] This measure of control, however, was insufficient for von Plehve.

More easily controlled was the weekly newspaper, *La Revue Russe*, published in Paris by Russian agents during 1903. Funded by the tsarist police and edited by Manuilov, this paper had been established by the ministry to counteract anti-Russian publicity.[82] Beginning in May it ran a series of articles and notices dealing with the Kishinev disorders and the worldwide reaction to them. One of these claimed that those papers which blamed the Russian government for the pogrom were funded largely by Jewish capital. Others sought to discredit the so-called "Kishinev dispatch," to justify the expulsion of *Times* reporter Braham, or merely to reproduce the official Russian version put forth by Lopukhin and von Plehve. Most interesting, perhaps, was an interview with the minister of interior reproduced from the New York *Herald*. In this interview, von Plehve not only rejected all allegations of government complicity, he even portrayed himself as a man sincerely interested in solving the "Jewish problem." He talked of plans to extend the territory where Jews were allowed to live, and he claimed to be in favor of large-scale Jewish emigration and improved access for Jews to certain closed professions. He came across, not as an anti-Semite, but rather as a practical statesman seeking solutions to a very complex problem.[83]

Unfortunately for the minister, *La Revue Russe* had a small circulation and limited credibility. It was a partisan publication, funded by the Russian government, and as such it had little impact on public opinion as a whole. By the end of the year, in fact, it would no longer be in print.[84]

Meanwhile, as the furor over the pogrom continued, the ministry began to focus its attention more explicitly on the connection between Russian Jews and the revolutionary movement. Von Plehve himself was convinced that the anti-government organizations were made up largely of Jews, and that impoverished conditions and government restrictions were driving even more young Jews into the revolutionary ranks.[85] And, although he favored Jewish emigration, the minister was increasingly concerned that the Russian Zionist movement harbored unreliable and seditious elements. In June, therefore, he issued a secret circular ordering the governors to prevent the Zionists from holding meetings and spreading propaganda.[86] In the foreign arena, working through Manuilov, the Department of Police put forth several press releases blaming extremist elements among the Jews for disrupting conferences in Saint Petersburg.[87] And the minister himself took advantage of a meeting with Odessa Jewish leaders to express his views directly.

This meeting did not make nearly as favorable an impression as had the earlier meeting with Kishinev Jews. On one hand, von Plehve did try to show concern for the plight of the Russian Jews, and claimed that he was working on plans to improve their situation. On the other hand, he made it clear that he would not tolerate Jewish involvement in anti-government activities. "I know that you yourselves are loyal subjects," he told his visitors, but he went on to complain that many younger Jews seemed to be abandoning their faith and joining the revolutionary movement. "In western Russia," he reportedly complained, "about ninety percent of the revolutionaries are Jews, and in Russia as a whole around forty percent." This, he went on, was intolerable. "If you do not hold back your young people from the revolutionary movement," he warned, "we will make your situation so unbearable that you will all have to leave Russia . . ." As might be expected, foreign press reports focused on the minister's threatening tone, and this meeting did little to improve the Russian image.[88]

Neither, for that matter, did the Russian response to the "Kishinev petition" drawn up by American Jews. While it was still circulating, in fact, the Russian ambassador made an attempt to head it off. In a statement to the U.S. press, Count Cassini described the petition as an unwarranted interference in Russia's internal affairs, and made it clear that his government would never agree to accept it. If this was intended to influence American opinion against the petition, however, it had the opposite effect. President Roosevelt instead was "angered" over what he regarded as the "impertinent action of the Russians" in "endeavoring to appeal to the people over our heads." Rather than dissuading him from forwarding the petition, then, the incident left him even more determined to see that it was sent. The Russian government, as expected, refused to receive it, but the damage had already been done.[89]

By late July, then, the imperial authorities had made little headway in their efforts to reverse the bad publicity engendered by the Kishinev pogrom. More than three months after the riots, although the story was fading from the headlines, the tsarist government was still being blamed for what had taken place. Unexpectedly, however, an opportunity soon arose that made it possible for the minister of interior to present himself and his government in a much more favorable light.

Toward the end of July, the minister received word that Dr. Theodor Herzl, the leader of the world Zionist movement, desired to meet with him. Having failed to gain an audience with the tsar, Herzl apparently decided to overlook von Plehve's reputation and approach him as a man who was in a position to aid the Zionist cause. The minister, besieged by criticism for his handling of the Kishinev affair, seized the opportunity to "make the acquaintance of so interesting a personality as Doctor Herzl," who was a revered and respected figure among the Russian Jews.[90]

In some respects, despite the vast chasm between the forces they represented, the Zionist leader and the tsarist minister had good reason to confer. Herzl, whose movement was devoted to the establishment of a Jewish homeland, and von Plehve, who was interested in resolving his country's "Jewish question," both had an interest in the large-scale emigration of Russian Jews. Herzl hoped that the Russians might provide a favorable climate for Jewish resettlement, toleration for Zionist activities, and perhaps even a diplomatic initiative to persuade the Turks to permit Jewish colonization of Palestine. Von Plehve hoped that Herzl might be able to divert the Russian Zionists away from seditious activity, focus their energies on emigration, and, if nothing else, distract the world's attention away from Kishinev.[91]

The two men met twice, once on July 26 and once on July 31, and their discussions were cordial and candid. Herzl pushed hard for Russian assistance for Jewish emigration, diplomatic support for a Jewish homeland, and extended rights for Russian Jews. Von Plehve acknowledged the difficult plight of Russian Jews, and expressed support for "the creation of an independent Jewish state, capable of absorbing several million Jews." He suggested a policy whereby Jews of "superior intelligence" would be encouraged to remain in Russia, while those of "little brains and less means" would be welcome to move elsewhere. To this extent, at least, he was in sympathy with the Zionist cause. But he also expressed concern about the new leaders of Russian Zionism, who seemed to be focusing more on political organization in Russia than on emigration to Palestine.[92]

The shadow of the Kishinev pogrom loomed prominently in these discussions. The minister, it was clear, was deeply concerned about Russia's public image and anxious to appear conciliatory. "It is easy enough," he told his visitor, "for foreign governments and public opinion abroad . . . to reproach us with the way we treat the Jews." "But," he went on, "if it were a question of these countries opening their gates to two or three million penniless Jews, they would sing a different tune."[93] He agreed to support Jewish emigration, but insisted that the expenses must be paid by wealthy Jews. He promised to consider extending Jewish residency rights into the Baltic provinces, and allowing Jews to form agricultural communities with some rights of private ownership. He further agreed to "press energetically" for a Russian initiative supporting a Jewish homeland in Palestine. He even provided Herzl with a letter promising assistance in any efforts that would lead to Jewish emigration. In return, he made clear, he hoped that his visitor would help restrain criticism of the Russian government, and divert attention away from Kishinev, at the upcoming World Zionist Congress.[94]

The results of this meeting proved more beneficial to the Russian minister than they did to the Zionist leader. Herzl was roundly criticized by fellow Jews for playing into the enemy's hand, and he found it difficult to control what was said and done at the Zionist Congress which met a short time later. The letter from von Plehve was generally regarded as useless, and in fact little actually came of the proposal for a Russian initiative with Turkey. Meanwhile, however, von Plehve had found a way to portray himself as a man of reason and a "friend of the Jews," and to dampen down the uproar over the Kishinev pogrom.[95]

A few weeks after the end of Herzl's visit, the Ministry of Interior took another step which seemed to show that it was serious about improving the lot of the Jews. On August 11, 1903, Police Director Lopukhin sent a circular letter on the Jewish question to the governors of the provinces within the Pale of Settlement. This circular, which eventually made its way into the foreign press, announced that the government was undertaking a thorough review of all regulations concerning the Jews. In order to facilitate this, the governors were asked to submit their opinions as to what changes in the existing laws were desirable. These opinions would then be considered by a special commission on Jewish legislation. Although the circular made it clear that the ministry was not interested in "radical reform," it did provide an opportunity for several governors to advocate some rather far-reaching changes.[96]

These efforts, of course, did not convince everyone that the Russian authorities were operating out of a spirit of goodwill. Especially among Jews, and among those generally hostile to the tsarist regime, a good deal of skepticism remained. Some saw the reception of Herzl as a clever trick designed merely to influence public opinion; others feared that the legislative review was intended merely as a pretext for increasing restrictions on Jews.[97]

On September 1, 1903, as if to justify this skepticism, a new pogrom occurred. This one took place in the city of Gomel, in the Belorussian province of Mogilev. Once again, accusing fingers were pointed at the Russian authorities, especially since local officials had sought to prevent Jewish self-defense. But this time the situation was different. For one thing, reports from Gomel did not accuse the central government of instigating the pogrom. For another thing, the Jews did manage to defend themselves: in fact, of the 20 persons who perished, eight were Christians. As a result, the Gomel riots came across more as a battle between Christians and Jews than as a one-sided slaughter in the likeness of Kishinev. And, in fact, they had far less impact on world opinion than the Kishinev tragedy did.[98]

By this time, too, the minister of interior had learned the value of meeting directly with world Jewish leaders. In October, von Plehve held a private meeting with Lucien Wolf, the head of the Joint Commission for the Aid of Jews of Eastern Europe. Wolf, an outspoken opponent of the Zionist movement, represented a far different segment of the world Jewish community than did Theodor Herzl. Despite this, von Plehve managed once again to make a favorable impression. He repeated much of what he had said to Herzl, including his recognition of the difficult lot of Russian Jews, his desire to improve their circumstances, and his hopes of assimilating the more talented ones. At the same time, however, he asserted that younger Jews were "giving themselves up entirely to the revolutionary movement," and that this justified the government's restrictive policies. Although he reiterated his support for Jewish emigration, this time the minister talked more about what might be done to expand the Pale of Settlement and open up areas for Jewish relocation within the Russian Empire. Wolf left Saint Petersburg convinced that von Plehve was serious in his determination to resolve the Jewish question and that, if he pursued "the course marked out by him," the minister would "deserve well of the Jewish people."[99]

By fall of 1903, then, the Russian authorities had managed to restore some of their credibility, and the Kishinev story had begun to fade from public view. The issues that had been raised by the worldwide reaction, however, refused to go away. Before long, in fact, the trial of the rioters, even though closed to the public, would once again focus attention on Kishinev. And the question of guilt, including that of the Russian government, would once again be raised.

CHAPTER 6

The Question of Guilt

By autumn of 1903, the city of Kishinev had begun to regain its normal outward appearance. With financial assistance from a variety of relief agencies, the city's Jews had managed to rebuild most of their homes and shops, and to reopen most of their businesses. The troops had been withdrawn, the mess had been cleaned up, and much of the damage had been repaired.

The internal wounds, however, were a long way from having healed. The question of guilt, and the problems of imposing justice, continued to cast a pall over the city's daily life. While the administrative authorities had been working to restore order, and the tsarist government had been struggling to defend its reputation, judicial officials were laboring to investigate the riots and bring charges against those who had taken part. In the long run, however, their efforts would be overshadowed by the widely held belief that the real culprit in the Kishinev affair was the Russian government itself.

Investigation and Indictment

During the course of the spring and summer, proceedings were instituted against most of the 800 persons who originally had been arrested. The majority were charged with relatively minor crimes: rioting, disturbing the peace, and carrying off possessions which had been thrown out of Jewish homes. Their cases were placed under the jurisdiction of the local justices of the peace, who eventually tried a total of 664 accused persons. Fines ranging from 25 to 300 rubles, depending upon the nature and severity of the crimes, were levied upon those convicted. Since even the lowest of these fines would have exceeded the typical worker's monthly wage, this was no small matter. Those who could not afford to pay were sentenced to prison terms ranging from seven days to a year. A number of cases were appealed, either by the defendants or the police, to the local congress of justices of the peace. According to official reports, the congress wound up deciding 98 cases involving 138 individuals. By late June, as a result of all this activity, 308 persons had been convicted and sentenced.[1]

The sentencing of these persons created several problems. One was the lack of jail space: there simply was not enough room to house so many individuals. Another had to do with the local economy: many of the convicts were people who made their living by agricultural labor or market gardening. To incarcerate them immediately, during the middle and late summer, would be to take them away from their fields and gardens when their labor was needed the most. It would also impose a hardship on their families, who would be left without income for much of the coming year. In early June, as a result, Acting Governor Ustrugov petitioned the Ministry of Interior for permission to delay the start of their prison terms until September 1, by which time most of the field work would be completed. This would both lessen the financial strain and help solve the problem of space. The new governor, Prince Urusov, eventually endorsed this proposal, with the condition that it only be applied on special request in individual cases. This arrangement won the approval of the ministers of interior and justice, and was formally confirmed by the emperor on July 9, 1903.[2]

Far more complex were the cases involving serious crimes like murder and assault. These had to proceed through the criminal court system: preliminary investigations had to be conducted, indictments issued, and trials arranged. On top of this there were numerous civil suits brought by Jews seeking restitution for the losses and damages they had suffered.

The main responsibility for investigating the riots and prosecuting the offenders fell on the shoulders of V. N. Goremykin, the procurator of the Kishinev Circuit Court. This talented and capable young official was the nephew of I. L. Goremykin, a former minister of interior and future prime minister of Russia. Procurator Goremykin was in no sense considered a friend of the Jews, and he in fact maintained a posture of coolness, professionalism, and impartiality toward all concerned. This attitude won him few friends. Russian "patriots" and local anti-Semites were disturbed that he prosecuted only Christians, and that he did not find some way to blame the Jews for what had taken place. His investigation, to them, seemed one-sided and partial. On the other hand, anti-government forces and Jews were upset that he focused only on the actual rioters, and that he did not seek to indict imperial officials and local dignitaries for encouraging and abetting the violence.[3]

Goremykin received considerable assistance and direction from A. I. Pollan, the procurator of the Odessa Chamber of Justice, who made a number of visits to Kishinev in the wake of the pogrom. Although he was critical of the authorities for not quickly suppressing the violence, Pollan also tended to downplay the reports of atrocities and to attribute the violence, not to government instigation, but to latent hostilities between local Christians and Jews.[4]

In order to sort out the evidence and bring charges against the suspects, 30 separate investigations were conducted by the prosecuting authorities. The work was time-consuming, complex, and controversial, and it was not always easy to separate truth from distortion and accurate accounts from exaggerations. Plaintiffs and witnesses sometimes had a tendency to overstate their losses, embellish their stories, or describe events they had not actually seen. The accused, quite naturally, sought to deny or depreciate their involvement. By October, in spite of these obstacles, the investigations were completed and indictments were handed down. The stage was set for the trials of the rioters.[5]

The formal bill of indictment, prepared by Goremykin, was a cautious document which adhered closely to the evidence and testimony compiled. It identified the inflammatory articles in *Bessarabets*, and the rumors of ritual murder in Dubossary, as the factors which "aggravated the hostile attitudes of local Christians toward the Jews" and thus served as the "most immediate causes" of the pogrom. It ignored the claim that the riots were precipitated by a Jewish carousel owner, and instead placed the blame squarely on the Christian crowd. It did imply, however, that Jewish self-defense efforts were in part responsible for the renewal of the disorders on

Monday. And it also concluded that the investigations had "not provided data which would indicate that the disorders were prepared ahead of time." Charges were brought only against the Christian rioters; no officials were indicted, and neither were any Jews.[6]

As a result, neither the anti-Semites nor the anti-government forces were satisfied with this document. *Novoe vremia*, the influential Saint Petersburg daily, published a long article criticizing the indictment and asking why only the Christians were accused, and not the "guilty Jews." It even suggested that this had occurred due to "strong Jewish influence throughout Russia and the world." Goremykin himself had to provide his superiors with an explanation, and defend himself against charges of partiality toward the Jews. At the same time, however, the leftist circles were also finding fault. The emigré journal *Liberation*, while praising the procurator for implicating Krushevan and ignoring the carousel story, nevertheless complained that Goremykin had "covered up some tracks" and not told the entire truth. The indictment, according to this critique, had wrongly portrayed Jewish defense efforts as attacks upon the Christians, and had overlooked clear evidence of prior preparation and government involvement.[7]

The questions of how and where to try the rioters also caused all sorts of concerns. Should the trial be open or closed to the public? Should it be held in Kishinev or moved to another location? How should the cases be combined, and in what order should they be treated?

In mid-June, Procurator Pollan sent a confidential memo to the Ministry of Justice arguing that the trial should be held behind closed doors. The pogrom, he argued, had engendered "false rumors" of government instigation. At first glance, he allowed, it might seem useful to disprove these rumors in a public trial; but in reality this would simply help publicize them and create a false impression among the common people. Since a number of plaintiffs were suing the government for insufficient protection, their lawyers were likely to focus attention on the actions of state officials. It would be most expedient, therefore, to try the case *in camera* and move it to a different town.[8]

Not everyone agreed with this judgment. Prince Urusov, the new governor, saw no reason either to exclude the public or to move the trials. In expressing his views to the Ministry of Justice, he gave his assurance that the trials could be held in Kishinev without any disruptions or disorders. In the end he was proven right: the case was tried in Kishinev, and there were no undue problems.[9]

At the insistence of the Ministry of Interior, however, the proceedings were closed to the public. In early July, when the ministers of justice and interior discussed this issue, von Plehve expressed strong support for Pollan's proposal. As a result, Minister of Justice Muraviev issued a formal order that the courtroom be closed. Later, once the sessions had begun, Prince Urusov appealed to Muraviev to rescind this order and open up the proceedings. The request was communicated to von Plehve, but the minister of interior remained adamant. "Opening the doors for the further consideration of these cases," he asserted, ". . . would only serve to support the false rumors that . . . there were revealed circumstances, discrediting the local authorities and the ministry of interior, which were concealed from the public by the government." The sessions remained closed throughout the duration of the trials.[10]

The effort to conceal what went on in the courtroom, however, was not entirely effective. Inside Russia, of course, the censorship prevented discussion of the actual proceedings. But the outside world was kept informed by individuals who attended gatherings with the lawyers each evening, then traveled to the border and conveyed what they had learned to members of the foreign press. As a result, detailed accounts of the trial were eventually published abroad. In the end, therefore, the attempt at information control accomplished little, and the secrecy only enhanced the impression that the authorities had something to hide.[11]

The Trials of the Rioters

The actual trials of the accused rioters began in Kishinev on November 6, 1903, six months to the day after the start of the pogrom. Because of the unwieldy number of defendants and plaintiffs, and perhaps to keep the proceedings from attracting too much attention, it was decided to divide the affair into several cases and try each one individually. There took place, therefore, a series of trials, conducted in succession over the next six months.

The first trial, however, was the one that attracted the most attention, and the one that proved most dramatic. This was the case of "Ivan Grigorzhevskii and others," a group of 39 persons accused of having committed various crimes, most of which were related to the attack on the apartment building at number 33 Gostinnii Street on the second day of the pogrom. Three Jewish men, an elderly woman named Rose Katsap, and a 16–year-old boy named Benjamin Baranovich had perished in the attack. The defendants included Kirill Gerchiu and Ivan Moroziuk, who were charged with having beaten to death several victims in the building's courtyard, and a number of other persons identified by witnesses as having taken part in the looting and violence. Some 53 injured parties, and over 500 witnesses, were also involved in the proceedings.[12] The drama in the courtroom, however, had little to do with the actual crimes committed or the role of those accused. Rather it focused on the causes of the pogrom, the origins of the violence, and the alleged responsibility of individuals and officials who were not actually on trial.

The presiding magistrate was Judge Vladimir Vasilievich Davydov, a chief justice who had been sent from Odessa to try the case, and who resided with the governor while in Kishinev. A member of the Russian landed nobility and a former justice of the peace, Davydov was experienced, intelligent, cautious, and prudent. In the beginning, he gave the attorneys relatively free reign in questioning witnesses and addressing broader issues of prior preparation and official inaction. But as time went on, perhaps due to pressure from above, he found it necessary to focus the sessions narrowly on the defendants and their activities, and to prevent the case from becoming an open forum for accusations against the government.[13]

The lawyers involved in the trial fell into three main categories. One group represented the Procurator's Office, whose job it was to prosecute the case against those who had been indicted. A second group represented the defendants, mostly lower-class Moldavians and Russians, who were charged with the various crimes. A third group, and the one which presented the greatest problem for the court, was composed of attorneys for the plaintiffs. They represented the Jews who had lost family members, had been seriously injured or maimed, or had suffered extensive property damage.

Although the trial was closed, and outsiders were technically barred, a number of additional persons were also present in the courtroom. As usual in such cases, there were formal representatives of each of the three social estates: a marshal of the nobility from Bender, a townsperson (the mayor) from Akkerman, and a peasant elder from the area around Kishinev. A gendarme officer, Captain Sviderskii, was appointed as an observer, and instructed by his superiors to keep a detailed daily diary of what went on in court. The governor, Prince Urusov, was also allowed to attend, and was provided with a special seat behind the presiding judges. Since the governor was respected in the Jewish community, the lawyers for the plaintiffs were willing to accept his presence, even as they objected to the attendance of other state officials.[14]

The chief prosecutor, N. F. Dzhibeli, was an assistant procurator from Odessa. As the government's main advocate, he sought simply to prove that the assembled defendants were responsible for the crimes that had been committed. Questions as to who had instigated the pogrom, and whether the authorities were to blame, were beyond his purview and mandate. From his perspective, these considerations could only serve to distract the court from its main function: deciding the guilt or innocence of the persons who were on trial. He tried, therefore, to focus the proceedings narrowly on the cases at hand.[15]

The lawyers for the defense, however, had other objectives. Since there was little doubt that crimes had been committed, and that their clients were somehow involved, their interest lay in placing the blame on someone else. Some of them, such as the staunch anti-Semite Aleksandr Semenovich Shmakov, tried to convince the court that the defendants were actually hapless victims whose actions had been provoked by Jewish aggression and oppression. Others, like the liberal lawyer Sergei Nikolaevich Shamonin, made common cause with the plaintiffs, arguing that the real criminals were not their clients but prominent persons who had engineered the pogrom from behind the scenes.[16]

The attorneys for the plaintiffs were, in some respects, the most illustrious group of all—and the most troublesome. They included Nikolai Platonovich Karabchevskii, the famous trial lawyer and champion of the oppressed, as well as Oskar Osipovich Gruzenberg,

Aleksandr Sergeevich Zarudny, and several other eminent jurists. From the beginning, they were less concerned about the actual defendants, whom they depicted as mere accomplices, than they were about the "real" villains who had not been charged with crimes. They sought to prove that the pogrom had been engineered beforehand by prominent local persons, and that these were the ones who should really be on trial. More importantly, perhaps, they were intent on proving that the government itself had caused the pogrom, by the direct involvement of some of its officials and the scandalous inaction of others.[17]

The proceedings began on a sour note which proved to be an omen of things to come. After the prosecutor had stated his case, describing the crimes in general terms and demanding that the criminals be punished, the time came for the witnesses to take their formal oath. At this point defense attorney Shmakov, in a gratuitous insult to the Jews, requested that the Jewish witnesses be required to take the oath *more judaico*, that is, on the premises of the synagogue with lighted candles. Otherwise, he claimed, their testimony was worthless and unreliable. The prosecutor objected, declaring that this was absurd and unheard of, and that oaths taken by Jews in a courtroom were every bit as valid as those taken in a synagogue. Speaking for the plaintiffs, Karabchevskii indicated that the witnesses would be willing to take the oath in the synagogue, despite the humiliation, if this would relieve doubts about the veracity of their testimony. The court, however, ruled for the prosecution, and the oaths were administered in the courtroom. Jewish witnesses were sworn in by a rabbi, and Christian witnesses by a priest.[18]

The first witness to be called was Karl Schmidt, the former mayor of Kishinev, who had still been in office at the time of the pogrom. Schmidt had little to offer concerning the behavior of the defendants: he admitted, in fact, that he had rushed home as soon as the trouble broke out on Sunday and stayed there throughout most of the pogrom. Instead he spoke about the climate in Kishinev before the riots, focusing largely on the role played by *Bessarabets* in stirring up anti-Jewish feelings. Until this newspaper had come along, he asserted, Christians and Jews had lived together in relative harmony. He also made reference to the unresponsiveness of police and soldiers during the actual rioting. His testimony suited well the purposes of those who wanted to focus the trial, not on the actual defendants, but on the prominent instigators and the authorities.[19]

After a one-day recess, the trial resumed on November 8 with Schmidt still on the stand. Defense attorney Shmakov, in an effort to shift some blame to the Jews, asked the witness if he was aware that the Jews monopolized commerce in Kishinev. The former mayor acknowledged this fact, but held the government responsible: having been expelled from the villages and deprived of other forms of livelihood, he asserted, the Jews had little choice but to make their living in business. When asked whether he had any evidence that the pogrom had been planned beforehand, Schmidt claimed that the rioters carried lists identifying which properties were Jewish and which were owned by Christians. No windows, he added, had been broken in Christian homes.[20]

Schmidt's testimony was followed by that of General Bekman, the garrison commander. Under questioning, Bekman admitted that there had been at least 5,000 soldiers at his disposal at the time of the pogrom, and that these should have been sufficient to quell the disorders quickly. When asked why this had not been done, however, he shifted the blame to von Raaben, declaring that the former governor had not authorized the military to employ deadly force until Monday afternoon. Only when it began to look as if the rioters might also attack Christians, Bekman implied, were the troops empowered to use their weapons and bring the disorders to an end.[21]

The third witness, a journalist named Feigin, claimed that the defendants had merely been used as tools by backstage agitators from among the educated classes. When he mentioned in this connection Pisarzhevskii, the young notary who had committed suicide a few months after the pogrom, the judge enjoined him against implicating persons who were presently not on trial. This exchange set off a heated debate in the courtroom. A. S. Zarudny, representing the plaintiffs, angrily protested that the influential culprits who had organized the violence were being protected by the court, while the poor wretches who had been indicted had to shoulder all the blame. He threatened to resign from the case if the court was going to keep the real criminals from being exposed. His colleague Karabchevskii and four of the defense attorneys spoke in his support, while prosecutor Dzhibeli and defense lawyer Shmakov vehemently opposed him. The court finally ruled against Zarudny, and the witness was ordered once again to avoid making reference to outside agitators and backstage organizers.[22]

The tone was thus set for the rest of the trial. Using every means at their disposal, the lawyers for the Jews, joined by some of the defense attorneys, sought to implicate prominent persons and government officials. The prosecuting attorneys and several defense lawyers, usually supported by the court, sought just as energetically to limit the discussion to the guilt or innocence of the defendants in the dock. Witness after witness was called and questioned, a confusing welter of testimonies and opinions was put forth, and the trial dragged on with no end in sight.

Despite the restraints placed upon them, some of the witnesses did manage to give testimony damaging to persons who were not on trial. The city's new mayor, Dr. Sitsinskii, took pains to implicate Krushevan, insisting that the inflammatory tone of *Bessarabets* had been a major cause of the pogrom. And he even involved von Plehve, noting that Christian patients had cited the government's subsidies to *Znamia* as evidence that the minister of interior approved of Krushevan's riots.[23] Another witness, the owner of the "Moscow" tavern, testified that proclamations issued by Pronin, inviting people to take part in the upcoming pogrom, had been distributed at his establishment prior to the riots. Pronin himself, in fact, was called to the stand to explain an article that he had recently published in *Znamia*. In this article—entitled "Who is Guilty?"—Pronin had blamed the Jews for starting the riots; in the courtroom, however, he was unable to substantiate his charges. He also admitted taking a trip to see Father John of Kronstadt, a highly regarded cleric who had at first condemned the pogrom, during which he convinced the holy man to issue a new statement criticizing the Jews and exculpating the Christian rioters. Although he claimed it was his duty "to help the minister of interior in his efforts to hold back Jewry," Pronin insisted that he had acted on his own.[24]

Various other witnesses complained about the authorities, accusing them of behavior ranging from total indifference to outright complicity. One shop owner told of how his business was ransacked in broad daylight, with policemen and soldiers looking on, and with Vice-Governor Ustrugov and Police Chief Khanzhenkov present at the scene.[25] Others raised questions about a police captain named Solovkin, who allegedly charged Jewish people five rubles a head for protection from the crowds.[26] Dr. Muchnik, the chairman of the committee formed to aid the Jewish victims, testified that Governor von Raaben had agreed to visit the scene of the disorders, only to change his mind after his visit from Okhrana Chief Levendal.[27]

Further testimony shed little more light. A. I. Stepanov, as head of the Christian artisans' association and a key anti-Jewish agitator, was called to testify about anti-Semitic articles he had published in Krushevan's *Znamia*. In the course of questioning, however, it became apparent that he was scarcely literate, and thus could not have written the diatribes that were printed under his name.[28] As the hearings continued, numerous other witnesses added details of the atrocities, descriptions of the social climate in Kishinev, and various accounts of what had taken place.[29]

Finally, after several weeks of confusing and conflicting testimony, government officials began to get impatient with the slow pace of the proceedings. Procurator Pollan reported to Minister of Justice Muraviev that the presiding judge was not managing the trial "with a firm hand." And Minister of Interior von Plehve complained that the trial was fostering anti-government agitation, and that "tendentious accounts" of the courtroom sessions were appearing in the foreign press. Consequently, on November 24, Muraviev sent a telegram to Judge Davydov asking him to speed things up "in the interests of the political order." Davydov was also instructed to restrict questioning of witnesses to the precise charges before the court, and to prevent criticism of the administrative order.[30]

The next day, in Kishinev, the trial reached a critical stage. At first the session was delayed for several hours, while the judges considered a request from several defense counselors that the proceedings be suspended and the case remitted for further investigation. Led by S. N. Shamonin, these attorneys argued that the original investigation was inadequate, and that new evidence about pogrom organization might well exonerate their clients. Later, when the hearings finally resumed, the court ruled that the new information was not sufficient to warrant a suspension of the trial. The request for adjournment was therefore denied.[31]

So the trial proceeded, but not in the same context as before. Shamonin and his colleagues, disturbed by the court's decision, declared that they could not continue to serve and asked to be relieved of their duties. This precipitated a crisis. In order to arrange for new lawyers, and to give the other attorneys a chance to discuss their response, the judges declared a recess which was extended until late afternoon.[32]

When the court reconvened, at 4:30 P.M. on November 26, A. S. Zarudny rose to speak in the name of the lawyers for the Jewish plaintiffs. In a wavering voice, he announced that he and his colleagues had unanimously concluded that a just verdict could be not be reached under the current circumstances. When Judge Davydov interrupted him, and instructed him not to speak in advance about the verdict, the agitated Zarudny deferred to his colleague O. O. Gruzenberg. The latter proceeded to explain that most of his fellow attorneys, finding it "juridically and morally impossible" to continue their participation, had decided to quit the case. He and several others, he added, had agreed to stay on, but they would play a much more modest role in the proceedings. Following his remarks, at approximately 6:00 P.M., the rest of the plaintiffs' attorneys rose and left the courtroom en masse.[33] The most dramatic stage of the Kishinev trial had suddenly come to an end.

The rest of the proceedings turned out to be anti-climactic. Further witnesses provided information about the rumors and leaflets that had circulated before Easter, and about various aspects of the pogrom itself. Despite the court's efforts, some even managed to make general remarks about the planning and preparation of the riots, and to implicate persons who were not actually on trial. In his concluding speech, however, Prosecutor Dzhibeli declared that the riots had not been planned beforehand, asserting rather that they had arisen spontaneously as a result of strident local anti-Semitism, fanned into flames by the articles in Krushevan's newspaper. Be that as it may, he concluded, the rioters must be punished, for attacks on life and property could never be condoned.[34] The court, for the most part, concurred: on December 7, when the verdicts were announced, 25 of the 37 defendants were found guilty on various counts and sentenced to terms ranging from six months to seven years. The stiffest sentences went to Kirill Gerchiu and Ivan Moroziuk, the two men convicted of murder, who got terms of hard labor for seven years and five years, respectively. The civil suits which had been brought by the various plaintiffs were denied.[35]

The Kishinev verdict was received with dismay by the Jewish community in Russia, and by its sympathizers in the West, but it did not have a major impact on the Russian public at large. There were some complaints about the leniency of the sentences, but there was no large public outcry. Indeed the subsequent trials, conducted during the first half of 1904, attracted little attention outside Kishinev. By this time Russia was at war with Japan, and the Kishinev affair was no longer a major story.[36]

The trials went on in relative obscurity for quite some time, with the results largely following the precedent set by the first set of verdicts. The second group of defendants, some 68 in all, were tried in a series of hearings lasting from February 8 through February 13, 1904. Prison sentences ranging from four months to four years were handed out to 29 of them, who were found guilty of having taken part in various beatings and killings. In a few cases, the convicted culprits were required to pay damages to the relatives of their victims. The bulk of the accused were acquitted, however, and most of the damage suits brought by the Jewish victims were rejected.[37]

Subsequent hearings and verdicts, conducted in April and May of 1904, followed pretty much the same pattern. One defendant was sentenced to five years in prison, and several others received four-year terms, for their role in the murders of several Kishinev Jews. On the whole, however, the penalties meted out were light, the claims of most plaintiffs were ignored, and a number of the defendants were found not guilty. By the time the trials finally wound to a close, they had ceased to attract any serious attention outside of Kishinev.[38]

The first trial, however, did end up having an important impact on world opinion. The reports that leaked out of the closed session portrayed the Russian government in a very unfavorable light. Long excerpts from the attorneys' speeches, some of which included direct allegations of official complicity, were also published abroad.[39] The most dramatic was that of Karabchevskii, who compared the Kishinev rioters to the soldiers of King Herod who had slaughtered Jewish infants at the time of Jesus' birth. Neither group, the lawyer insisted, had acted on its own; both were simply fulfilling criminal orders issued from above.[40]

As a result of these remarks, and others like them, the widespread impression of official complicity was strengthened and confirmed. In the eyes of the Kishinev court, it was the convicted rioters and murderers who were responsible for the massacre. In the eyes of the foreign press, however, and in much of the outside world, the Russian government stood convicted as the real author of the pogrom.[41]

The Evidence of Official Complicity

The accusation that officials in Saint Petersburg had engineered an anti-Jewish riot in Bessarabia seemed neither incongruous nor illogical to contemporaries or to later historians.[42] After all, repression of Jews had long been part of Russian state policy, enshrined in numerous statutes, regulations, and decrees. The situation in Russia was difficult and the Jews, many of whom were prominent either in the commercial economy or in the revolutionary movement, provided an easy target and an obvious scapegoat. And the evidence of government involvement in the Kishinev disorders was persuasive and compelling. It included the anti-Semitic reputations of certain key officials, the favoritism shown by imperial authorities to anti-Jewish instigators, the reticence of local police and soldiers to move against the rioters, the questionable behavior of the government in the wake of the pogrom, the lenient treatment of local officials suspected of involvement, and subsequent revelations made by highly placed observers.

Even before the Kishinev pogrom, some of the most prominent figures in the Russian government were known to regard the Jews with scarcely concealed antipathy. Tsar Nicholas II himself had little love for his Jewish subjects, whom he considered to be infidels and troublemakers. Grand Duke Sergei Aleksandrovich, the emperor's uncle and governor-general of Moscow, was a reputed anti-Semite who had been associated with the brutal expulsion of the

Jews from Moscow in 1891. Viktor K. von Wahl, the commander of gendarmes, had come to be regarded as a Jew-hater during his earlier tenure as governor of Vilnius, where at one point he had been shot and wounded by a revenge-minded young Jew.[43]

It was the minister of interior, however, who was linked most directly with state-sponsored anti-Semitism. In the course of his career, V. K. von Plehve had acquired a reputation as a ruthless authoritarian, a crafty intriguer, an unprincipled careerist, and a dedicated anti-Semite. He had been director of the imperial police during the pogroms of 1881–1882 and, since these had been widely attributed to police connivance, he had long been suspected as a pogrom instigator. In 1890, having taken over as head of the Pahlen commission on Jewish legislation, he had put forth a plan for more extensive and permanent restrictions on the Jews. Not long thereafter, he had played an influential role in drafting the laws which restricted Jewish participation in rural and municipal self-government.[44] And, as recently as January of 1903, he had openly admitted that he considered "Jewry" to be "inimical to the national well-being of Russia."[45] With such an attitude and reputation, he appeared to be quite capable of plotting a pogrom.

Furthermore, the events preceding the Easter riots had seemed to show that the central government and the Ministry of Interior were interested in fostering anti-Jewish violence in Kishinev. Despite its irresponsible reporting and inflammatory articles, the newspaper *Bessarabets* had neither been censured nor warned by the ministry. Instead, it had received rather favorable treatment from the Main Office on Affairs of the Press—the branch of the ministry responsible for censorship of publications. Its publisher, Krushevan, had been given a government subsidy to begin publishing the *Znamia* in Saint Petersburg, thus providing a new rostrum for his vicious propaganda. And Pronin, Krushevan's accomplice and collaborator, had made several trips to Saint Petersburg, openly bragging about his close relationship with the minister of interior. Clearly, it seemed, the ministry was supportive of Krushevan and Pronin, and approved of their anti-Semitic activities.[46]

The behavior of the local authorities on the eve of the pogrom had also appeared to fit into this pattern. Vice-Governor Ustrugov, the Jew-hater who handled most of the governor's duties, had bent over backward to tolerate the activities of men like Krushevan and Pronin. Okhrana Chief Levendal, the shadowy police agent sent to Kishinev to combat revolution, had reportedly met often with Pronin and his associates during the months before Easter. Meanwhile, rumors had spread openly about a secret imperial decree calling for a three-day "punishment" of the Jews, and handbills had appeared urging Christian workers to seek revenge against the Jewish "exploiters." Despite complaints from the Jewish community, neither the governor nor the police had taken any steps to stop this, thus lending credence to the notion that some sort of imperial policy calling for mistreatment of Jews actually did exist, and that the tsar himself approved of anti-Semitic violence.[47]

The riots themselves had shown signs of prior planning and official connivance. The violence had begun as if by prearranged signal, and the crowds had reportedly been led by persons who could point out the Jewish properties. Icons had appeared in the windows of Christian buildings, making it easy for the rioters to distinguish between Christian and Jewish shops and homes. Many rioters had behaved as if they were following government instructions and expecting no interference from the police. And, in fact, the local police had done little to stop the massacre, while some were actually reported to have encouraged the rioters. Even the soldiers had remained inactive until late on the second day, seeming more concerned with protecting Christian properties than with stopping the disturbance. The vice-governor and the police chief had witnessed some of the violence but had done little or nothing to stop it. And the governor himself had remained out of sight, having decided, after conferring with Baron Levendal, not to visit the scene of the disorders. It hardly seemed likely that they would have behaved this way without support and encouragement from Saint Petersburg.[48]

All of these circumstances had pointed in the direction of possible government involvement. More direct evidence surfaced a bit later, with the London *Times'* publication of the "Kishinev dispatch" from von Plehve to von Raaben, allegedly transmitted twelve days before the pogrom. This document seemed to prove that the central government had known in advance about the impending riots, and had instructed the local authorities not to interfere. No wonder the police and soldiers had refrained from using their weapons against the rioting mob! And, although the Russian government had eventually denied the authenticity of this communication, its handling of the matter had seemed to confirm its culpability. The long delay in responding to the report, and the subsequent expulsion from Russia of a *Times* correspondent, had given the dispatch even greater credibility than it otherwise might have borne.[49]

Meanwhile, the imperial government had been conducting itself almost as if it were a criminal conspiracy trying to hide its guilt. Its report on the pogrom, published several weeks after the event, had glossed over the evidence of prior planning and official inaction, and had even tried to fault the Jews for some of the violence. Shortly thereafter, the Ministry of Interior had sent instructions to the governors, advising them to prevent the formation of self-defense societies among the Jews. The censorship office, meanwhile, had forbidden publication of stories about the massacre, and had actually censured journals which dared to print articles sympathetic to the Jewish victims. Efforts of Kishinev Jews to secure state financial relief were consistently disallowed, while Christian peasants arrested in connection with the riots were released from jail to tend their fields. Finally, as if to confirm the fact that it wished to conceal the true origins of the riots, the government had ordered that the pogrom trials must be closed to the public.[50]

The minister of interior, on several occasions, had actually seemed to go out of his way to justify the pogrom. In private, a short time after the riots, von Plehve had told the minister of war that the Jews needed to be "taught a lesson" because they were "conceited" and "stood in the forefront of the revolutionary movement."[51] In public, a few months later, he had threatened a Jewish delegation that he would make their situation "unbearable" if they did not keep their young people out of the revolutionary movement. Not only had the minister been unrepentant; he had also seemed to hint that future violence might be forthcoming against the Jews unless they changed their ways.[52]

On top of all this, the local officials who had countenanced the riots, and the local agitators who had instigated them, were treated remarkably well. Governor von Raaben, it is true, was dismissed and disgraced, but he was an obvious scapegoat. Police Chief Khanzhenkov also lost his job. The others, however, suffered no such indignities. Vice-Governor Ustrugov, who bore far more responsibility than von Raaben for the anti-Jewish atmosphere in Kishinev, was merely transferred to another province with no decline in rank. Baron Levendal, whose name would surface repeatedly during the pogrom trials, was moved away from Kishinev to another official post before the proceedings began. He seems to have been neither censured nor reprimanded for his activities. Pavolachi Krushevan, who had moved to Saint Petersburg even before the pogrom, was never indicted or brought to trial, despite the fact that his daily *Bessarabets* had been implicated directly as a major cause of the riots. Indeed, Krushevan's new Saint Petersburg newspaper, *Znamia*, continued to publish anti-Jewish articles in the wake of the pogrom. Georgii Pronin, who narrowly escaped indictment for his role, continued his anti-Semitic activities for a full year after the riots, until he was temporarily expelled from Kishinev by the governor.[53] If anything, the imperial government behaved as if it was more interested in shielding these people than in exposing or punishing them.

Further evidence against the government was added some years later, when the memoirs of state officials eventually were published. It was revealed by Prince Urusov, for example, that before the pogrom Baron Levendal had sent a report to the Department of Police in Saint Petersburg warning of impending disorders—and still the government had taken no steps to forestall possible violence.[54] Later, it was made known by Sergei Witte, and confirmed by A. A. Lopukhin, that anti-Semitic organizations received state funding, and that anti-Jewish proclamations were printed by the police, during the revolutionary years of 1905 and 1906.[55] Although these things took place a few years after the Kishinev riots, the pattern seemed consistent: if such things were done in 1905, was it not likely that similar things had been done in 1903?

Count Witte, in fact, went so far as to lay the blame for the pogrom squarely upon the shoulders of the minister of interior. According to Witte's memoirs, von Plehve had earlier been "the guiding spirit and the real author of all the anti-Jewish laws and administrative measures" taken during the 1880s and 1890s.[56] Once he had become minister of interior, Witte went on, von Plehve had begun "looking for a psychological turning point in the revolutionary mood of the masses," and had actually "sought it in Jewish pogroms." Finally, as if to preclude any further doubt, the former finance minister plainly asserted that the Kishinev pogrom had been "arranged with the connivance of von Plehve."[57]

All this evidence produced a convincing theory about the origins of the Kishinev pogrom. Faced with rising popular discontent, a growing revolutionary movement, increasing radical activity among Jews, and the tsar's own anti-Semitism, von Plehve and von Wahl allegedly decided to encourage anti-Jewish violence. This way they could simultaneously divert popular hostility and punish the Jews. Working through local agents like Levendal and Ustrugov, they encouraged private citizens like Krushevan and Pronin to stir up the masses against their Jewish neighbors. The latter published articles and pamphlets, spread rumors about secret tsarist orders to "beat the Jews," and began to organize the rioters. Von Plehve and Levendal then acted to neutralize the governor, encouraging him not to use force and to avoid the scene of the turmoil. Later, when the pogrom created an international furor, they made a scapegoat of von Raaben, firing him to cover up their own guilt.

This interpretation, reinforced by various reports, accounts, and reminiscences, eventually became enshrined in standard historical works dealing with the Jewish question in late imperial Russia.[58] It has, in fact, much to recommend it. It is persuasive and logical, and it is based on extensive, albeit circumstantial, evidence. It provides an attractive explanation, not just for the Kishinev massacre, but also for the other pogroms which surfaced from time to time in late imperial Russia. It treats the Kishinev pogrom, not as an isolated incident, but as part of a broader pattern of state-sponsored violence and intimidation. It is not, however, entirely convincing.

The Role of the Russian Government

A closer look at all this material shows that the case against the Russian government, in many respects, is not as strong as it at first appears. It is based largely on impression, conjecture, and circumstantial evidence, and it fails to take into account the limits of state power and the overriding official interest in maintaining internal order.

For one thing, the government's failure to forestall or foreshorten the massacre does not mean that it approved. Legally, the state's authority was extensive; in practice, its power was rather limited. In fact, Kishinev was but one of a number of trouble spots where effective control was lacking. In 1902, for example, officials had been unable to prevent serious peasant riots in Ukraine and bloody railway strikes around Rostov-on-the-Don; in both cases, they had had great difficulty restoring order. In Ufa province, only weeks before the pogrom, it had taken the army to disperse a mob of strikers, and even then 45 persons had died in the melee. In summer of 1903, a few months after the Kishinev riots, massive general strikes spread throughout the southern provinces, much to the frustration of the imperial authorities. In September, despite government instructions ordering local officials to prevent new disorders, a major pogrom occurred at Gomel.[59] In the final analysis, the maintenance of order was in the hands of the local police, who were as a rule badly trained, poorly paid, little respected, and seriously understaffed. They could be supplemented, when necessary, by military troops, but these were no better educated, motivated, or prepared for such duties. On occasion, under determined and experienced leadership, the police and troops could be effective in preventing or stopping disorders. But, as often as not, the leaders were confused, unmotivated, and lacking in initiative, especially when it came to protecting and defending the Jews.[60]

For another thing, the connections between instigators in Kishinev and officials in Petersburg were tenuous at best. Kishinev was 900 miles from the capital, in a remote corner of the empire; contact and control were not easily maintained. State subsidies for Krushevan's Saint Petersburg paper did not necessarily imply support for a pogrom in Kishinev; nor, for that matter, did they protect this gazette from government censure a month after the Easter riots.[61] Pronin's claims of intimacy with high officials must be regarded with great skepticism, especially since he was always anxious to inflate his own importance. Ustrugov, as a vice-governor, would have had little direct contact with the minister of interior, nor did his repression of the Jews win official approval. His decisions, in fact, were regularly overturned by the Ruling Senate, and later he narrowly escaped indictment for refusing to comply with the Senate's rulings. Even Baron Levendal was not necessarily linked directly with von Plehve and von Wahl. His background, it is true, was in the gendarmes, but as Okhrana Chief he would have come under the purview of the "Special Section" of the Department of Police. His direct supervisors would have been Sergei Zubatov, head of the Special Section, and A. A. Lopukhin, director of the Police Department. Neither was considered an anti-Semite; indeed, at the time of the pogrom they were actively sponsoring several Jewish worker associations. And Levendal himself, whatever his faults, had made an effort to warn the department beforehand of the dangerous situation, complaining that the governor and police chief were paying him no heed.[62]

More importantly, perhaps, the main pieces of "proof" do not hold up well under scrutiny. Neither the "Kishinev dispatch" nor the Witte memoirs can be considered reliable sources. The dispatch, if authentic, shows that the minister of interior knew of impending trouble and advised against using armed force to stop it; this does not prove he wanted a bloodbath. Not long before the pogrom, in fact, stung by criticism of the recent slaughter of strikers in Ufa province, he had asked the minister of war whether it might be possible for troops to use less deadly force in quelling such disturbances.[63] He may well have been anxious to avoid a similar disaster in Kishinev.

Furthermore, it is quite possible that there never was any dispatch. No original was ever found, either in Saint Petersburg or Kishinev. The only evidence of its existence was the English version published by the London *Times*, which admitted in the same issue that the paper could not "vouch that it is authentic."[64] Rumor later held that the original had been sold by the governor's office to journalist Michael Davitt, who visited Kishinev in May of 1903. In his book on the pogrom, however, Davitt made no mention of this, and instead claimed to have found no evidence of government complicity in the riots. His personal papers, moreover, show no trace of any such document, and no copy was found in the records of the Ministry of Interior.[65] Von Raaben himself made no reference to any dispatch, either in his private letters to the minister of interior or in his subsequent testimony before the Ruling Senate. Yet, based on his handling of the pogrom, he had been fired from his job and deprived of his pension. In his later efforts to restore his good name, he assumed full responsibility for his actions, maintaining that under the circumstances he had taken the steps that he had then deemed most appropriate. He made no attempt whatever to claim that his actions had been based on instructions from above. If the "dispatch" existed, it hardly seems likely that he would have overlooked this obvious means of explaining and justifying his behavior.[66]

Witte's memoirs, meanwhile, are full of contradictions. The former finance minister, who had spent his career battling the Ministry of Interior, had an intense hostility toward von Plehve which colored and distorted his recollections. His account is neither reliable nor consistent on Kishinev. At one point he implicates the minister of interior; at another point he writes that he "would not go so far as to say that von Plehve engineered these pogroms personally." In fact, although he is clearly anxious to blame his rival, he seems to have had no real first-hand knowledge of what went on in Kishinev.[67]

Other officials, in their memoirs, denied government involvement and called the dispatch a forgery. "Obviously there never was any such letter," wrote the minister of interior's chancellor, whose office had supposedly transmitted it.[68] The director of the ministry's rural section insisted that the letter was apocryphal, and that "the government took no part in organizing Jewish pogroms."[69] Police Director Lopukhin claimed that "as a result of my painstakingly conducted investigation, this letter was shown to be a forgery." Lopukhin also exonerated von Plehve, asserting that he was "deeply convinced that it is unjust to attribute to him the organization of the Kishinev pogrom."[70]

These men, as officials of the ministry in question, were hardly unbiased witnesses. Still, as memoirists writing years after the event, they could and did deal candidly with the venalities of the high officials they served. None had much love for von Plehve or von Wahl; they could easily have implicated these men had they felt justified in doing so. Lopukhin, it is true, might have been reticent to expose state complicity for fear of indicting himself. But the police director, according to reliable accounts, was an opponent of anti-Semitism: he argued within the ministry for an end to anti-Jewish restrictions and later helped expose police attempts to encourage anti-Jewish activity. Indeed, regarding Kishinev, he did not hesitate to fault the government: through its anti-Jewish policies, he admitted, it had helped to cause the pogrom, even though it had not consciously set out to do so.[71]

Perhaps the most objective testimonies are those of Michael Davitt, the Irish nationalist turned journalist who investigated the riots, and Prince S. D. Urusov, who replaced von Raaben as governor of Bessarabia. Neither man actually witnessed the riots, but both became familiar with the details of the case. Both were considered fair and honest men, sympathetic toward the Jews, and extremely critical of the imperial authorities. Davitt, in fact, took pains to refute the official version of events, to emphasize the criminal inactivity of the local authorities, and to contend forcefully that the pogrom had been prearranged.[72] But he also insisted that there was no reason for him "to implicate the Government at Saint Petersburg in a responsibility for the outbreak." "I failed to discover any evidence," he maintained, ". . . which could even indirectly bring home to the Government the charge of guilty connivance in the *Bessarabetz* plot."[73]

Prince Urusov was in an even better position to comment. Although he did not arrive in Bessarabia until two months after the pogrom, he did come to know most of the principals, and he did get to attend the closed trial of the rioters. He also won the confidence of Kishinev's Jews, spoke out strongly against anti-Jewish legislation, and gained a reputation for honesty and integrity. Later, in the State Duma, he would accuse the government of fostering anti-Semitism and, in his memoirs, he would hold the government accountable for the conditions that led to the pogrom.[74] But he also denied the authenticity of the "Kishinev dispatch," calling it "spurious" and "apocryphal." And he rejected the notion that the ministry had engineered the massacre: "In examining . . . the secret papers of the Kishinev case in the Central Police Bureau in Saint Petersburg, I found not a thing to justify the assumption that the ministry of interior found it expedient to permit a Jewish massacre, or even an anti-Jewish demonstration, in Kishinev."[75]

There is, in fact, little reason to believe that ministry officials wanted a pogrom. Von Plehve's comments to the minister of war and threats to the Jewish delegation show that he was angered by the prominent role of Jewish youth in the revolutionary movement. But they by no means prove that he or his colleagues were anxious to encourage riots. Their highest priority was to *maintain* order, not disrupt it. For some time, policies had been designed to minimize contact between Jews and peasants, based on the premise that it led to discontent and turmoil. Behind this premise was the notion that the masses were at once easy prey for Jewish exploitation and prone to violent anti-Semitism. The government repressed the Jews in an effort to restrict their influence, preserve order, and protect the simple peasants, not to incite the masses to anti-Semitic violence.[76]

For that matter, there is no reason to believe that Petersburg officials had fomented pogroms in the past. Although the pogroms of 1881–1882 were sometimes attributed to Minister of Interior Ignat'ev and Police Director von Plehve, these riots in fact began before either man had settled into his job. Furthermore, the officials were at first clearly stunned and alarmed, seeing these pogroms as part of the same terrorist movement that had recently murdered the tsar. Their behavior during and after the riots may have been confused and ineffective, but it was hardly conspiratorial: they sought to restore order without alienating the Christian masses. Eventually, it is true, they had concluded that the Jews, by exploiting the common folk, had helped to bring this violence upon themselves. The net result had been the May Laws of 1882, which had sought to eliminate the "cause" of the pogroms by inhibiting Jewish exploitation. Despite their absurdity, these policies had seemed successful: for two decades thereafter, no major pogroms had occurred.[77]

By the time of Kishinev, moreover, the Ministry of Interior had begun to reconsider its views about the value of the anti-Jewish laws. Experience had shown, von Plehve admitted in 1902, that anti-Jewish legislation had actually been detrimental to state interests.[78] In January of 1903, the minister further elaborated these views:

[T]he Jewish population, crowded into the cities, does not have sufficient wages. Impoverished Jews, living in unsanitary conditions, present a danger for public health and order; while young Jews, raised without proper supervision, are always open to revolutionary propaganda. New restrictive measures could make matters still worse.

Later he went on to argue that "any steps toward relief of the Jews . . . , so as to eliminate their difficult economic plight, must be supported."[79]

Even before this, in fall of 1902, the ministry had decided to liberalize Jewish residence rules, and to permit Jews to purchase farmland in some areas. In May of 1903, as a consequence of this decision, a number of new places were opened to Jewish habitation, and in August the ministry began soliciting opinions from governors and mayors on the revision of Jewish legislation. In January of 1904, Jewish leaders were called in to express their views, and the governors were assembled to do likewise. A commission was set up to revise Jewish legislation and, by summer of 1904, a number of "needless" limitations were removed.[80] These changes do not mean the ministry had a change of heart—numerous restrictions remained. They do, however, seem inconsistent with the notion of a government anxious to foment pogroms.

At any rate, by the time of the Kishinev riots, Saint Petersburg had already begun to reconsider its policies toward Jews. Persuaded that repressive measures were merely driving young Jews into revolutionary activity, the Ministry of Interior was starting to soften the restrictions. The Department of Police, meanwhile, was helping Jewish workers in Minsk, Odessa, and Vilnius to form mutual aid societies and labor organizations.[81] Faced with the growing specter of worker agitation, peasant unrest, and revolutionary terrorism, officials were hoping to *prevent* turmoil, not to promote it. Given these priorities, it seems unlikely that they would seek to incite violent rioting among the lower classes.

All this, of course, by no means exonerates the government. It is still possible, albeit improbable, that von Plehve and von Wahl were somehow involved in seeking to instigate the pogrom, and that they consciously employed Baron Levendal as a secret agent to encourage and support the work of Pronin and Krushevan—and to discourage interference by local authorities. Then, perhaps, in order to cover up the evidence, the "dispatch" and any other relevant materials were systematically destroyed. It is also possible, however, that they were totally uninvolved, and that the local instigators acted entirely on their own, implying to their cronies—and to the potential rioters—that the tsar and the high officials favored an Easter massacre. The evidence does not entirely preclude either possibility.

The evidence does suggest, however, that a third alternative is much more probable than either of these two scenarios. The Ministry of Interior, it is quite apparent, was aware of the activities of Krushevan and Pronin, and approved of their general thrust. Bessarabia, after all, was an unstable region, with a growing revolutionary movement, a population that was predominantly Moldavian, and a large Jewish minority living mostly in the cities. Krushevan, Pronin, and Stepanov were each actively involved in trying to spread Russian patriotism and loyalty to the tsarist empire among the Christian masses. They were especially active in their attempts to win the loyalty of the urban working classes, which seemed most susceptible to revolutionary propaganda. It was the policy of the Ministry of Interior, and its Department of Police, to encourage and sponsor patriotic assemblies and mutual support activities among the urban workers to serve as a counterforce to the activities of revolutionary parties. It was also state policy to support and encourage the publication of conservative newspapers and journals which favored the autocratic government and its policies. Imperial activities in Kishinev, in the six months before the Easter pogrom, clearly fit this pattern.

The decision to establish a branch of the Okhrana in Kishinev, at the end of 1902, shows that the ministry and police were seriously concerned about the situation there. Baron Levendal, like the chiefs of other Okhranas, no doubt received instructions to encourage patriotic elements among the local populace, especially those with influence among the working classes. In Kishinev, of course, these persons were also the leaders of the anti-Semitic movement. They were engaged in "defending" the Christian workers against the Jewish "exploiters," and spreading anti-Jewish libels among the lower classes. Some, in fact, were actively encouraging the use of violence against the Jews. Local officials, influenced by their own anti-Semitic attitudes, did little to stop this. Defense of the Jews, and protection of their property, was scarcely a high priority.

As Easter approached, Levendal finally reported to Saint Petersburg that the situation in Kishinev was growing rather tense. The Dubossary murder, and the inflammatory articles in *Bessarabets*, had engendered anger and fear, and the dangerous atmosphere was being reinforced by rumors, leaflets, and posters. The local judicial authorities, and the official provincial newspaper, made a concerted effort to refute the claims of ritual murder and discredit the *Bessarabets* articles, while the local police and military officials did make plans for increased patrols over the Easter holidays. But the governor and police chief largely ignored the warnings, and the Ministry of Interior, having no reason to anticipate a massacre, ordered no extraordinary measures to prevent disorder or violence. Only on the second day of the pogrom, when the ministry learned that the situation had gotten completely out of hand, did it order the sort of crackdown needed to bring the violence to an end. By this time, unfortunately, it was too late to prevent extensive property damage and loss of life.

Even if the Russian government did not actively instigate the riots, then, it still must bear a large share of the responsibility for them. Whether or not government officials actually wanted a pogrom, they nevertheless helped set the stage by fostering narrow Russian chauvinism and official anti-Semitism, and by giving aid and support to the local zealots and agitators. The anti-Jewish legislation, the state's repressive policies, and the favoritism shown to anti-Semites all contributed to the general impression that anti-Jewish activity was not only condoned but rewarded. In this atmosphere, it is easy to see how ambitious local officials might seek to advance their careers by repressing the Jews, or how local peasants and townsfolk could believe that anti-Jewish violence reflected the will of the tsar.

CHAPTER 7

The Causes and Legacy of the Easter Riots

The Easter riots in Kishinev made an enormous impression, both in Russia and abroad. For much of 1903, worldwide attention was focused on an area that had hitherto been rather obscure. Eventually, however, the Kishinev pogrom and the concerns it raised tended to fade into the background, overshadowed by other more pressing, developments. Still, the events of April 1903 could hardly be forgotten, even if they no longer received constant public attention. The causes of the pogrom, and its long-term implications, remained a matter of controversy and concern, long after reports about the riots and their repercussions had disappeared from the newspapers and faded from public view.

The Reasons for the Riots

The traditional explanation for the outbreak of the riots was simple and clear: the Kishinev pogrom happened because the Russian government wanted it to happen. Those who spread and publicized anti-Jewish libels, those who organized and led the disorders, those who actually took part in the vandalism and murder, and those who failed to take effective measures to put an end to the violence were all, in this interpretation, accomplices of the government in its unsavory scheme. But if, as the evidence presented above suggests, government leaders did not consciously seek to instigate the pogrom, then the problem of causation becomes somewhat more complicated, and much more problematic.

The fact is that tensions and anxieties had existed in Bessarabia, between Christians and Jews, long before the Kishinev riots took place. Many of these were based upon age-old hostilities, rooted in religious rivalry and cultural differences that inspired mistrust and suspicion. Outlandish rumors and absurd libels—including time-worn legends about Jewish ritual murders—were readily accepted by certain elements among the Christian population. Orthodox Christian clergy had at times contributed to this atmosphere, depicting the Jews as aliens and infidels, and even lending credibility to anti-Jewish slanders. Political leaders, when it had served their purposes, had not been averse to preying upon this mentality, and historical Moldavia had been no stranger to repression and persecution of Jews.

By the early twentieth century, these tensions and anxieties were being exacerbated by several relatively recent developments. One of these was the legal discrimination against the Jews perpetrated and encouraged by the imperial Russian government. The Pale of Settlement, the May Laws of 1882, the restrictions on Jewish residence, the quotas on Jewish participation in higher education, local government, and various professions—all of these sent a clear and unmistakable message to Jew and Christian alike. The Jews were not only *different*, they were *dangerous*: they were a hostile, alien force against which the Christian population had to be "protected." The legal status of the Jews gave the distinct impression that Jews could and should be regarded as a threat, and that every Jew was a potential exploiter, criminal, and enemy. If the legal system treated Jews as dangerous subversives, it is hardly surprising that common people did the same—and that they were encouraged to do so by career-minded officials and ambitious private persons who identified closely with the established order. For many such persons, hostility toward the Jews became almost synonymous with legality and order.

A second factor was the rise of nationalism and national self-consciousness within the Russian Empire. From the perspectives of both the official nationalism of imperial Russia and the emergent nationalism of the subject nationalities, the Jews were outsiders. They were not really Russians, but neither were they Ukrainians or Moldavians. They were not really citizens, not really part of the "nation," not really "us." Most other nationalities at least had a homeland, a place where they were recognized as indigenous natives. Nowhere, except perhaps in their own neighborhoods and ghettos, did the Jews really fit. It is little wonder that many Jews felt alienated in the land of their birth, and that many non-Jews saw anti-Semitism as a component of patriotism and national pride.

A third contributing factor was the social and economic climate in the city of Kishinev itself. The forces of urbanization and population growth had transformed a sleepy provincial town into a growing metropolis, complete with ethnic neighborhoods and slums, widespread poverty and unemployment, and social conflicts and clashes. The steady increase in the Jewish population, to the point where the Jews had become the city's largest ethnic group, was unsettling and threatening to both Moldavians and Russians. The domination of the town's commerce by Jewish individuals intensified concerns about "Jewish exploitation," and aroused resentments among some Christian businessmen. The preponderance of Jews in the skilled trades fostered fears and hostilities among the Christian artisans, who frequently found it difficult to hold their own. And the growing number of impoverished Jews, who were often willing to work for subsistence wages, posed a threat to the unskilled workers among the non-Jewish population.

These tensions, and the factors that precipitated them, were not in themselves the causes of the Easter pogrom. Indeed, the atmosphere in Kishinev at the beginning of the twentieth century was not necessarily more volatile than that of any number of other cities and, as various observers pointed out, Christians and Jews generally managed to live and work together with reasonable calm, despite the underlying anxieties. But the climate in Kishinev did help set the stage for the pogrom: it provided both the fuel and the conditions which would support a conflagration, given the proper preparation.

Prominent local persons, mostly from the private sector, did the preparatory work. Publisher Krushevan, the region's most notorious anti-Semite, bore a major share of the responsibility for the violence that took place. Krushevan was not always on the scene as the fires were being lit: he spent much of 1903 in Saint Petersburg nurturing the *Znamia*, his fledgling newspaper. But his Kishinev paper, the

Bessarabets, was nonetheless quite active in spreading vile slanders about the Jews and inculcating fear among the Christian populace. And Krushevan's press apparently served as the source of at least some of the scurrilous handbills and posters that actively encouraged anti-Semitic violence in the weeks before the pogrom. Pronin and Stepanov, the self-styled leaders and defenders of the Christian workers, were also active in this effort, as were a number of other local lights. Their activities were countenanced, and to some extent even supported, by Vice-Governor Ustrugov and various police officials.

But the most important single event which galvanized the forces of hatred and fear into action was the murder of young Mikhail Rybachenko in the town of Dubossary. The mysterious circumstances of the lad's disappearance, the rumors that surrounded this tragedy, and the fact that it occurred as the Jewish Passover approached all combined to conjure up age-old legends about Jewish ritual murders. Then, even as the local investigation was disproving the libelous rumors, the *Bessarabets* gave credence to them by publishing sensational accounts. The atmosphere in Kishinev was thus transformed: among the Christians who believed these libels, resentment was turned into anger and fear was turned into rage. Kishinev authorities, using the official local newspaper, tried to discredit the rumors of ritual murders and calm the agitated population; the *Bessarabets* was even induced to print a retraction. But by that time the damage had been done, and the level of hostility had been stepped up several notches.[1]

In this atmosphere, as Easter approached, the agitators spread rumors that the tsar himself favored strong action against the Jews, and that Christians who enriched themselves at Jewish expense during Eastertide could expect to go unpunished. Printed proclamations, circulated by the instigators among the lower classes, tended to verify the legend that the emperor had proclaimed a three-day period during which Christians could take vengeance against their Judaic neighbors. Despite the anxious pleas of local Jewish leaders, neither the governor nor the bishop was willing to take extraordinary measures to discredit the rumors or to protect the Jews. The stage was set for the pogrom.

The outbreak of violence on Easter Sunday afternoon, then, was no accident. Despite the official account, there seems to have been no single incident which triggered the riots: indeed, several groups of rabble-rousers appear to have formed themselves and begun their vandalism almost simultaneously. The reports that some groups had leaders who were able to point out which establishments were Jewish, and the circumstance that Christians knew enough to protect their property by marking it with crosses and icons, showed at least some level of prior arrangement. The violence was not entirely indiscriminate, and not entirely spontaneous.

Still, it would be misleading to portray the Kishinev pogrom as a well-planned, well-coordinated, preconceived attack against the Jews. The early originators of the violence were buoyed up by the festive mood, and some by excessive drink; they were more engaged in wanton vandalism than in organized behavior. At first they limited themselves mainly to window-breaking and sporadic looting, engaging in very little violence against persons. But as time went on their behavior lost all sense of discipline and order. Those who instigated the pogrom may have helped initiate the riots, but they appear to have exercised little influence over the crowds once the pogrom was under way.

This is amply demonstrated by the events of the second day. On Monday, April 7, what had begun as an attack on property turned into an attack on persons, and all semblance of reason or restraint quickly vanished. Some of the change may have resulted from rumors that Jews were attacking Christians, which helped engender both fear and ferocity among the various rioters. But the Jewish attempts at self-protection were isolated and defensive: they hardly constituted a counterattack in any sense of the word. And the actions of the Christian mob showed little fear of resistance or reprisal. If anything, it was the apparent passivity of the police and the soldiers that influenced the crowd's behavior. The fact that those who stoned and looted were rarely dispersed or arrested gave rise to a widespread perception that one could plunder and beat the Jews without fear of serious consequence. In the minds of many rioters, this must have confirmed the rumors and proclamations that had spread during the previous weeks: the officials indeed seemed willing to permit mistreatment of Jews. The mob violence created its own momentum, and the lack of external restraint only added to its force. The more the crowds got away with, the more violent they became. Only when the soldiers and police began to act decisively, and make numerous arrests, did it become apparent that some might well be punished. When this happened, the majority of the rioters soon abandoned their pursuits. The pogrom ended, not so much because it was effectively crushed by authorities, but rather because their long-delayed action served to destroy the myth of official sanction and approval. The rioters could no longer be sure that they would get away with murder.

This is not to say that the local authorities were conscious accomplices to the crime, or that the troops and police were purposely restricted from interfering in the disorders. The behavior of the officials was more suggestive of confusion than of coordination: neither the governor nor the garrison commander was fully sure of how to respond, and each seems to have expected the other to assume more effective command. Given this lack of leadership, combined with their own fears and prejudices, few patrolmen or soldiers were willing to risk their necks or act boldly in defense of the vilified Jews. Several made an effort to confront the rampaging crowds; some actually urged on the rioters; most simply sought to avoid confrontation until decisive orders were issued. When the orders finally came they proceeded to do their duty, and the disorders were brought to an expeditious end.

The Kishinev pogrom, then, was neither a spontaneous outburst against the Jewish "exploiters" nor a well-planned and well-coordinated attack organized and supported by government officials. It was rather the result of a systematic campaign of vilification and distortion actively pursued by local anti-Semites, who published articles, spread rumors, and issued proclamations about Jewish "crimes" and the duty of patriotic Russians and Moldavians to resist them. It was set within the context of the social, religious, and economic tensions present in a multi-ethnic city with a growing Jewish population, a commercial environment in which Jews played a prominent role, and a large underclass of semi-literate Christians who were susceptible to anti-Jewish propaganda. It was aided by the attitudes of government officials, who rigorously enforced the legal restrictions against Jews while often showing favoritism to anti-Semites, whom they regarded as stable and patriotic elements within the Kishinev community. The riots themselves were initiated by a loosely organized bunch of hooligans, whose original goal seems to have been to "teach the Jews a lesson" by damaging and vandalizing Jewish properties. On the second day, when it became evident that the forces of law and order were offering little resistance, the crowds lost all sense of restraint, and the violence intensified into wanton pillage, beating, and murder.

The Impacts of the Pogrom

The immediate impact of the Easter riots was serious enough: numerous homes and businesses were damaged, 51 people were dead, and hundreds of others were left injured, maimed, widowed, orphaned, unemployed, or homeless. The long-term implications, however, were even more extensive. The effects of the massacre on the Russian Jewish community, the imperial Russian government, and on overall relations between Christians and Jews were sweeping and profound.

One major impact of the pogrom was a legacy of bitterness and mistrust between the Kishinev Jews and their Christian neighbors. For some time after the riots, in fact, Jewish proprietors and employers were very hesitant to engage Christian artisans and workers, partly out of fear, no doubt, and partly out of resentment over what had occurred. Since the Jews played such a prominent role in local business, this meant that large numbers of Christian workers were left without work, increasing their hostility toward the Jews and depressing the local economy.[2] Further resentments surfaced among the Christian population when indictments were handed down for crimes committed during the riots and no Jews were charged with any wrongdoing.[3] These circumstances, combined with the recurrent rumors of renewed disorders, kept tensions at a simmering point long after life in Kishinev, at least on the surface, appeared to have returned to normal.

Almost a year after the pogrom, as Easter of 1904 approached, it became evident that tensions and antagonisms had by no means disappeared. Rumors and fears of a new massacre began to circulate, and Jews began to prepare in various ways to defend themselves. The situation, in fact, became quite tense. But the efforts of the new governor, buttressed by a strongly worded telegram from the minister of interior, were enough to galvanize the local police into taking extensive precautionary measures. Pronin was expelled from the city by administrative order until the holidays had passed, and vigorous steps were taken to prevent the circulation of pogrom-inciting literature and to counter the scurrilous rumors. Police patrols were stepped up, and special "obligatory resolutions" were published prohibiting things such as loitering, forming groups on the streets, or carrying firearms. The holiday passed without serious incident.[4] Within a few months, the last trials of the indicted rioters wound to an end, and the case of the Kishinev pogrom was formally brought to a close.

Even then, however, relations between Jews and Christians remained tense, and the possibility of renewed violence continued to exist. The tumultuous events of 1905—defeats suffered by Russian troops in East Asia, the growing revolutionary ferment, the specter of worker strikes and government repression, and the confusion and dislocation which resulted from all this—had their impact on Kishinev as well. Following the Manifesto of October 17, in which the tsar guaranteed civil liberties and promised to grant legislative powers to an elected State Duma, a wave of demonstrations swept through the cities of southern and western Russia, including Kishinev. Here, as elsewhere, "patriotic" organizations and elements took advantage of the situation to launch renewed attacks against the Jews. On October 18, 1905, a new pogrom occurred in Kishinev, taking the lives of at least 29 Jews and causing extensive damage. This riot, however, was only part of a much broader trend; it was largely obscured by the dramatic events taking place in the capital, and by the devastating pogroms that occurred simultaneously in Kiev, Odessa, and elsewhere. It achieved neither the prominence nor the notoriety of the Easter massacre of 1903.[5]

Another major impact of the 1903 pogrom was its effect on Jewish consciousness. Dreams that progressive forces might make it possible for Russian Jews to live in peace with their Christian neighbors had been rudely shattered, not just in Kishinev but throughout the Pale of Settlement. The Kishinev pogrom reinforced and underscored a central reality: it was very dangerous to be a Jew in the Russian Empire.

Many Jews responded to this reality by leaving their Russian homes and seeking better fortunes and greater security in the West. A new wave of Jewish emigration, similar to that which had occurred after the pogroms of 1881–1882, began. In the months that followed the riots, hundreds of Jews left Kishinev: according to reports in *Bessarabets*, the police granted exit visas to more than 500 Jews and their families during the first four and a half months after the riots.[6] Elsewhere in the Pale of Settlement, the story was similar. In Paris, the Alliance Israélite Universelle, one of several organizations that provided emigration aid, reported that the Kishinev and Gomel pogroms had created a "veritable panic" among Russian Jews, and that in certain months of 1903 more than 6,000 of them had arrived in New York and Philadelphia alone.[7]

For some Jews, however, the lure of the West seemed to be a false hope: although anti-Semitism may have been less violent in Western Europe and America, it was nonetheless all too evident in these places as well. According to the Zionists, Jews would never be safe anywhere in the world unless and until they had a homeland of their own. But the promise of Zion was too far in the future for the Kishinev Jews: no homeland existed in 1903, and none was likely to exist for quite some time. Besides, the Zionist movement at the time was badly split over the possibility that the British might provide a colony for Jews in Uganda: some wanted to pursue this as a way station; others insisted that no place other than Palestine would be acceptable. In the wake of the Easter pogrom, several proposals were put forth which would have created a settlement of Kishinev Jews in Palestine and brought Jewish orphans there from Kishinev. Nothing, however, ever came of these proposals.[8]

For other Jews, emigration was more of an escape than a solution. All it did was to play into the hands of the anti-Semites, who were only too happy to see large numbers of Jews depart, and leave the millions who stayed behind in an even more precarious position. To the members of the Jewish Bund, and to Jews who joined other revolutionary groups, the only sensible response was to join hands with the Russian radicals and work for the overthrow of the tsarist regime. To these people, and to the Russians who supported them, the Kishinev disorders represented not so much an expression of popular anti-Semitism as an extension of state policy. Once the autocratic government was overthrown, they dared to hope, the source and impetus for pogroms would be removed. Using such arguments the Bund and other rebel groups sought, with some success, to attract more Jews to their cause in the wake of the Kishinev riots.[9]

The recourses of emigration, Zionism, or revolution, whatever their merits, were either unattainable or unacceptable to most Russian Jews. To them, whatever the long-term solution might be, the short-term need was to organize themselves for defense in case new pogroms should arise. As a result, the main legacy left by the Kishinev riots in the Russian Jewish community was the formation of self-defense groups, armed, organized, and ready to do combat with any group of ruffians who might seek to attack the Jews.

For some Jews, in fact, the absence of any organized self-defense in Kishinev, and the inadequate efforts made by local Jews to protect their families, were a source of national shame. The notion that Jewish males had behaved in a cowardly fashion, although not entirely accurate, became part of the Kishinev lore. Especially influential in this regard was Hayyim Bialik's widely read poem, "The City of Slaughter," which contains a brutal indictment of Kishinev's Jewish men:

> Note also, do not fail to note,
> In that dark corner, and behind that cask,
> Crouched husbands, bridegrooms, brothers,
>   peering from the cracks,
> Watching the sacred bodies struggling underneath
> The bestial breath,
> Stifled in filth, and swallowing their blood!
> The lecherous rabble portioning for booty,
> Their kindred and their flesh!
> Crushed in their shame, they saw it all;
> They did not stir nor move. . .
> Perhaps, perhaps, each watcher had it in his
>   heart to pray:
> A miracle, O Lord—and spare my skin this day![10]

The poem was patently unfair to those Jewish husbands and fathers who had sought, in various ways, to protect their families and restrain the rampaging crowds, but it did serve to highlight the helplessness of the Kishinev Jews. Thus the lesson of Kishinev for

Jews was very clear: since neither the authorities, nor the police, nor the military forces could be relied upon to protect them, they would have to defend themselves. Within weeks after the pogrom, in city after city within the Pale of Settlement, Jewish self-defense groups were formed. Before long, in fact, the Ministry of Interior was warning the governors to prevent the organization of such associations.[11] But these warnings were ineffective: in September of 1903, at the time of the pogrom in Gomel, Jewish groups actively fought back against the rioting crowds and inflicted a heavy toll on their Christian attackers. The Jewish Bund played a major role in organizing this opposition, and as a result gained credibility as an effective force for protecting Russian Jews.[12] By 1905, when the next major wave of pogroms swept through the Pale of Settlement, Jewish self-defense was conspicuous almost everywhere.[13] It may not have stopped the attacks, but it did make them much more costly. The Kishinev experience, and the shame it engendered, helped to transform the Jews from passive victims to active and militant resisters.

Meanwhile, the Russian government and its policies were also suffering as a result of the Kishinev pogrom. The widespread belief that Saint Petersburg officials had planned and orchestrated the massacre undermined the credibility of the tsarist autocracy, both inside and outside of Russia. Radical groups seized upon the opportunity to portray the tsar's regime as a criminal force which brutalized its own subjects.[14] This, of course, made it easier to recruit disenchanted persons to the revolutionary fold, and to justify acts of violence, terror, and sedition.

The most ironic example of this was the case of Evno Azef. By 1903, as a talented and effective undercover Okhrana agent, Azef had worked his way into a position of influence in the terrorist wing of the Socialist Revolutionary Party. As a result, he was in a position to learn in advance of terrorist activities, including assassination attempts upon Russian officials, and warn the tsarist police in advance. But Azef was also a Jew, and as such he was profoundly troubled by the Kishinev pogrom and the government's reputed role. Shortly after the pogrom, when he became the effective leader of the terrorist wing, he made an important decision: he would help to organize and direct an assassination attempt against Minister of

Interior von Plehve, who had been so widely identified as the author of the pogrom. In July of 1904, under the guidance and direction of Azef, this mission was successfully completed: von Plehve was murdered on the streets of Saint Petersburg on his way to visit the tsar.[15]

Likewise, in the arena of world opinion, the reputation of the Russian government suffered a severe setback. A whole host of articles and books, published in Europe and North America, defamed the autocratic regime, accused it of criminal behavior, and blamed it for the massacres.[16] Relations between Russia and the United States were severely strained as a result of the widespread public indignation in major American cities, and the role played by the U.S. government in attempting to transmit the protest petition to Emperor Nicholas II. Even in France, which was Russia's formal ally, protests were held and dismay expressed about the reports from Kishinev.[17] In 1904, when Russia found itself at war, it received very little sympathy from the Western public and the Western press, despite the fact that the war was initiated by Japan's surprise attack. Much of this, it is true, can be attributed to the international situation at the time, but the anti-Russian climate clearly had been intensified by the reports of government complicity in the riots at Kishinev.

The most tragic impact of the Kishinev massacre, however, was perhaps the example it set. It represented the first major pogrom of the twentieth century, and it received a vast amount of publicity and notoriety. By standards set later in the century, it is true, it was a relatively modest affair: far more massive attacks against the Jews would eventually make it seem mild. At the time, however, it was a major event, and it shocked much of the world. But it also helped to demonstrate how easy it was for a few militant anti-Semites, taking advantage of religious antagonisms, economic rivalries, and age-old superstitions and fears, to organize a brutal attack against the Jewish community. It showed that anti-Semitic publications and effective propaganda could be used to arouse the Christian people against their Jewish neighbors. It showed that respectable middle-class Christians, who might not think of engaging in riots themselves, were unlikely to lift a finger to prevent attacks upon Jews. It showed that Christian police, soldiers, and law enforcement officials, who were often so rigid and efficient in enforcing anti-Jewish laws, were at best ineffective and at worst downright hostile when it came to defending the Jews. It showed that Christian religious leaders could be counted upon to sit by in silence, rather than raise their voices on behalf of the Jewish people. It laid things out for the whole world to see how terribly vulnerable were the Jews who lived in Christian Europe, and how few Christians could be expected to come to their aid in the event of a monstrous attack. This, sadly, was an important part of the legacy of the Easter riots in Kishinev.

Notes

1. The Jewish Question in Russia

1. Dennis Prager and Joseph Telushkin, *Why the Jews? The Reason for Antisemitism* (New York: Simon and Schuster, 1983), 27–36.
2. Ibid., 27–45, 83–110; James Parkes, *Antisemitism* (Chicago: Quadrangle Books, 1963), 57–60; Edward H. Flannery, *The Anguish of the Jews: Twenty-three Centuries of Antisemitism* (New York: Paulist Press, 1985), 7–38.
3. Parkes, 60–62; Prager and Telushkin, 90–93.
4. Flannery, 28–46; Paul E. Grosser and Edwin G. Halperin, *Anti-Semitism: Causes and Effects* (New York: Philosophical Library, 1983), 49–54; Jules Isaac, *The Teaching of Contempt: Christian Roots of Anti-Semitism* (New York: Holt, Rinehart and Winston, 1964), 39–52.
5. Malcolm Hay, *Europe and the Jews: The Pressure of Christendom on the People of Israel for 1900 Years* (Boston: Beacon Press, 1961), 12–32; Isaac, 44–45, 111–112; Prager and Telushkin, 93–96.
6. Isaac, 109–117; Prager and Telushkin, 92–93; Hay, 21–31; Flannery, 42–54.
7. *Povest' vremennykh let*, ed. V. P. Adrianov-Perets, 2 vols. (Moscow: Izdatel'stvo Akademii Nauk SSSR, 1950), 1:60. See also *The Russian Primary Chronicle: Laurentian Text*, trans. Samuel H. Cross and Olgerd Sherbovitz-Wetzor (Cambridge, MA: Mediaeval Academy of America, 1953), 96–98.
8. Simon M. Dubnov, *History of the Jews in Russia and Poland from the Earliest Times until the Present Day*, trans. Israel Friedlander, 3 vols. (Philadelphia: Jewish Publication Society of America, 1916–1920), 1:30–31; George P. Fedotov, *The Russian Religious Mind*, 2 vols. (New York: Harper and Row, 1960), 1:86–91; John D. Klier, *Russia Gathers Her Jews: The Origins of the "Jewish Question" in Russia, 1772–1825* (De Kalb: Northern Illinois University Press, 1986), 23.

9. Salo W. Baron, *The Russian Jew under Tsars and Soviets* (New York: Macmillan, 1964), 5; Klier, 22–23; Fedotov, 1:91–92.

10. Baron, 6–7; Klier, 24–25.

11. Dubnov, 1:242–3; Klier, 25–28; Baron, 7–8.

12. Bernard D. Weinryb, *The Jews of Poland: A Social and Economic History of the Jewish Community in Poland from 1100 to 1800* (Philadelphia: Jewish Publication Society of America, 1972), 24–30, 32–39, 41–48; Klier, 4–8.

13. Israel Friedlander, *The Jews of Russia and Poland* (New York and London: G. P. Putnam's Sons, 1915), 42–54; Klier, 8–11; Weinryb, 41–48; 56–70.

14. Weinryb, 33–44; Klier, 10–12.

15. Dubnov, 1:144–53; Weinryb, 133–155, 181–203; Klier, 13–15; Friedlander, 72–81.

16. Richard Pipes, "Catherine II and the Jews: The Origins of the Pale of Settlement," *Soviet Jewish Affairs* 5, no. 2 (1975): 14–17; Klier, 75–76, 140; Baron, 18, 32–33.

17. Hans Rogger, *Jewish Policies and Right-Wing Politics in Imperial Russia* (Berkeley: University of California Press, 1986), 115–120; Mark Vishniak, "Antisemitism in Tsarist Russia: A Study in Government-Fostered Antisemitism," in *Essays on Antisemitism*, ed. Koppel S. Pinson (New York: n.p., 1942), 126–127.

18. Klier, 134–145.

19. Michael Stanislawski, *Tsar Nicholas I and the Jews: The Transformation of Jewish Society in Russia, 1825–1855* (Philadelphia: Jewish Publication Society of America, 1983), 185–188; Friedlander, 129–147; Dubnov, 2:13–66; Vishniak, 126–127.

20. Rogger, 120–126; Baron, 39–41; Dubnov, 2:154–177.

21. N. Kh. Bunge, "The Years 1881–1894: A Memorandum," ed. George E. Snow, *Transactions of the American Philosophical Society* 71, Part 6 (1981): 26–27; Dubnov, 2:184–192, 198–202; Rogger, 127–131; Stephen M. Berk, *Year of Crisis, Year of Hope: Russian Jewry and the Pogroms of 1881–1882* (Westport, CT: Greenwood Press, 1985), 45–48; Baron, 41–42.

22. I. Michael Aronson, *Troubled Waters: The Origins of the 1881 Anti-Jewish Pogroms in Russia* (Pittsburgh: University of Pittsburgh Press, 1990), 26–27, 42–43, 220–223; Aronson, "Geographical and Socioeconomic Factors in the 1881 Anti-Jewish Pogroms in Russia," *Russian Review* 39 (January 1980): 21–22; Berk, 48–53.

23. Aronson, *Troubled Waters*, 227–230; Aronson, "Geographical and Socioeconomic Factors," 26–27.

24. I. D. Sosis, "K istorii antievreiskogo dvizheniia v tsarskoi Rossii," *Trudy Belorusskogo Gosudarstvennogo Universiteta v g. Minsk*, no. 6–7 (1925): 181–186; Mark S. Simpson, "The *Svyaschonnaya druzhina* and Jewish Persecution in Tsarist Russia," *New Zealand Slavonic Journal* no. 2

(1978):17–23, 25; Aronson, *Troubled Waters*, 44–61; Berk, 35–44. See also "Dokladnaia zapiski grafa P. I. Kutaisova," in *Materialy dlia istorii antievreiskikh pogromov v Rossii*, ed. S. M. Dubnov and G. Ia. Krasnyi-Admoni, 2 vols. (Petrograd and Moscow: Tipografiia "Kadima" and Gosudarstvennoe izdatel'stvo, 1919, 1923), 2:183–528.

25. Iulii I. Gessen, "Graf N. P. Ignat'ev i 'Vremennya pravila' o evreiakh 3 maia 1882 goda," *Pravo*, no. 30 (27 July 1908): 1631–1633; Bunge, 27–28; Rogger, 133–144; *Polnoe sobranie zakonov rossiiskoe imperii*, 33 vols., 3rd ed. (Saint Petersburg: Gosudarstvennaia tipografiia, 1885–1916), 2, no. 834 (3 May 1882).

26. *Obzor postanovlenii vysshei kommisii po peresmotru deistvuiushchikh o evreiakh v imperii zakonov (1883–1888)* (Saint Petersburg: [Gosudarstvennaia tipografiia], 1888), 88–112; G. B. Sliozberg, *Dela minuvshikh dnei: Zapiski russkago evreia*, 3 vols. (Paris: Imprimerie Pascal, 1933–1934), 1:255–257; Dubnov, 2:362–370; Bunge, 30–31; Rogger, 144–151.

27. Baron, 48–49; Dubnov, 2:384–386, 401–404; Sergei Iu. Witte, "Evreiskii vopros pri vvedenii piteinoi monopolii: Vsepoddanneishii doklad," *Evreiskaia starina* 8 (1915), 406–409; Rogger, 66–69, 154–156. For a detailed account of the anti-Jewish measures, see Leo Errera, *The Russian Jews: Extermination or Emancipation?* (New York: Macmillan, 1894; reprint, Westport, CT: Greenwood Press, 1975), 32–99.

28. Dubnov, 2:373–377; Zoza Szajkowski, "How the Mass Migration to America Began," *Jewish Social Studies* 4 (October 1982): 291–297; Walter Laqueur, *A History of Zionism* (New York: Holt, Rinehart and Winston, 1972), 103–108; Henry J. Tobias, *The Jewish Bund in Russia from Its Origins to 1905* (Stanford: Stanford University Press, 1972), 22–48.

29. Bunge, 29–33; Rogger, 109–112, 174–175; I. Michael Aronson, "Russian Bureaucratic Attitudes toward the Jews, 1881–1894" (Ph.D. dissertation, Northwestern University, 1973), 296–317.

2. Kishinev

1. George F. Jewsbury, *The Russian Annexation of Bessarabia, 1774–1828* (New York: East European Monographs, 1976), 7–54.

2. Ibid., 57, 67; A. Zashchuk, *Materialy dlia geografii i statistiki Rossii: Bessarabskaia oblast'* (Saint Petersburg: n.p., 1862), 10–11, 147–148, 151–181.

3. Jewsbury, 77–79, 95–96, 142–161; *Pervaia vseobshchaia perepis' naselenie rossiiskoe imperii, 1897*, vol. 3, *Bessarabskaia guberniia* (Saint Petersburg: Izdanie tsentral'nago statisticheskago komiteta ministerstva vnutrennikh del, 1905), x-xi.

4. Jewsbury, 66–74; V. S. Zelenchuk, *Naselenie Bessarabii i podnestrov'ia v XIX v.* (Kishinev: "Shtiintsa," 1979), 148–160; *Istoriia Kishineva*,

comp. Kishinevskii gosudarstvennyi universitet kafedra istorii SSSR (Kishinev: Izdatel'stvo "Kartia Moldoveniaske," 1966), 47–50, 99–101.

5. *Pervaia vseobshchaia perepis'*, 3:xi, 74–93; Andrei Popovici, *The Political Status of Bessarabia* (Washington, DC: Ransdell Inc., 1931), 102–105, 109; Zelenchuk, 168, 174, 205–206.

6. *Pervaia vseobshchaia perepis'*, 3:xi-xii; Prince S. D. Urusov, *Memoirs of a Russian Governor*, trans. Herman Rosenthal (London and New York: Harper and Brothers, 1908), 14.

7. Afanasii Lukich Odud, *Kishinev: Economiko-geograficheskii ocherk* (Kishinev: Gosudarstvennoe izdatel'stvo "Kartia Moldoveniaske," 1964), 23, 25; Jewsbury, 134; Y. Zlatova and V. Kotel'nikov, *Across Moldavia* (Moscow: Foreign Languages Publishing House, 1959), 26; A. S. Konstantinov, *Kishinev: ekonomicheskii ocherk* (Kishinev: "Kartia Moldoveniaske," 1966), 11–12.

8. Odud, 29–32; *Istoriia Kishineva*, 14–40; Jewsbury, 134–141; F. F. Vigel', "Zamechanii na nyneshnee sostoianie Bessarabii," *Russkii arkhiv* Book 1, Part 2 (1893): 25–26.

9. Urusov, 96–98; Konstantinov, 22–23; Michael Davitt, *Within the Pale: The True Story of Anti-Semitic Persecutions in Russia* (New York: A. S. Barnes, 1903; reprint, New York: Arno Press, 1975), 158–159.

10. Konstantinov, 12–13, 18–21; Zlatova and Kotel'nikov, 26–27; *Istoriia Kishineva*, 83–87.

11. *Pervaia vseobshchaia perepis'*, 3:2–3; *Istoriia Kishineva*, 49, 101.

12. Konstantinov, 22–23; Davitt, 158–159.

13. *Pervaia vseobshchaia perepis'*, 3:80–81; *Istoriia Kishineva*, 49, 101; Davitt, 155.

14. *Pervaia vseobshchaia perepis'*, 3:228–231; Zelenchuk, 154; Anthony Babel, *La Bessarabie: Etude historique, ethnographique et économique* (Paris: Librairie Félix Alcan, 1926), 229–231; P. Cazaco, *Notes sur la Bessarabie* (Bucharest: "Cartea Romaneasca," 1926), 20–21; Popovici, 84–88.

15. *Pervaia vseobshchaia perepis'*, 3:178–179; *Istoriia Kishineva*, 99–101; Urusov, 25, 37–38, 59–61.

16. Jewsbury, 67–68; Zelenchuk, 171–178; Aronson, "Geographical and Socioeconomic Factors," 21–26.

17. *Pervaia vseobshchaia perepis'*, 3:2–3, 112–119, 178–179; *Istoriia Kishineva*, 49, 101; Zelenchuk, 168–171; Urusov, 161–165.

18. Urusov, 19, 25, 100–101, 112, 161–162; Davitt, 93–94; Louis Guy Michael, *More Corn for Bessarabia* (East Lansing: Michigan State University Press, 1983), 76–81.

19. *Istoriia Kishineva*, 132–145; *Istoriia Moldavskoi SSSR*, ed. L. V. Cherepnin, et al., 2 vols. (Kishinev: Izdatel'stvo "Kartiia Moldoveniaske," 1965), 1:527–530, 532–533; *Pervaia v Rossii podpol'naia tipografiia Leninskoi gazety "Iskra*," comp. Institut istorii partii pri TsK KP Moldavii (Kishinev: Izdatel'svto "Kartiia Moldoveniaske," 1970), 4–6; Maurice

Laporte, *Histoire de l'Okhrana: La police secrète des tsars, 1880–1917* (Paris: Payot, 1935), 51; V. D. Novitskii, "Zapiska gen. Novitskago," *Sotsialist-revoliutsionner*, no. 2 (1910): 73–74, 79–80.

20. Popovici, 103–117; Emanuel Turczynski, "The Background of Romanian Fascism," in *Native Fascism in the Successor States 1918–1945*, ed. Peter F. Sugar (Santa Barbara, CA: n.p., 1971), 105–106.

21. E. Schwarzfeld, "The Jews of Roumania from the Earliest Times to the Present Day," in *American Jewish Year Book 5662* (Philadelphia: Jewish Publication Society of America, 1901), 28–50, passim; *Materialy*, 2:183–185, 531.

22. Urusov, 147–148; Schwarzfeld, 63–84; Stephen Fischer-Galati, "Romanian Nationalism," in *Nationalism in Eastern Europe*, ed. Peter Sugar and Ivo Lederer (Seattle: University of Washington Press, 1969), 385–386; Turczynski, 104–107; *Bessarabets*, March 22, 1903, p. 1; November 14, 1903, p. 2.

23. Zashchuk, 171–173; Zelenchuk, 63–64, 158, 201–205; *Encyclopedia Judaica*, 16 vols. (Jerusalem: Macmillan, 1971), 14:386–387; 4:704; *Jewish Encyclopedia*, 12 vols. (New York and London: Funk and Wagnalls, 1916), 10:512–513.

24. Zelenchuk, 64, 158, 205–206; *Encyclopedia Judaica*, 4:704.

25. Zelenchuk, 203–206; *Encyclopedia Judaica*, 4:705–706.

26. *Pervaia vseobshchaia perepis'*, 3:3, 36–39, 178–179; Zelenchuk, 203–206; Zashchuk, 171–173; *Evreiskaia entsiklopediia*, 16 vols. (Saint Petersburg: Brokgauz-Efron, 1906–1913), 9:504–505; *Encyclopedia Judaica*, 10:1063–1064.

27. *Jewish Encyclopedia*, 7:512; *Encyclopedia Judaica*, 10:1063–64; *Pervaia vseobshchaia perepis'*, 3:178–179; Urusov, 158–165; Davitt, 155–156, 162–163, 181.

28. *Jewish Encyclopedia*, 7:512; *Encyclopedia Judaica*, 10:1063–64; *Evreiskaia entsiklopediia*, 9:504–505.

29. Urusov, 33–34, 147–148, 153–154.

30. *Polnoe sobranie zakonov*, 3rd ed., 12, no. 8708 (June 11, 1892); *Jewish Encyclopedia*, 7:512; Tobias, 7–10; Urusov, 73–74, 79–80, 145–147, 169–170.

31. *Istoriia Moldavskoi SSSR*, 1:522; *Istoriia Kishineva*, 137.

3. Agitation and Provocation

1. Urusov, 45–46, 79–80; Davitt, 158–159; *Materialy*, 1:217.

2. Urusov, 10, 46; M. B. Slutskii, *V skorbnye dni: Kishinevskii pogrom* (Kishinev: Tipografiia M. Averbukha, 1930), 43–44; B. A. Trubetskoi, *Iz istorii periodicheskoi pechati Bessarabii (1854–1916)* (Kishinev: Izdatel'stvo "Kartiia Moldoveniaske," 1968), 41; Davitt, 97–98; *Encyclopedia Judaica*, 10:1281.

3. Slutskii, 44; Urusov, 46, 79; Davitt, 97, 99; Heinz-Dietrich Lowe, *Anti-*

semitismus und reaktionäre Utopie: Russischer Konservatismus im Kampf gegen den Wandel von Staat und Gesellschaft, 1890–1917 (Hamburg: Hoffman und Campe, 1978), 59–60; Bessarabets, 3 January 1903, 2.

4. Slutskii, 44–45; Bessarabets, 24 January 1903, 2; 8 February 1903, 2; 9 February 1903, 3; 11 February 1903, 2; 13 February 1903, 3; 14 February 1903, 3; 19 February 1903, 2, 3; 20 February 1903, 3; 27 February 1903, 2.

5. Norman Cohn, Warrant for Genocide: The Myth of the Jewish World-Conspiracy and the Protocols of the Elders of Zion (Chico, CA: Scholars Press, 1981), 65–66; Lowe, 64.

6. Slutskii, 47.

7. Ibid., 46–47; Urusov, 47; Bessarabets, 8 February 1904, 3.

8. Urusov, 47, 76; Bessarabets, 5 July 1903, 3.

9. Urusov, 47–49; Bessarabets, 17 April 1903, 3; Materialy, 1:264–268, 328–330; Osvobozhdenie, no. 13/37 (2 December 1903): 227.

10. Urusov, 15, 17; Slutskii, 49; Materialy, 1:344–346.

11. Slutskii, 49–51; Urusov, 15–17.

12. Slutskii, 52–53; Urusov, 12, 16, 28–30.

13. Urusov, 12, 16, 33–34, 145–146; Slutskii, 53.

14. Davitt, 97–99, 137; Slutskii, 52–53; Urusov, 28–34, 145–146, 157–158; Osvobozhdenie, no. 22 (8 May 1903): 379; Materialy, 1:217.

15. Materialy, 1:204, 208; Davitt, 124, 195–196; Davitt Papers, Trinity College Dublin (TCD) MS 9578:34.

16. Slutskii, 53–54; Materialy, 1:148–149, 274.

17. Bessarabets, 17 April 1903, 3; 21 April 1903, 3; 27 January 1904, 3; 10 May 1904, 3; Isidore Singer, Russia at the Bar of the American People: A Memorial of Kishinef (New York: Funk and Wagnalls, 1904), 265.

18. Slutskii, 2–3

19. Laporte, 51; A. P., "Departament politsii v 1892–1908gg.: Iz vospominanii chinovnika," Byloe, no. 5–6/27–28 (November-December 1917): 20; Novitskii, "Zapiska," 73–74, 75.

20. Istoriia Kishineva, 137–141.

21. P. P. Zavarzin, Zhandarmy i revoliutsionery: Vospominaniia (Paris: Payot, 1930), 70–71; Slutskii, 54–55; Urusov, 81–82; Lowe, 63; Materialy, 1:319.

22. Urusov, 56–61, 84–85.

23. Slutskii, 111–112.

24. Ibid., 44–45; Bessarabets, 3 February 1903, 2; 11 February 1903, 2; 19 February 1903, 2; 9 February 1903, 3; 13 February 1903, 3; 14 February 1903, 3; 20 February 1903, 3; 25 February 1903, 3; 4 March 1903, 2, 3; 6 March 1903, 3; 11 March 1903, 3; 15 March 1903, 3; 16 March 1903, 2; 19 March 1903, 3; 23 March 1903, 3.

25. B. A. Henry, Les Massacres de Kichinev (Paris: "Siecle," 1903), 8; Materialy, 1:5–6.

26. Materialy, 1:1–2, 6, 28–29, 32–37.

27. Hay, 122–134; Flannery, 99–101, 116–117, 120–121; *Encyclopedia Judaica*, 4:1120–1124.
28. Baron, 9, 25, 28, 34; Dubnov, 2:72–84, 150–153, 203–205; *Encyclopedia Judaica*, 4:1129–1130. For a detailed study of the "blood-libel" phenomenon see Alan Dundes, ed., *The Blood Libel Legend: A Casebook in Anti-Semitic Folklore* (Madison: The University of Wisconsin Press, 1991).
29. *Materialy*, 1:5–7.
30. Ibid., 126–129.
31. *Bessarabets*, 4 March 1903, 2.
32. Ibid., 9 March 1903, 3; 11 March 1903, 2.
33. *Materialy*, 1:7–8; *Novoe vremia*, 6 March 1903, 1; 7 March 1903, 5; 8 March 1903, 13; 12 March 1903, 4; 22 March 1903, 13.
34. *Materialy*, 1:42.
35. *Novoe vremia*, 23 March 1903, 6; *Bessarabskiia gubernskiia vedomosti*, 22 March 1903, 4; 5 August 1903, 3.
36. *Materialy*, 1:7–8; Slutskii, 1–2.
37. *Materialy*, 1:7–8; *Bessarabets*, 17 March 1903, 3; 19 March 1903, 3; *Osvobozhdenie*, no. 12/36 (24 November 1903): 208.
38. *Bessarabskiia gubernskiia vedomosti*, 20 March 1903, 1; 22 March 1903, 2.
39. Slutskii, 1, 3; Davitt, 213; *Osvobozhdenie*, no. 13/37 (2 December 1903): 226; Singer, 263; "Les Massacres de Kischinef," *Bulletin annuel de l'Alliance Israélite Universelle* (AIU) 65 (1903): 14–15, 23; Urusov, 80–82.
40. Slutskii, 1; *Kishinevskii pogrom*, comp. by editors of "Osvobozhdenie" (Stuttgart: Verlag und Druck von J. H. W. Dietz, 1903), 1–2.
41. Slutskii, 1–2; *Bessarabets*, 6 April 1903, 4.
42. Slutskii, 2–3.
43. *Materialy*, 1:135, 208–209.
44. *Bessarabets*, 22 March 1903, 1; 23 March 1903, 3; 24 March 1903, 3; 25 March 1903, 1; 29 March 1903, 2; 31 March 1903, 2; 2 April 1903, 2; 6 April 1903, 4.
45. Slutskii, 1–2; *Materialy*, 1:135.
46. Urusov, 81–82; V. D. Novitskii, *Iz vospominanii zhandarma* (Leningrad: "Priboi," 1929), 209.
47. *Materialy*, 1:209, 211; *Bessarabets*, 6 April 1903, 4; *Osvobozhdenie*, no. 13/37 (2 December 1903): 226; no. 12/36 (24 November 1903): 208; Slutskii, 3.

4. Pogrom!

1. "Kishinevskii pogrom: Obvinitel'nyi akt," supplement to *Osvobozhdenie*, no. 9/33 (19 October 1903): 1; *Materialy*, 1:210.

2. "Obvinitel'nyi akt," 1; *Materialy*, 1:204–205.

3. "Obvinitel'nyi akt," 1.

4. Ibid.; Leo Motzkin ("A. Linden"), ed., *Die Judenpogrome in Russland*, 2 vols. (Cologne and Leipzig: Jüdischer Verlag, 1910), 2:11.

5. "Obvinitel'nyi akt," 1; *Kishinevskii pogrom*, 2; Motzkin, 2:11–12.

6. *Materialy*, 1:135–136; "Obvinitel'nyi akt," 4; *Novoe vremia*, 29 April 1903, 1.

7. *Materialy*, 1:204, 208; *Osvobozhdenie*, no. 13/37 (2 December 1903): 227.

8. Davitt, 135; *Materialy*, 1:165.

9. "Obvinitel'nyi akt," 1.

10. Ibid.

11. Davitt, 135–136.

12. "Obvinitel'nyi akt," 1.

13. Ibid.; *Materialy*, 1:205–206, 210; V. H. C. Bosanquet and C. S. Smith, *Despatch from His Majesty's Consul-General at Odessa, forwarding a Report on the Riots at Kishiniev* (London: Harrison and Sons, 1903), 2; Slutskii, 5.

14. "Obvinitel'nyi akt," 1; Slutskii, 5; *Osvobozhdenie*, no. 13/37 (2 December 1903): 225. Although Sitsinskii's testimony refers to the "first day" of the pogrom, it seems likely that the two dead Jews and two dead Christians were brought to the hospital on Monday rather than Sunday. Both the bill of indictment and Dr. Slutskii (the senior surgeon at the Jewish hospital), report that there were no deaths or serious injuries on Sunday, and the indictment indicates that only two Christians perished during the entire pogrom—at least one of them on Monday. "Obvinitel'nyi akt," 1, 2; Slutskii, 5.

15. "Obvinitel'nyi akt," 1; *Osvobozhdenie*, no. 13/37 (2 December 1903): 226–227; *Materialy*, 1:206.

16. "Obvinitel'nyi akt," 1; *Materialy*, 1:206; Davitt, 196; *Kishinevskii pogrom*, 4.

17. "Obvinitel'nyi akt," 1–2.

18. *Materialy*, 1:205–206, Urusov, 57–58, 78–81; "Obvinitel'nyi akt," 1–2.

19. *Materialy*, 1:153–156, 165–166; "Obvinitel'nyi akt," 2, 3.

20. "Obvinitel'nyi akt," 2; *Materialy*, 1:206–207; *Kishinevskii pogrom*, 9–10.

21. "Obvinitel'nyi akt," 3; *Materialy*, 1:273; Dov Volchonsky, "The First Pogrom of the XX Century," [Hebrew] *He-Avar* 20: 184.

22. *Kishinevskii pogrom*, 2–3, 8–9; "Obvinitel'nyi akt," 1–2.

23. "Obvinitel'nyi akt," 2; *Materialy*, 1:206–207.

24. "Obvinitel'nyi akt," 2; *Materialy*, 1:157, 206–207.

25. *Materialy*, 1:153–156, 165–166; "Obvinitel'nyi akt," 2, 3.

26. "Obvinitel'nyi akt," 2, 3; *Materialy*, 1:151.

27. *Materialy*, 1:151–2; "Obvinitel'nyi akt," 2.

28. *Materialy*, 1:152–156, 165–166; "Obvinitel'nyi akt," 2, 3.

29. *Materialy*, 1:153–156, 165–166; "Obvinitel'nyi akt," 2, 3; Davitt, 130–131, 218–221, 225–226; *Osvobozhdenie*, no. 13/37 (2 December 1903): 228; no. 14/38 (25 December 1903): 259–260.
30. V. G. Korolenko, "House No. 13: An Episode in the Massacre of Kishinev," *Contemporary Review* 85 (February 1904): 268; *Materialy*, 1:152; "Obvinitel'nyi akt," 3.
31. Korolenko, 271, 273; *Materialy*, 1:156–157.
32. Korolenko, 268, 270, 273–277; *Materialy*, 1:156–158; Motzkin, 16–17.
33. "Obvinitel'nyi akt," 2, 3; *Materialy*, 1:159–160.
34. *Materialy*, 1:151, 161–165; "Obvinitel'nyi akt," 2, 3.
35. "Obvinitel'nyi akt," 2–3; *Materialy*, 1:161–164; Korolenko, 271–272; Davitt, 131–133, 166–167, 219.
36. "Obvinitel'nyi akt," 3.
37. Ibid., 1–2.
38. *Materialy*, 1:213–214; *Osvobozhdenie*, no. 12/36 (24 November 1903): 208.
39. *Materialy*, 1:205.
40. Ibid., 205, 209, 211; Slutskii, 30, 49–51.
41. *Materialy*, 1:339–341.
42. D. N. Liubimov, "Russkaia smuta nachala deviatisotykh godov, 1902–1906," Manuscript in archives of the Hoover Library, Stanford, California, 81; *Materialy*, 1:130.
43. *Materialy*, 1:211.
44. Slutskii, 13.
45. *Materialy*, 1:205, 211–212; "Obvinitel'nyi akt," 1; Liubimov, 82–83.
46. Slutskii, 30–31.
47. Ibid., 30–31; *Osvobozhdenie*, no. 13/37 (2 December 1903): 225.
48. *Materialy*, 1:341–342, 344.
49. Ibid., 207–208; *Osvobozhdenie*, no. 13/37 (2 December 1903): 227; Slutskii, 8–9.
50. *Materialy*, 1:212; Lowe, 58; Slutskii, 8–9.
51. *Materialy*, 1:211, 214–215, 341–343; Slutskii, 11–12.
52. Slutskii, 31; *Materialy*, 1:131, 206, 292.
53. *Materialy*, 1:345.
54. Slutskii, 30; Davitt, 133; *Kishinevskii pogrom*, 3–4.
55. *Kishinevskii pogrom*, 3.
56. *Materialy*, 1:211–212.
57. Ibid., 131.
58. Liubimov, 81; Davitt, 186–187; *Times* (London), 25 June 1903, 5; Urusov, 6; *Materialy*, 1:131.
59. *Materialy*, 1:211–212.
60. Ibid.; "Obvinitel'nyi akt," 2; Richard Gottheil, "Kishineff," *The Forum* 35 (July-September 1903): 154–155.
61. "Obvinitel'nyi akt," 2–3; *Materialy*, 1:211–212.
62. *Materialy*, 1:139, 214; "Obvinitel'nyi akt," 3.

63. *Bessarabets*, 8 December 1903, 3; 28 February 1904, 3; 26 April 1904, 4; 6 May 1904, 4.
64. *Novoe vremia*, 7 November 1903, 1; *Bessarabets*, 8 December 1903, 3; 28 February 1904, 3; 26 April 1904, 4; 6 May 1904, 4.
65. *Kishinevskii pogrom*, 2; *Revoliutsonnaia Rossiia*, no. 23 (1 May 1903): 2; Roubanovich, "Les massacres de Kichinev," *Pages libres*, no. 124 (16 May 1903): 425.
66. Volchonsky, 183–184; *Kishinevskii pogrom*, 9–10; *Bessarabets*, 8 December 1903, 3; 28 February 1904, 3; 26 April 1904, 4; 6 May 1904, 4.
67. "Obvinitel'nyi akt," 1, 2; *Materialy*, 1:206–207.
68. Calculations are based on the data published in *Bessarabets*, 8 December 1903, 3; 28 February 1904, 3; 26 April 1904, 4; 6 May 1904, 4; and in *Pervaia vseobshchaia perepis'*, 3:112–119.
69. *Bessarabets*, 8 December 1903, 3; 28 February 1904, 3; 26 April 1904, 4; 6 May 1904, 4; *Pervaia vseobshchaia perepis'*, 3:228–231.
70. *Bessarabets*, 8 December 1903, 3; 28 February 1904, 3; 26 April 1904, 4; 6 May 1904, 4.
71. Slutskii, 10–15; *L'Univers Israélite* 58, no. 33 (8 May 1903): 206–207.
72. Slutskii, 17–18, 118–119; "Obvinitel'nyi akt," 2.
73. *Materialy*, 1:333; "Obvinitel'nyi akt," 2; Slutskii, 17, 19.
74. *Materialy*, 1:144, 166.
75. Davitt, 129–133, 217–222; *L'Univers Israélite* 58, no. 33 (8 May 1903): 206; Korolenko, 268–272.

5. Repercussions and Reverberations

1. *Materialy*, 1:132–133.
2. Ibid., 131–132, 136–139.
3. Ibid., 137–138.
4. Slutskii, 36.
5. Ibid., 37–38; *Materialy*, 1:133–134; *Novoe vremia*, 17 April 1903, 5; 19 April 1903, 16.
6. Urusov, 77–78; "Obvinitel'nyi akt," 4; *Novoe vremia*, 19 April 1903, 1; *New York Times*, 6 June 1903, 3.
7. *Novoe vremia*, 16 April 1903, 13; 17 April 1903, 5.
8. *Novoe vremia*, 17 April 1903, 5; 19 April 1903, 13; Slutskii, 37; "Dokladnaia zapiska Evreiskago Obshchestva," in *Kishinevskii pogrom*, 19–21; Davitt, 208–216.
9. Slutskii, 37.
10. Ibid.; *Kishinevskii pogrom*, 10–11.
11. "Tsirkuliara ministra vnutrennykh del gubernatoram, gradonachal'nikam i oberpolitsiimeisteram," supplement to *Osvobozhdenie*, no. 9/33 (19 October 1903): 4; *Novoe vremia*, 29 April 1903, 1; *Kishinevskii pogrom*, 9 (n.1).

12. "Tsirkuliara ministra," 4; *Novoe vremia*, 29 April 1903, 1; Slutskii, 38; *Bessarabets*, 30 April 1903, 1.
13. "Tsirkuliara ministra," 4; *Novoe vremia*, 29 April 1903, 1.
14. *Materialy*, 1:204, 208; Slutskii, 38; Davitt, 183, 189–190.
15. "Tsirkuliara ministra," 4; *Novoe vremia*, 29 April 1903, 1; Slutskii, 38; *Osvobozhdenie*, no. 9/33 (19 October 1903): 166.
16. *Novoe vremia*, 29 April 1903, 1.
17. *Times* (London), 25 June 1903, 5; Davitt, 187–188.
18. Liubimov, 82–83; Davitt, 188; *Times* (London), 20 June 1903, 7; 21 June 1903, 5; 25 June 1903, 5.
19. *Novoe vremia*, 29 April 1903, 1; *Bessarabets*, 30 April 1903, 1–2; 4 May 1903, 2; Slutskii, 41–42.
20. Urusov, 12–13; Davitt, 107–108; Slutskii, 36–37; *Bessarabets*, 21 April 1903, 3; *Materialy*, 1:131–132; 133, 138.
21. *Materialy*, 1:227, 230–231.
22. Ibid., 226; *Novoe vremia*, 14 May 1903, 13.
23. *Materialy*, 1:227.
24. Ibid., 225; *Times* (London), 18 August 1903, 3.
25. *Materialy*, 1:234, 243–244.
26. Ibid., 253–258, 260, 182–191, 236–242, 244–251; *Bessarabets*, 17 April 1903, 3; 27 April 1903, 3; 28 April 1903, 3.
27. *Kishinevskii pogrom*, 21; Slutskii, 38–39.
28. *Bessarabets*, 10 April 1903, 3; *Novoe vremia*, 13 April 1903, 6.
29. *Novoe vremia*, 11 April 1903, 1.
30. *Times* (London), 24 April 1903, 5; *New York Times*, 24 April 1903, 6.
31. Alliance Israélite Universelle (AIU) Archives, URSS dossier, IV.B, docs. 5460, 5546, 5710; "Souscription en faveur des israélites de Kischineff," *Bulletin mensuel de l'AIU* 31 (April 1903): 51–52; Cyrus Adler, ed., *The Voice of America on Kishineff* (Philadelphia: The Jewish Publication Society of America, 1904), 468.
32. Adler, 467–468; *New York Times*, 9 May 1903, 3; Philip E. Schoenberg, "The American Reaction to the Kishinev Pogrom of 1903," *American Jewish Historical Quarterly* 63 (September 1973): 263–264.
33. *Novosti*, 14 and 15 April, 1903; *Sankt Petersburgskiia vedomosti*, 25 April 1903; cited in *Bulletin mensuel de l'AIU* 31 (April 1903): 40–44.
34. *New York Times*, 28 April 1903, 6; Schoenberg, 262; *Times* (London), 2 May 1903, 8.
35. *Times* (London), 6 May 1903, 7.
36. Ibid., 18 May 1903, 10.
37. Ibid., 9.
38. Ibid., 10.
39. Davitt Papers, TCD MSS 9501, 5298, 5299; *New York American*, 13 May 1903, 1.
40. Davitt Papers, TCD MS 9670:39; MS 9672:35; T. W. Moody, *Davitt and Irish Revolution, 1846–1882* (Oxford: Clarendon Press, 1981), 548–549;

New York American, 13 May 1903, 1; Francis Sheehy-Skeffington, *Michael Davitt: Revolutionary, Agitator, and Labour Leader* (London: T. Fisher Unwin, 1908; reprint, London: MacGibbon & Kee, 1967), 184–185.

41. Cuthbert W. Dale, "The Story of Michael Davitt," *Men and Women*, 11 July 1903.

42. Davitt Papers, TCD MS 9578:10–20, 36–42; Schoenberg, 272.

43. Davitt Papers, TCD MS 9670:28–35; *New York American*, 5 June 1903; *New York American and Journal*, 14 June 1903, 51.

44. Davitt Papers, TCD MSS 9670:30, 32, 35, 36; William Curtis Stiles, *Out of Kishineff: The Duty of the American People to the Russian Jew* (New York: G. W. Dillingham, 1903), 294–299; Leo Errera, *Les Massacres de Kichinev* (Brussels: Falk fils, 1903), 15–16. Articles and editorials appeared in many papers, including the *Irish Times*, 10 June 1903, *Chicago Citizen*, 13 June 1903, and *L'Européen*, 23 June 1903 (see Errera, *Les Massacres*, 16 (n.1); Davitt Papers, TCD MS 9670:35).

45. *Kishinevskii pogrom*, 22–26; *Bulletin annuel de l'AIU* 65 (1903): 25–26; Volchonsky, 188–189; Errera, *Les Massacres*, 26–27.

46. *Bulletin annuel de l'AIU* 65 (1903): 27; Davitt, 270–271; Errera, *Les Massacres*, 28–29.

47. *Bulletin annuel de l'AIU* 65 (1903): 27–29; Davitt, 272–275; Errera, *Les Massacres*, 29–30.

48. Korolenko, 266–280.

49. *Kishinevskii pogrom*, 27–29.

50. See *Osvobozhdenie*, nos. 22 (8 May 1903) through 39–40 (19 January 1904), passim.

51. F. S. Zuckerman, "Self-imagery and the Art of Propaganda: V. K. von Plehve as Propagandist," *Australian Journal of Politics and History* 28, no. 1 (1982): 73; *Kishinevskii pogrom*, 30–37; *Bulletin annuel de l'AIU* 65 (1903): 33–39; Raffaello Prato, *I massacri di Kiscineff* (Rome: Carlo Mariani, 1903).

52. *Kishinevskii pogrom*, 37; *Bulletin annuel de l'AIU* 65 (1903): 29.

53. Adler, xvii-xxiii; Schoenberg, 268–274. See also *Kishinev Massacre: Proceedings of a Meeting of Citizens of New York* (New York: The American Hebrew, 1903), 3, 11–13.

54. Singer, 112, 114.

55. Taylor Stults, "Roosevelt, Russian Persecution of Jews, and American Public Opinion," *Jewish Social Studies* 33 (1971): 17; Theodore Roosevelt, *The Letters of Theodore Roosevelt*, vol. 3, *The Square Deal, 1901–1903*, ed. Elting E. Morison (Cambridge: Harvard University Press, 1951), 477 (n.1); Schoenberg, 276.

56. Singer, 124–129; Schoenberg, 277–278.

57. Singer, 130–135, 140; Adler, 478–481; Stults, 19–21.

58. *Novoe vremia*, 29 April 1903, 1; *Times* (London), 12 May 1903, 5; V. B. Nabokov, "Kishinevskaia krovovaia bania," *Pravo*, no. 18 (27 April 1903): 1281–1285; *Osvobozhdenie*, no. 1/25 (18 June 1903): 15; E. P.

Semenoff, *The Russian Government and the Massacres* (London: John Murray, 1906), 36–37.

59. Adler, xii-xiii; *New York Times*, 19 May 1903, 2.

60. Adler, xii.

61. *Materialy*, 1:219–223; *Osvobozhdenie*, no. 22 (8 May 1903): 319; V. I. Gurko, *Features and Figures of the Past: Government and Opinion in the Reign of Nicholas II*, trans. Laura Matveev (Stanford: Stanford University Press, 1939), 248; *New York Times*, 28 May 1903, 2; *Novoe vremia*, 14 May 1903, 1; *Times* (London), 22 May 1903, 3; Stiles, 37–38.

62. Sliozberg, 3:50–56; Edward H. Judge, *Plehve: Repression and Reform in Imperial Russia, 1902–1904* (Syracuse: Syracuse University Press, 1983), 24–25, 32–37, 104–5.

63. *Novoe vremia*, 22 May 1903, 4; 23 May 1903, 1; 24 May 1903, 2; Rogger, 79–80.

64. *Novoe vremia*, 4 June 1903, 1; Slutskii, 74–78; Urusov, 1, 9; *La Revue Russe*, 25 June 1903, 3.

65. *Novoe vremia*, 4 June 1903, 1; Urusov, 1–2, 6–7.

66. Urusov, 3–5, 10–12.

67. Ibid., 12–13, 18–20; Slutskii, 74–75.

68. Urusov, 20–23; Slutskii, 77–78.

69. Urusov, 23–24; Slutskii, 77, 79.

70. *Bessarabets*, 29 June 1903, 3; 2 September 1903, 3; *L'Univers Israélite* 59, no. 9 (20 November 1903): 268.

71. *Novoe vremia*, 5 June 1903, 2; *Bessarabets*, 6 June 1903, 3; 9 June 1903, 2; 12 June 1903, 2; Slutskii, 43; *Osvobozhdenie*, no. 1/25 (18 June 1903): 1–2.

72. *Kishinevskii pogrom*, 2; *Osvobozhdenie*, no. 9/33 (19 October 1903): 167; *Materialy*, 1:176; *Bessarabets*, 5 July 1903, 3.

73. Urusov, 17–18, 23–24, 26, 27, 33–35; Zavarzin, 50, 70; *Bessarabets*, 20 July 1903, 3; 3 August 1903, 3; 4 October 1903, 3; Slutskii, 77–79, 83.

74. *New York Times*, 5 May 1903, 2; *Novoe vremia*, 13 May 1903, 4.

75. *Materialy*, 1:219–220, 223–224; *Novoe vremia*, 17 May 1903, 2; *New York Times*, 28 May 1903, 2.

76. *New York Times*, 29 May 1903, 1; 30 May 1903, 3; *Novoe vremia*, 22 May 1903, 2.

77. Zuckerman, 73–74, 81 (n.28).

78. *New York Times*, 6 June 1903, 3.

79. Davitt, 182–186; Zuckerman, 74; Rogger, 172–173; *Times* (London), 13 June 1903, 7.

80. Davitt, 186–188; Zuckerman, 74–75; *Times* (London), 25 June 1903, 5.

81. Zuckerman, 74; V. K. Agafonov, *Zagranichnaia okhranka* (Petrograd: Izdatel'stvo "Kniga," 1918), 61.

82. Zuckerman, 81 (n.21); Agafonov, 61; K. Betskii and P. Pavlov, *Russkii rokambol': Prikliucheniia I. F. Manasevicha-Manuilova* (Leningrad: Izdatel'stvo "Byloe," 1925), 38–40.

83. *La Revue Russe*, 14 May 1903, 2; 28 May 1903, 1; 4 June 1903, 4; 18 June 1903, 8; 25 June 1903, 2–3. See also *Archives Israélites de France* 64, no. 26 (25 June 1903): 203.
84. Zuckerman, 81 (n.21).
85. A. F. Koni, "Sergei Iul'evich Vitte," *Sobranie sochinenii* (Moscow: Izdatel'stvo "Iuridicheskaia literatura," 1968), 5:273–274; Rogger, 79.
86. Plehve, 412–414; *Osvobozhdenie*, no. 7/31 (18 September 1903): 125.
87. Zuckerman, 74–75.
88. Ibid., 75–76; *Osvobozhdenie*, no. 1/25 (18 June 1903): 15; *New York Times*, 22 July 1903, 7.
89. Schoenberg, 279; Roosevelt, 3:508 (n.2), 509.
90. Theodor Herzl, *The Complete Diaries of Theodor Herzl*, trans. Harry Zohn, 5 vols. (New York and London: Herzl Press and Thomas Yoseloff, 1960), 4:1493–1494, 1509–1510; Herzl, *The Diaries of Theodor Herzl*, ed. and trans. Marvin Lowenthal (New York: Dial Press, 1956), 387.
91. Herzl, *Complete Diaries*, 4:1520, 1532–1533; Judge, 108.
92. Herzl, *Complete Diaries*, 4:1535; Herzl, *Diaries*, 390–391.
93. Herzl, *Diaries*, 399.
94. Ibid., 399–400, 401; Rogger, 80–81; S. Ginzburg, "Poezdka Teodora Gertslia v Peterburg," in *Evreiskii Mir*, comp. Union of Russian Jews, Sbornik 2 (New York: Grenich Printing Corp., 1944), 205–206; *Archives Israélites de France* 65, no. 35 (27 August 1903): 276.
95. Herzl, *Diaries*, 400, 406, 411; Ginzburg, 208–209; Louis Greenberg, *The Jews in Russia: The Struggle for Emancipation*, 2 vols. (New Haven: Yale University Press, 1944, 1951), 2:180; Dubnov, 3:84; *Osvobozhdenie*, no. 5/29 (19 August 1903): 87–88.
96. *Osvobozhdenie*, no. 8/32 (2 October 1903): 149; Urusov, 142, 176–177.
97. *Osvobozhdenie*, no. 5/29 (19 August 1903): 87–88; no. 8/32 (2 October 1903): 149–150; Greenberg, 2:180; Lowe, 55.
98. *Osvobozhdenie*, no. 8/32 (2 October 1903): 133–136; Dubnov, 3:86–90; *New York Times*, 2 October 1903, 5; Liubimov, 86–87. See also *Gomel'-skii protsess: Podrobnyi otchet* (Saint Petersburg: Tipografiia t-va "Ob-shchestvennaia Pol'za," 1907), v-x.
99. Lucien Wolf, "M. de Plehve and the Jewish Question," *Times* (London), 6 February 1904, 6. See also Shlomo Lambroza, "The Pogrom Movement in Tsarist Russia, 1903–1906" (Ph.D. dissertation, Rutgers University, 1981), 81–83; A. I. Braudo, "Beseda V. K. Pleve s L. Volf'om (1903)," *Evreiskaia starina* 9 (1916): 121–125.

6. The Question of Guilt

1. *Materialy*, 1:178–179.
2. Ibid., 169–170, 179–180, 181, 258.
3. Urusov, 83–85; Slutskii, 92–93; *Osvobozhdenie*, no. 9/33 (19 October 1903): 166–7.

4. *Materialy,* 1:132–133, 134–140, 171–174.

5. Ibid., 179; Urusov, 25, 74, 76.

6. "Obvinitel'nyi akt," 1–4.

7. *Novoe vremia,* 16 October 1903, 2–3; Urusov, 85; Slutskii, 92–93; *Osvobozhdenie,* no. 9/33 (19 October 1903): 166.

8. *Materialy,* 1:170.

9. Urusov, 74–75.

10. Ibid.; *Materialy,* 1:323–324, 324 (n.1).

11. Slutskii, 96; *Osvobozhdenie,* no. 12/36 (24 November 1903): 207–209; no. 13/37 (2 December 1903): 225–229; no. 14/38 (25 December 1903): 259–262; no. 15–16/39–40 (19 January 1904): 270–274; Urusov, 75.

12. Singer, 249–251; "Obvinitel'nyi akt," 3–4.

13. *Materialy,* 1:272–3, 318; Singer, 248–9, Slutskii, 96–97; Urusov, 74–76.

14. *Materialy,* 1:272–3; Singer, 248–249; Urusov, 74–76.

15. *Materialy,* 1:273–4, *Bessarabets,* 10 October 1903, 3; Singer, 250, 257.

16. *Materialy,* 1:272–273, 288; Singer, 250.

17. *Materialy,* 1:272, 274; Singer, 250.

18. *Osvobozhdenie,* no. 12/36 (24 November 1903): 208; Singer, 251–252.

19. *Osvobozhdenie,* no. 12/36 (24 November 1903): 208; *Materialy,* 1:214–218.

20. *Osvobozhdenie,* no. 12/36 (24 November 1903): 209.

21. Ibid.; Singer, 256–257; *Materialy,* 1:211–213.

22. *Osvobozhdenie,* no. 12/36 (24 November 1903): 209; Singer, 257.

23. *Osvobozhdenie,* no. 13/37 (2 December 1903): 225, 227; Singer, 258.

24. *Materialy,* 1:263–270; *Osvobozhdenie,* no. 13/37 (2 December 1903): 227.

25. Singer, 267; *Osvobozhdenie,* no. 13/37 (2 December 1903): 228.

26. Singer, 264, 268; *Osvobozhdenie,* no. 14/38 (25 December 1903): 260–261.

27. *Osvobozhdenie,* no. 13/37 (2 December 1903): 225.

28. Singer, 265; *L'Univers Israélite* 59, no. 12 (December 1903): 373.

29. *Osvobozhdenie,* no. 12/36 (24 November 1903): 207–208; no. 13/37 (2 December 1903): 225–229; no. 14/38 (25 December 1903): 259–260.

30. *Materialy,* 1:317–318.

31. Ibid., 286–287, 289–290; *Bulletin annuel de l'AIU* 65 (1903): 48–49.

32. *Materialy,* 1:290.

33. Ibid., 290–291; *Osvobozhdenie,* no. 14/38 (25 December 1903): 262; *Times* (London), 16 December 1903, 7.

34. *Materialy,* 1:291–292; Singer, 281–282; *Osvobozhdenie,* no. 15–16/39–40 (19 January 1904): 270–271.

35. *Bessarabets,* 8 December 1903, 4; 27 May 1904, 4; *Novoe vremia,* 9 December 1903, 2; Singer, 283.

36. *Times* (London), 26 December 1903, 3; *Novoe vremia,* 10 February 1904, 2; Slutskii, 91, 97; Urusov, 82–83.

37. *Novoe vremia,* 10 February 1904, 2; *Bessarabets,* 8 February 1904, 3; 11

February 1904, 4; 12 February 1904, 4; 13 February 1904, 4; 14 February 1904, 4; 28 February 1904, 3; Urusov, 82–83.

38. *Bessarabets*, 21 April 1904, 4; 26 April 1904, 4; 2 May 1904, 4; 6 May 1904, 4; 27 May 1904, 4; Urusov, 83.

39. *Times* (London), 21 November 1903, 7; 28 November 1903, 7; 16 December 1903, 7; 19 December 1903, 7; 25 December 1903, 4; 26 December 1903, 3; 31 December 1903, 3; 9 January 1904, 5; *Bulletin annuel de l'AIU* 65 (1903): 42–51; *Osvobozhdenie*, no. 14/38 (25 December 1903): 261–262; no. 15–16/39–40 (19 January 1904): 271–274; Singer, 272–280.

40. *Osvobozhdenie*, no. 13/37 (2 December 1903): 229; no. 14/38 (25 December 1903): 261.

41. Urusov, 76–77.

42. See, for example, *Times* (London), 18 May 1903, 9; 20 May 1903, 7; 22 May 1903, 3; *New York Times*, 18 May 1903, 1; 31 May 1903, 5; 22 June 1903, 1; Slutskii, 56–63; E. P. Semenoff, *The Russian Government and the Massacres* (London: John Murray, 1906), 36–50; Sliozberg 3:63–64; G. Ia. Krasnyi-Admoni, "Staryi rezhim i pogromy," in *Materialy*, 1:xvi–xxxii; Dubnov, 3:72–74, 76–78; Greenberg, 2:50–52.

43. Edward J. Bing, ed., *The Secret Letters of the Last Tsar* (New York: Longmans, Green and Co., 1938), 30, 187–188; Dubnov, 2:399–402; Eliyahu Feldman, "Plehve and the Kishinev Pogrom of 1903," [Hebrew] *He'-Avar* 12: 148 (n.56); *Novoe vremia*, 8 May 1902, 4; Urusov, 82.

44. Judge, 24–25, 32–37, 94, 104–105; Gurko, 47–48, 107–113; Sergei Iu. Witte, *Vospominaniia: Tsarstvovaniia Nikolaia II*, 2 vols. (Berlin: Knigoizdatel'stvo "Slovo," 1922), 1:28–29, 188, 192–194, 233; Sliozberg 2:165–168; 3:52–55; Rogger, 69; P. A. Zaionchkovskii, *Rossiiskoe samoderzhavie v kontse XIX stoletiia* (Moscow: Izdatel'stvo "Mysl'," 1970), 134–135; Tsentral'nyi Gosudarstvennyi Istoricheskii Arkhiv SSSR (TsGIA), f. 1162, op. 6, d. 419, ll. 170, 171; Dubnov, 2:380–382, 385–386, 399–402.

45. Koni, 5:273.

46. *Novoe vremia*, 6 March 1903, 1; 7 March 1903, 5; 8 March 1903, 13; *Materialy*, 1:11–12, 14, 40–42, 44; Slutskii 43–45; Urusov, 46–47, 76, 79–80; *New York Times*, 13 June 1903, 9; Greenberg, 2:50–51.

47. *Osvobozhdenie*, no. 13/37 (2 December 1903): 225; no. 14/38 (25 December 1903): 262; *Materialy*, 1:xxix, 319; Slutskii, 1–4, 52–55; Urusov, 12, 16–17, 33–34, 79–82; Davitt, 125–129, 133–134, 210–216; *Bulletin annuel de l'AIU* 65 (1904): 13–25; *Kishinevskii pogrom*, 2–12.

48. Singer, 267; *Osvobozhdenie*, no. 13/37 (2 December 1903): 225, 228; no. 14/38 (December 25, 1903): 262; Slutskii 5–9, 54–55; Davitt, 125–129, 133–134, 210–216; *Bulletin annuel de l'AIU* 65 (1904): 13–25; *Kishinevskii pogrom*, 2–12; *Materialy*, 1:xxix, 319; Urusov, 81–82.

49. *Materialy*, 1:219–223; *Times* (London), 18 May 1903, 10; 22 May 1903, 3; *New York Times*, 28 May 1903, 2; Gurko, 248.

50. *Novoe vremia*, 29 April 1903, 1; *Materialy*, 1:169–170, 179–180, 181, 258, 323–324, 333–334; Urusov, 74–75.

51. A. N. Kuropatkin, "Dnevnik," *Krasnyi arkhiv* 2 (1922): 43.
52. *Osvobozhdenie*, no. 1/25 (18 June 1903): 15; *New York Times*, 22 July 1903, 7.
53. *Times* (London), 25 June 1903, 5; Davitt, 187–188; Urusov, 18, 24, 46–49, 79–80; Singer, 265; *Materialy*, 1:263–270, 274; *Bessarabets*, 4 October 1903, 3; Slutskii, 79–81.
54. Urusov, 5–6, 81–82.
55. Witte, *Vospominaniia*, 1:316; 2:63, 72–74; A. A. Lopukhin, *Otryvki iz vospominanii* (Moscow: Gosudarstvennoe izdatel'stvo, 1923), 76, 86–89.
56. Witte, *Vospominaniia*, 1:192.
57. Ibid., 193.
58. For examples of this interpretation see Dubnov, 3:68–71; Greenberg, 2:50–52; Sliozberg 3:56–60, 63–65, 69; Krasnyi-Admoni, 1:xviii-xxxi; Slutskii, 56–63.
59. *Krest'ianskoe dvizhenie v Poltavskoi i Khar'kovskoi guberniakh v 1902 g.* (Kharkov: Khar'kovskoe knizhnoe izdatel'stvo, 1961), xvi-xix, 55–56, 67–78, 82–93; *Novoe vremia*, 29 April 1902, 2; 30 November 1902, 2; 16 March 1903, 2; Gurko, 246; *Vseobshchaia stachka na iuge Rossii v 1903 godu: Sbornik dokumentov* (Moscow: Gosudarstvennoe izdatel'stvo politicheskoe literatury, 1938), 33, 42–48, 90–92; "Obvinitel'nyi akt," 2–4; Dubnov, 3:84, 88–90; *Gomel'skii protsess*, ii-viii; Rogger, 31 (n.29).
60. Shlomo Lambroza, "The Tsarist Government and the Pogroms of 1903–06," *Modern Judaism* 7, no. 3 (1987): 292–293; Neil Weissman, "The Regular Police in Tsarist Russia, 1900–1914," *Russian Review* 44 (January 1985): 47–63, 67–68; *Materialy*, 1:209–210.
61. *Novoe vremia*, 13 May 1903, 4; 20 June 1903, 1.
62. Urusov, 5–6, 33, 77–78; Zavarzin, 50–54, 70–71; Jeremiah Schneidermann, *Sergei Zubatov and Revolutionary Marxism* (Ithaca: Cornell University Press, 1976), 220–221, 228–229.
63. *Times* (London), 18 May 1903, 10; Kuropatkin, 40.
64. *Times* (London), 18 May 1903, 9, 10.
65. Feldman, 138, 139 (n.16); Davitt, 137, 141–142, 202–206; Davitt Papers, TCD MSS 9501–9681; *Materialy*, 1:xviii-xix.
66. *Materialy*, 1:335–356; Urusov, 15, 78.
67. Witte, *Vospominaniia*, 1:192, 193. For a discussion of Witte's reliability on this issue see Feldman, 141–144.
68. Liubimov, 85.
69. Gurko, 247, 248–249.
70. Lopukhin, 15, 16.
71. Urusov, 78, 175–177; A. S. Tager, *The Decay of Czarism* (Philadelphia: Jewish Publication Society of America, 1935), 9–10. See also L. M. Aizenberg, "Na slovakh i na dele: po povodu memuarov Vitte i Lopukhina," *Evreiskaia letopis'* 3 (1924): 41–42.

72. Davitt, 189–201.
73. Ibid., 137, 202–203.
74. Slutskii 78, 80–84; Dubnov, 3:93–97; Semenoff, 149–160; Urusov, 5–6, 9, 15, 75–76, 81–83, 165–166, 176–177.
75. Urusov, 77–78.
76. See discussions in Rogger, 133–175; Lambroza, "Tsarist Government," 291–293; Lambroza, "Plehve, Kishinev and the Jewish Question: A Reappraisal," *Nationalities Papers* 23, no. 2 (1981): 122–123.
77. *Materialy*, 2:5–20, 47–48, 88–89, 172–173; Rogger, 28–31; Berk, 40–43, 57–64, 72–76. For a detailed discussion of the government's behavior with regard to the pogroms of 1881–1882 see Aronson, *Troubled Waters*, 125–176, 217–235.
78. I. I. Ianzhul, "Vospominaniia o perezhitom i vidennom," *Russkaia starina* 144 (1910): 488–490.
79. *Osvobozhdenie*, no. 19 (19 March 1903): 340; Koni, 5:272, 273–274.
80. *Grazhdanin*, 7 November 1902, 15–16; *Novoe vremia*, 24 May 1903, 2; 18 January 1904, 4; 7 July 1904, 4; Urusov, 142, 165–166, 171, 175; Dubnov, 3:92–93; *Osvobozhdenie*, no. 8/32 (2 October 1903): 149–150; no. 19/43 (7 March 1904): 337.
81. I. Kh. Ozerov, *Politika po rabochemu voprosu v Rossii za poslednie gody* (Moscow: Tipografiia t-va I. D. Sytina, 1906), 224–228; N. A. Bukhbinder, "Nezavissimaia evreiskaia rabochaia partiia," *Krasnaia letopis'*, no. 2–3 (1922): 208–221, 230–232, 281–283; Bukhbinder, "O Zubatovshchine," *Krasnaia letopis'*, no. 4 (1922): 300–320, 326–328.

7. The Causes and Legacy of the Easter Riots

1. *Bessarabskiia gubernskiia vedomosti*, 20 March 1903, 2; 22 March 1903, 2; *Bessarabets*, 4 March 1903, 2; 9 March 1903, 3; 11 March 1903, 2; 19 March 1903, 3; *Materialy*, 1:7–8; "Obvinitel'nyi akt," 1.
2. Urusov, 12; *Bessarabets*, 21 April 1903, 3.
3. Urusov, 85.
4. Ibid., 48–50, 54–55; *Bessarabskiia gubernskiia vedomosti*, 20 March 1904, 1–2.
5. Motzkin, 85–89; Semenoff, 242–246; Lambroza, "Pogrom Movement," 149–150.
6. *Bessarabets*, 29 June 1903, 6; 2 September 1903, 3.
7. *Bulletin annuel de l'AIU* 66 (1904): 7.
8. Herzl, *Diaries*, 407–410; Volchonsky, 191–192.
9. Volchonsky, 193; *Kishinevskii pogrom*, 22–23; Tobias, 222–224.
10. Hayyim Nahman Bialik, "The City of Slaughter," trans. Abraham M. Klein, in *Selected Poems of Hayyim Nahman Bialik*, ed. Israel Efros, rev. ed. (New York: Histadruth Ivrith of America, 1965), 118–119. Reprinted by permission of the publisher.
11. *Novoe vremia*, 29 April 1903, 1.

12. Lambroza, "Pogrom Movement," 101–102, 230–239; *Osvobozhdenie*, no. 8/32 (2 October 1903): 134; Dubnov, 3:88–90; Tobias, 222–230.
13. Volchonsky, 193; Lambroza, "Pogrom Movement," 131, 136, 138, 142–143, 149–150, 244–260; Tobias, 313–316.
14. See, for example, *Revoliutsionnaia Rossiia*, no. 23 (1 May 1903): 2–3; no. 25 (1 June 1903): 10–11; *Osvobozhdenie*, no. 22 (8 May 1903): 377–380; 24 (2 June 1903): 451–452.
15. Nikolaevskii, 68–69, 87–88; L. A. Rataev, "Evno Azef: Istoriia ego predatel'stva," *Byloe*, no. 2/24 (1917): 198; Boris V. Savinkov, *Vospominaniia terrorista* (Khar'kov: Izdatel'stvo "Proletarii," [1926]), 13, 56–57.
16. See, for example, Cyrus Adler, ed., *The Voice of America on Kishineff* (Philadelphia, 1904); Isidore Singer, *Russia at the Bar of the American People* (New York, 1904); William Curtis Stiles, *Out of Kishineff* (New York, 1903); Leo Errera, *Les Massacres de Kichinev* (Brussels, 1903); E. P. Semenoff, *The Russian Government and the Massacres* (London, 1906); Raffaello Prato, *I massacri di Kiscineff* (Rome, 1903); "Les Massacres de Kischinef," *Bulletin annuel de l'AIU* 65 (1903): 13–52.
17. Schoenberg, 268–283; *Osvobozhdenie*, no. 24 (2 June 1903): 452; *Bulletin annuel de l'AIU* 65 (1903): 29–41.

Bibliographical Note

The most important and abundant source of information about the Kishinev pogrom is the first volume of *Materialy dlia istorii antievreiskikh pogromov v Rossii*, edited by S. M. Dubnov and G. Ia. Krasnyi-Admoni and published in Petrograd in 1919. This collection contains a vast assortment of documents pertaining to the murder and "blood libel" in Dubossary, the Easter riots in Kishinev, the subsequent investigation and trial, and other related matters. Taken mostly from the files of the imperial Russian Ministry of Justice and Department of Police, the assortment includes numerous reports and a vast amount of correspondence between government officials on the scene in Bessarabia and their superiors in Saint Petersburg. Although these materials were published largely to demonstrate the Russian government's responsibility for the pogroms, they fall short of conclusively proving that tsarist officials consciously instigated the riots. They do, however, provide a wealth of information on every aspect of the Kishinev affair, and fascinating insights into the mentality of those who had to deal with it.

Other useful materials concerning the pogrom may be found in *Kishinevskii pogrom*, a small collection of articles and documents compiled by editors of the emigré journal *Osvobozhdenie* and published in Stuttgart in 1903. It contains copies of the memorandum drawn up by leading Kishinev Jews giving their account of the Easter riots, as well as several other accounts of the pogrom and a number of proclamations and resolutions issued by various groups in the wake of the disturbances. The journal *Osvobozhdenie* itself published a number of valuable reports, including the text of the bill of indictment drawn up by Procurator Goremykin and long excerpts from the proceedings of the closed-door sessions of the trials of the rioters. The editors of *Osvobozhdenie*, like the editors of *Materialy dlia istorii antievreiskikh pogromov v Rossii*, may have been more interested in implicating the imperial government than in providing an objective assessment; nevertheless, by obtaining and publishing materials that were otherwise unavailable, they provided an extremely valuable resource for later historians.

Other periodical publications are also quite helpful in providing information on various aspects of the Kishinev affair. Of particular value is the *Bessarabets*, the anti-Semitic daily newspaper published in Kishinev by the notorious Krushevan. By virtue of its regular anti-Jewish diatribes, its apocryphal accounts of Jewish "crimes" and "conspiracies," and its sensational reporting of the Dubossary murder, it provides a powerful perspective on the ugly atmosphere in Kishinev which it helped to create. And by its publication of various official reports, its accounts of appointments and dismissals in the local government agencies, and its detailed information on the names, ages, occupations, and social status of the accused rioters who were brought to trial, it supplies insights into the composition and mentality of both the local government and the rioting crowds.

Another local newspaper, the *Bessarabskiia gubernskiia vedomosti*, provides a much more balanced portrayal of developments in Kishinev. An official publication which came out several times a week, it shows (among other things) that there was an effort made by responsible local persons to counteract the impact of the Dubossary "blood libel." It also published a number of official documents and reports, as did the *Novoe vremia*, a widely circulated Saint Petersburg daily newspaper that tended to be hostile to the Jews and to republish and spread the scurrilous accounts emanating from Dubossary and Kishinev. Less valuable, but useful nevertheless, were accounts and stories printed in publications like *Revoliutsionnaia Rossiia*, *Pravo*, and *Grazhdanin*. Further documents and recollections touching upon the Kishinev massacre were eventually published in journals like *Evreiskaia letopis'*, *Evreiskaia starina*, *Byloe*; and *Krasnyi arkhiv*.

Foreign newspapers and journals, in the wake of the pogrom, published a flood of information, reports, and proclamations. Among the most prominent in this regard were the *Times* of London, which became involved in a running dispute with the Russian government by printing the text of the alleged "Kishinev dispatch," and the *New York American*, which hired the Irish nationalist Michael Davitt to travel to Kishinev and send back on-the-scene reports. Jewish publications, like *Archives Israélites de France*, *L'Univers Israélite*, and the *Bulletins* of the Alliance Israélite Universelle, also provided extensive coverage. Of particular interest is *La Revue Russe*, a short-lived gazette published in Paris by agents of the Russian Ministry of Interior, which sought to influence foreign opinion on behalf of the tsarist government.

The memoirs of involved individuals also provide an important supplement to the official documents and periodical accounts. Especially valuable are the reminiscenses of Dr. M. B. Slutskii *(V skorbnye dni: Kishinevskii pogrom)*, senior surgeon at the Jewish hospital in Kishinev, Prince S. D. Urusov *(Memoirs of a Russian Governor)*, the man who became governor of Bessarabia in the wake of the Easter riots, and Michael Davitt *(Within the Pale)*, the Irish nationalist who traveled to Kishinev on behalf of the *New York American*. Of less pertinence, but useful in illuminating various aspects of the Kishinev story, are the memoirs of tsarist officials like V. I. Gurko, D. N. Liubimov, A. A. Lopukhin, V. D. Novitskii, P. P. Zavarzin, A. N. Kuropatkin, and S. Iu. Witte. The recollections of liberal activists I. I. Ianzhul and A. F. Koni supply glimpses into the thinking of several tsarist ministers. And the diaries of Zionist leader Theodor Herzl provide information about the influence of the Kishinev pogrom upon the Zionist movement, as well as a fascinating account of Herzl's personal visits with key imperial officials several months after the riots.

In the aftermath of the Kishinev pogrom, a number of books appeared which dealt in various ways with the Easter riots and their impact. Among these are *Out of Kishineff* by William Curtis Stiles, *Les Massacres de Kichinev* by Leo Errera, *The Voice of America on Kishineff* edited by Cyrus Adler, *Russia at the Bar of the American People* by Isidore Singer, *The Russian Government and the Massacres* by E. P. Semenoff, *Les Massacres de Kichinev* by B. A. Henry, and *I massacri di Kiscineff* by Raffaello Prato. Largely polemical in tone and condemnatory of the Russian government, these works shed little light on what actually happened in Kishinev, but they do provide an important indication of the outside world's reactions to the riots. Some of them also contain useful documents, such as the partial transcript of the Kishinev trials which is printed in Isidore Singer's work, and the text of the American protest petition which is supplied by Cyrus Adler.

Pertinent documents and data may also be found in a number of other places. Volume III of the Imperial Russian Census of 1897 *(Pervaia vseobshchaia perepis' naselenie rossiiskoe imperii, 1897)* provides extensive information about the population of Kishinev and Bessarabia at the end of the nineteenth century, including impressive charts on religion, ethnicity, social status, occupation, age, and literacy. It can be supplemented by the works of F. F. Vigel', A. Zashchuk, and V. S. Zelenchuk, which provide statistics on the region's population earlier in that century. The archives of the Alliance Israélite Universelle contain numerous documents relating to the assistance given to Kishinev Jews and the substantial emigration that followed the pogrom. The personal papers of Michael Davitt, located at Trinity College in Dublin, supplement and expand upon the information and impressions supplied in Davitt's book. The report on the Kishinev riots made by the British vice-consul at Odessa (V. H. C. Bosanquet) gives details of the riots from the perspective of a foreign official. And official publications like the resolutions of the Pahlen Commission *(Obzor postanovlenii vysshei kommisii po peresmotru deistvuiushchikh o evreiakh v imperii zakonov [1883–1888])* and the collection of laws of the Russian Empire *(Polnoe sobranie zakonov rossiiskoe imperii)* shed light on the legal status of Russian Jews.

Several literary works also have a bearing on the Kishinev story. The most prominent of these is V. G. Korolenko's "House Number 13" *(Dom No. 13)*, a short story describing in detail the massacre of Jews living in a single building on Asia Street. Influential too was "The City of Slaughter," the poem by H. N. Bialik which, among other things, decried the lack of resistance to the massacre on the part of Kishinev's Jews.

With regard to historical studies, there have been a number of works which deal in part with the Kishinev pogrom. The most influential, no doubt, has been S. M. Dubnov's three-volume *History of the Jews in Russia and Poland from the Earliest Times until the Present Day* which discusses in some depth the riots of 1903. Other useful histories of Russian Jews include Israel Friedlander's *The Jews of Russia and Poland*, Louis Greenberg's *The Jews in Russia: The Struggle for Emancipation*, and G. B. Sliozberg's, *Dela minuvshikh dnei: Zapiski russkago evreia*, a combined memoir and historical account. As might be expected, these works tend to focus on the harsh treatment accorded to the Jews by the Russian government, and to place the Kishinev massacre squarely within that context.

More recent studies of Russian anti-Semitism have provided a somewhat different perspective. Outstanding among these are the various articles of Hans Rogger, reprinted in the collection *Jewish Policies and Right-Wing Politics in Imperial Russia*, which provide perceptive insights into the thinking of Russian officials on the so-called "Jewish question." Although Rogger by no means exculpates the tsarist government or excuses its treatment of the Jews, he does argue convincingly that it is unlikely that imperial officials consciously sought to instigate pogroms. Similar conclusions have been reached by I. Michael Aronson and Stephen M. Berk in their works on the pogroms of 1881–1882. As for the Kishinev pogrom itself, the insightful articles of Rogger, Eliyahu Feldman, and Shlomo Lambroza, along with my own biography of V. K. von Plehve, have cast considerable doubt on the long-held theory that it was organized and engineered by the Ministry of Interior.

There are a number of other interesting studies which illuminate different aspects of the Kishinev affair. Among these are Heinz-Dietrich Lowe's *Antisemitismus und reaktionäre Utopie*, Leo Motzkin's *Die Judenpogrome in Russland*, and Dov Volchonsky's article on "The First Pogrom of the XX Century." As for the government's response, especially noteworthy is F. S. Zuckerman's "Self-imagery and the Art of Propaganda," which describes V. K. Plehve's artful attempts to counteract the anti-Russian wave of world opinion which followed the Kishinev riots.

The histories of Kishinev and Bessarabia are dealt with in a variety of works. Most valuable, perhaps, is *Istoriia Kishineva*, compiled by the department of history at Kishinev State University. Interestingly, although it contains a very detailed account of the city's growth and development, it says almost nothing about the 1903 pogrom. Also of interest are *Istoriia Moldavskoi SSSR* edited by L. V. Cherepnin, et al., *Kishinev: Economikogeograficheskii ocherk*, by A. L. Odud, *Kishinev: ekonomicheskii ocherk* by A. S. Konstantinov, *Iz istorii periodicheskoi pechati Bessarabii (1854–1916)* by B. A. Trubetskoi, and George F. Jewsbury's *The Russian Annexation of Bessarabia, 1774–1828.*

Finally, although they do not deal specifically with Kishinev or its pogrom, a number of works elucidate subjects which had a profound influence on the developments of 1903. Studies by I. Michael Aronson, John D. Klier, Michael Stanislawski, and I. D. Sosis, for example, provide excellent material on the development of the "Jewish question" in Russia. The works of V. K. Agafonov, N. A. Bukhbinder, Maurice Laporte, B. I. Nikolaevskii, and Neil Weissman supply a variety of insights into the functioning of the imperial and local police. And books on anti-Semitism, such as those by Edward H. Flannery, Paul Grosser and Edwin Halperin, Dennis Prager and Joseph Telushkin, Malcolm Hay, Jules Isaac, James Parkes, and Alan Dundes, contribute to an understanding of the roots and causes of this sordid and destructive cancer which has so long afflicted Western society.

Bibliography

Adler, Cyrus, ed. *The Voice of America on Kishineff*. Philadelphia: The Jewish Publication Society of America, 1904.

Agafonov, V. K. *Zagranichnaia okhranka*. Petrograd: Izdatel'stvo "Kniga," 1918.

Aizenberg, L. M. "Na slovakh i na dele: po povodu memuarov Vitte i Lopukhina." *Evreiskaia letopis'* 3 (1924): 24–43.

Alliance Israélite Universelle (AIU) Archives. Paris. URSS dossier.

A. P. "Departament politsii v 1892–1908gg.: Iz vospominanii chinovnika." *Byloe*, no. 5–6/27–28 (November-December 1917): 17–24.

Aronson, I. Michael. "Geographical and Socioeconomic Factors in the 1881 Anti-Jewish Pogroms in Russia." *Russian Review* 39 (January 1980): 18–31.

———. "Russian Bureaucratic Attitudes toward the Jews, 1881–1894." Ph.D. dissertation, Northwestern University, 1973.

———. *Troubled Waters: The Origins of the 1881 Anti-Jewish Pogroms in Russia*. Pittsburgh: University of Pittsburgh Press, 1990.

Babel, Anthony. *La Bessarabie: Etude historique, ethnographique et économique*. Paris: Librairie Félix Alcan, 1926.

Baron, Salo W. *The Russian Jew under Tsars and Soviets*. New York: Macmillan, 1964.

Berk, Stephen M. *Year of Crisis, Year of Hope: Russian Jewry and the Pogroms of 1881–1882*. Westport, CT: Greenwood Press, 1985.

Bessarabets. Kishinev. 1903–1904.

Bessarabskiia gubernskiia vedomosti. Kishinev. 1903–1904.

Betskii, K., and P. Pavlov. *Russkii rokambol': Prikliucheniia I. F. Manasevicha-Manuilova*. Leningrad: Izdatel'stvo "Byloe," 1925.

Bialik, Hayyim Nahman. "The City of Slaughter." Translated by Abraham M. Klein. In *Selected Poems of Hayyim Nahman Bialik*, edited by Israel Efros. Rev. ed. New York: Histadruth Ivrith of America, 1965.

Bing, Edward J., ed. *The Secret Letters of the Last Tsar*. New York: Longmans, Green and Co., 1938.

Bosanquet, V. H. C., and C. S. Smith. *Despatch from His Majesty's Consul-General at Odessa, forwarding a Report on the Riots at Kishiniev*. London: Harrison and Sons, 1903.

Braudo, A. I. "Beseda V. K. Pleve s L. Volf'om (1903)." *Evreiskaia starina* 9 (1916): 121–125.

Bukhbinder, N. A. "Nezavissimaia evreiskaia rabochaia partiia." *Krasnaia letopis'*, no. 2–3 (1922): 208–284.

———. "O Zubatovshchine." *Krasnaia letopis'*, no. 4 (1922): 289–335.

Bulletin annuel de l'Alliance Israélite Universelle. Paris. 1903.

Bulletin mensuel de l'Alliance Israélite Universelle. Paris. 1903–1904.

Bunge, N. Kh. "The Years 1881–1894: A Memorandum." Edited by George E. Snow. *Transactions of the American Philosophical Society* 71, Part 6 (1981): 18–72.

Cazaco, P. *Notes sur la Bessarabie*. Bucharest: "Cartea Romaneasca," 1926.

Cohn, Norman. *Warrant for Genocide: The Myth of the Jewish World-Conspiracy and the Protocols of the Elders of Zion*. Chico, CA: Scholars Press, 1981.

Dale, Cuthbert W. "The Story of Michael Davitt." *Men and Women*, 11 July 1903.

Davitt, Michael. *Within the Pale: The True Story of Anti-Semitic Persecutions in Russia*. New York: A. S. Barnes, 1903; reprint, New York: Arno Press, 1975.

Davitt Papers. Trinity College Dublin (TCD). MSS 9501–9681.

"Dokladnaia zapiska Evreiskago Obshchestva." In *Kishinevskii pogrom*, comp. by editors of *Osvobozhdenie*, 19–21. Stuttgart: Verlag und Druck von J. H. W. Dietz, 1903.

Dubnov, Simon M. *History of the Jews in Russia and Poland from the Earliest Times until the Present Day*. Translated by Israel Friedlander. 3 vols. Philadelphia: Jewish Publication Society of America, 1916–1920.

Dundes, Alan, ed. *The Blood Libel Legend: A Casebook in Anti-Semitic Folklore*. Madison: The University of Wisconsin Press, 1991.

Encyclopedia Judaica. 16 vols. Jerusalem: Macmillan, 1971.

Errera, Leo. *Les Massacres de Kichinev*. Brussels: Falk fils, 1903.

———. *The Russian Jews: Extermination or Emancipation?* New York: Macmillan, 1894; reprint, Westport, CT: Greenwood Press, 1975.

Evreiskaia entsiklopediia. 16 vols. Saint Petersburg: Brokgauz-Efron, 1906–1913.

Fedotov, George P. *The Russian Religious Mind*. 2 vols. New York: Harper and Row, 1960.

Feldman, Eliyahu. "Plehve and the Kishinev Pogrom of 1903." [Hebrew] *He'-Avar* 12: 137–150.

Fischer-Galati, Stephen. "Romanian Nationalism." In *Nationalism in Eastern Europe*, ed. Peter Sugar and Ivo Lederer, 373–395. Seattle: University of Washington Press, 1969.

Flannery, Edward H. *The Anguish of the Jews: Twenty-three Centuries of Antisemitism*. New York: Paulist Press, 1985.

Friedlander, Israel. *The Jews of Russia and Poland*. New York and London: G. P. Putnam's Sons, 1915.

Gessen, Iulii I. "Graf N. P. Ignat'ev i 'Vremennya pravila' o evreiakh 3 maia 1882 goda." *Pravo*, no. 30 (27 July 1908): 1631–1685.

Ginzburg, S. "Poezdka Teodora Gertslia v Peterburg." In *Evreiskii Mir*, comp. Union of Russian Jews, Sbornik 2, 197–209. New York: Grenich Printing Corp., 1944.

Gomel'skii protsess: Podrobnyi otchet. Saint Petersburg: Tipografiia t-va "Obshchestvennaia Pol'za," 1907.

Gottheil, Richard. "Kishineff." *The Forum* 35 (July-September 1903): 149–160.

Grazhdanin. Saint Petersburg. 1902.

Greenberg, Louis. *The Jews in Russia: The Struggle for Emancipation*. 2 vols. New Haven: Yale University Press, 1944, 1951.

Grosser, Paul E., and Edwin G. Halperin. *Anti-Semitism: Causes and Effects*. New York: Philosophical Library, 1983.

Gurko, V. I. *Features and Figures of the Past: Government and Opinion in the Reign of Nicholas II*. Translated by Laura Matveev. Stanford: Stanford University Press, 1939.

Hay, Malcolm. *Europe and the Jews: The Pressure of Christendom on the People of Israel for 1900 Years*. Boston: Beacon Press, 1961.

Henry, B. A. *Les Massacres de Kichinev*. Paris: "Siècle," 1903.

Herzl, Theodor. *The Complete Diaries of Theodor Herzl*. Translated by Harry Zohn. 5 vols. New York and London: Herzl Press and Thomas Yoseloff, 1960.

———. *The Diaries of Theodor Herzl*. Edited and translated by Marvin Lowenthal. New York: Dial Press, 1956.

Ianzhul, I. I. "Vospominaniia o perezhitom i vidennom." *Russkaia starina* 144 (1910): 258–272, 485–500.

Isaac, Jules. *The Teaching of Contempt: Christian Roots of Anti-Semitism*. New York: Holt, Rinehart and Winston, 1964.

Istoriia Kishineva. Compiled by Kishinevskii gosudarstvennyi universitet kafedra istorii SSSR. Kishinev: Izdatel'stvo "Kartia Moldoveniaske," 1966.

Istoriia Moldavskoi SSSR. Edited by L. V. Cherepnin, et al. 2 vols. Kishinev: Izdatel'stvo "Kartiia Moldoveniaske," 1965.

Jewish Encyclopedia. 12 vols. New York and London: Funk and Wagnalls, 1916.

Jewsbury, George F. *The Russian Annexation of Bessarabia, 1774–1828*. New York: East European Monographs, 1976.

Judge, Edward H. *Plehve: Repression and Reform in Imperial Russia, 1902–1904*. Syracuse: Syracuse University Press, 1983.

Kishinev Massacre: Proceedings of a Meeting of Citizens of New York. New York: The American Hebrew, 1903.

Kishinevskii pogrom. Compiled by editors of *Osvobozhdenie.* Stuttgart: Verlag und Druck von J. H. W. Dietz, 1903.

"Kishinevskii pogrom: Obvinitel'nyi akt." Supplement to *Osvobozhdenie,* no. 9/33 (19 October 1903): 1–4.

Klier, John D. *Russia Gathers Her Jews: The Origins of the "Jewish Question" in Russia, 1772–1825.* De Kalb: Northern Illinois University Press, 1986.

Koni, A. F. "Sergei Iul'evich Vitte." *Sobranie sochinenii,* 5: 238–277. Moscow: Izdatel'stvo "Iuridicheskaia literatura," 1968.

Konstantinov, A. S. *Kishinev: ekonomicheskii ocherk.* Kishinev: "Kartia Moldoveniaske," 1966.

Korolenko, V. G. "House No. 13: An Episode in the Massacre of Kishinev." *Contemporary Review* 85 (February 1904): 266–280.

Krasnyi-Admoni, G. Ia. "Staryi rezhim i pogromy." In *Materialy dlia istorii antievreiskikh pogromov v Rossii,* ed. S. M. Dubnov and G. Ia. Krasnyi-Admoni, 1: xvi–xxxii. Petrograd: Tipografiia "Kadima," 1919.

Krest'ianskoe dvizhenie v Poltavskoi i Khar'kovskoi guberniakh v 1902 g. Kharkov: Khar'kovskoe knizhnoe izdatel'stvo, 1961.

Kuropatkin, A. N. "Dnevnik." *Krasnyi arkhiv* 2 (1922): 5–117.

Lambroza, Shlomo. "Plehve, Kishinev and the Jewish Question: A Reappraisal." *Nationalities Papers* 23, no. 2 (1981): 117–127.

———. "The Pogrom Movement in Tsarist Russia, 1903–1906." Ph.D. dissertation, Rutgers University, 1981.

———. "The Tsarist Government and the Pogroms of 1903–06." *Modern Judaism* 7, no. 3 (1987): 287–296.

Laporte, Maurice. *Histoire de l'Okhrana: La police secrète des tsars, 1880–1917.* Paris: Payot, 1935.

Laqueur, Walter. *A History of Zionism.* New York: Holt, Rinehart and Winston, 1972.

Liubimov, D. N. "Russkaia smuta nachala deviatisotykh godov, 1902–1906." Manuscript in archives of the Hoover Library, Stanford, California.

Lopukhin, A. A. *Otryvki iz vospominanii.* Moscow: Gosudarstvennoe izdatel'stvo, 1923.

Lowe, Heinz-Dietrich. *Antisemitismus und reaktionäre Utopie: Russischer Konservatismus im Kampf gegen den Wandel von Staat und Gesellschaft, 1890–1917.* Hamburg: Hoffman und Campe, 1978.

"Les Massacres de Kischinef." *Bulletin annuel de l'Alliance Israélite Universelle* 65 (1903): 13–52.

Materialy dlia istorii antievreiskikh pogromov v Rossii. Edited by S. M. Dubnov and G. Ia. Krasnyi-Admoni. 2 vols. Petrograd and Moscow: Tipografiia "Kadima" and Gosudarstvennoe izdatel'stvo, 1919, 1923.

Mendes-Flohr, Paul R., and Jehuda Reinharz. *The Jew in the Modern World: A Documentary History.* New York: Oxford University Press, 1980.

Michael, Louis Guy. *More Corn for Bessarabia.* East Lansing: Michigan State University Press, 1983.

Moody, T. W. *Davitt and Irish Revolution, 1846–1882*. Oxford: Clarendon Press, 1981.

Motzkin, Leo. ("A. Linden"), ed. *Die Judenpogrome in Russland*, 2 vols. Cologne and Leipzig: Jüdischer Verlag, 1910.

Nabokov, V. B. "Kishinevskaia krovovaia bania." *Pravo*, no. 18 (27 April 1903): 1281–1285.

New York American. New York. 1903.

New York Times. New York. 1903.

Nikolaevskii, Boris I. *Istoriia odnogo predatelia: Terroristy i politicheskaia politsiia*. Berlin: Petropolis, 1932.

Novitskii, V. D. *Iz vospominanii zhandarma*. Leningrad: "Priboi," 1929.

———. "Zapiska gen. Novitskago." *Sotsialist-revoliutsionner*, no. 2 (1910): 53–113.

Novoe vremia. Saint Petersburg. 1902–1904.

"Obvinitel'nyi akt." See "Kishinevskii pogrom: Obvinitel'nyi akt."

Obzor postanovlenii vysshei kommisii po peresmotru deistvuiushchikh o evreiakh v imperii zakonov (1883–1888). Saint Petersburg: [Gosudarstvennaia tipografiia], 1888.

Odud, Afanasii Lukich. *Kishinev: Economiko-geograficheskii ocherk*. Kishinev: Gosudarstvennoe izdatel'stvo "Kartia Moldoveniaske," 1964.

Osvobozhdenie. Stuttgart, Paris. 1903–1904.

Ozerov, I. Kh. *Politika po rabochemu voprosu v Rossii za poslednie gody*. Moscow: Tipografiia t-va I. D. Sytina, 1906.

Parkes, James. *Antisemitism*. Chicago: Quadrangle Books, 1963.

Pervaia v Rossii podpol'naia tipografiia Leninskoi gazety "Iskra." Compiled by Institut istorii partii pri TsK KP Moldavii. Kishinev: Izdatel'svto "Kartiia Moldoveniaske," 1970.

Pervaia vseobshchaia perepis' naselenie rossiiskoe imperii, 1897. Vol. 3, *Bessarabskaia guberniia*. Saint Petersburg: Izdanie tsentral'nago statisticheskago komiteta ministerstva vnutrennikh del, 1905.

Pipes, Richard. "Catherine II and the Jews: The Origins of the Pale of Settlement." *Soviet Jewish Affairs* 5, no. 2 (1975): 3–20.

Plehve, V. K. "Tsirkuliar o sionisme i evreiskom natsional'nom dvizhenii (1903 g.)." *Evreiskaia starina* 7 (1915): 412–414.

Polnoe sobranie zakonov rossiiskoe imperii. 33 vols. 3rd ed. Saint Petersburg: Gosudarstvennaia tipografiia, 1885–1916.

Popovici, Andrei. *The Political Status of Bessarabia*. Washington, DC: Ransdell Inc., 1931.

Porath, Jonathan D., ed. *The Jews in Russia: The Last Four Centuries*. New York: United Synagogue of America, 1974.

Povest' vremennykh let. Edited by V. P. Adrianov-Perets. 2 vols. Moscow: Izdatel'stvo Akademii Nauk SSSR, 1950.

Prager, Dennis, and Joseph Telushkin. *Why the Jews? The Reason for Antisemitism*. New York: Simon and Schuster, 1983.

Prato, Raffaello. *I massacri di Kiscineff*. Rome: Carlo Mariani, 1903.

Rataev, L. A. "Evno Azef: Istoriia ego predatel'stva." *Byloe*, no. 2/24 (1917): 187–210.

Revoliutsonnaia Rossiia. Tomsk, Geneva. 1903.

La Revue Russe. Paris. 1903.

Rogger, Hans. *Jewish Policies and Right-Wing Politics in Imperial Russia*. Berkeley: University of California Press, 1986.

Roosevelt, Theodore. *The Letters of Theodore Roosevelt*. Vol. 3, *The Square Deal, 1901–1903*, ed. Elting E. Morison. Cambridge: Harvard University Press, 1951.

Roubanovich. "Les massacres de Kichinev." *Pages libres*, no. 124 (16 May 1903): 417–436.

The Russian Primary Chronicle: Laurentian Text. Translated by Samuel H. Cross and Olgerd Sherbovitz-Wetzor. Cambridge, MA: Mediaeval Academy of America, 1953.

Savinkov, Boris V. *Vospominaniia terrorista*. Khar'kov: Izdatel'stvo "Proletarii," [1926].

Schneidermann, Jeremiah. *Sergei Zubatov and Revolutionary Marxism*. Ithaca: Cornell University Press, 1976.

Schoenberg, Philip E. "The American Reaction to the Kishinev Pogrom of 1903." *American Jewish Historical Quarterly* 63 (September 1973): 262–283.

Schwarzfeld, E. "The Jews of Roumania from the Earliest Times to the Present Day." In *American Jewish Year Book 5662*, 25–62. Philadelphia: Jewish Publication Society of America, 1901.

Semenoff, E. P. *The Russian Government and the Massacres*. London: John Murray, 1906.

Sheehy-Skeffington, Francis. *Michael Davitt: Revolutionary, Agitator, and Labour Leader*. London: T. Fisher Unwin, 1908; reprint, London: MacGibbon & Kee, 1967.

Simpson, Mark S. "The *Svyaschonnaya druzhina* and Jewish Persecution in Tsarist Russia." *New Zealand Slavonic Journal*, no. 2 (1978): 17–26.

Singer, Isidore. *Russia at the Bar of the American People: A Memorial of Kishinef*. New York: Funk and Wagnalls, 1904.

Sliozberg, G. B. *Dela minuvshikh dnei: Zapiski russkago evreia*. 3 vols. Paris: Imprimerie Pascal, 1933–1934.

Slutskii, M. B. *V skorbnye dni: Kishinevskii pogrom*. Kishinev: Tipografiia M. Averbukha, 1930.

Sosis, I. D. "K istorii antievreiskogo dvizheniia v tsarskoi Rossii." *Trudy Belorusskogo Gosudarstvennogo Universiteta v g. Minsk*, no. 6–7 (1925): 176–188; no. 12 (1926): 82–94.

"Souscription en faveur des israélites de Kischineff." *Bulletin mensuel de l'Alliance Israélite Universelle* 31 (April 1903): 51–52.

Stanislawski, Michael. *Tsar Nicholas I and the Jews: The Transformation of Jewish Society in Russia, 1825–1855*. Philadelphia: Jewish Publication Society of America, 1983.

Stiles, William Curtis. *Out of Kishineff: The Duty of the American People to the Russian Jew.* New York: G. W. Dillingham, 1903.

Stults, Taylor. "Roosevelt, Russian Persecution of Jews, and American Public Opinion." *Jewish Social Studies* 33 (1971): 13–22.

Szajkowski, Zoza. "How the Mass Migration to America Began." *Jewish Social Studies* 4 (October 1982): 291–310.

Tager, A. S. *The Decay of Czarism.* Philadelphia: Jewish Publication Society of America, 1935.

Times. London. 1903–1904.

Tobias, Henry J. *The Jewish Bund in Russia from Its Origins to 1905.* Stanford: Stanford University Press, 1972.

Trubetskoi, B. A. *Iz istorii periodicheskoi pechati Bessarabii (1854–1916).* Kishinev: Izdatel'stvo "Kartiia Moldoveniaske," 1968.

Tsentral'nyi Gosudarstvennyi Istoricheskii Arkhiv SSSR (TsGIA). Leningrad.

"Tsirkuliara ministra vnutrennykh del gubernatoram, gradonachal'nikam i oberpolitsiimeisteram." Supplement to *Osvobozhdenie*, no. 9/33 (19 October 1903): 4.

Turczynski, Emanuel. "The Background of Romanian Fascism." In *Native Fascism in the Successor States 1918–1945*, ed. Peter F. Sugar, 101–111. Santa Barbara, CA: n.p., 1971.

L'Univers Israélite. Paris. 1903–1904.

Urusov, Prince S. D. *Memoirs of a Russian Governor.* Translated by Herman Rosenthal. London and New York: Harper and Brothers, 1908.

Vigel', F. F. "Zamechanii na nyneshnee sostoianie Bessarabii." *Russkii arkhiv* Book 1, Part 2 (1893): 1–36.

Vishniak, Mark. "Antisemitism in Tsarist Russia: A Study in Government-Fostered Antisemitism." In *Essays on Antisemitism*, ed. Koppel S. Pinson, 121–144. New York: n.p., 1942.

Volchonsky, Dov. "The First Pogrom of the XX Century." [Hebrew] *He'-Avar* 20: 176–194.

Vseobshchaia stachka na iuge Rossii v 1903 godu: Sbornik dokumentov. Moscow: Gosudarstvennoe izdatel'stvo politicheskoe literatury, 1938.

Weinryb, Bernard D. *The Jews of Poland: A Social and Economic History of the Jewish Community in Poland from 1100 to 1800.* Philadelphia: Jewish Publication Society of America, 1972.

Weissman, Neil. "The Regular Police in Tsarist Russia, 1900–1914." *Russian Review* 44 (January 1985): 45–68.

Witte, Sergei Iu. "Evreiskii vopros pri vvedenii piteinoi monopolii: Vsepoddanneishii doklad." *Evreiskaia starina* 8 (1915): 405–410.

———. *Vospominaniia: Tsarstvovaniia Nikolaia II.* 2 vols. Berlin: Knigoizdatel'stvo "Slovo," 1922.

Wolf, Lucien. "M. de Plehve and the Jewish Question." *Times* (London), 6 February 1904, 6.

Zaionchkovskii, P. A. *Rossiiskoe samoderzhavie v kontse XIX stoletiia*. Moscow: Izdatel'stvo "Mysl'," 1970.

Zashchuk, A. *Materialy dlia geografii i statistiki Rossii: Bessarabskaia oblast'*. Saint Petersburg: n.p., 1862.

Zavarzin, P. P. *Zhandarmy i revoliutsionery: Vospominaniia*. Paris: Payot, 1930.

Zelenchuk, V. S. *Naselenie Bessarabii i podnestrov'ia v XIX v.* Kishinev: "Shtiintsa," 1979.

Zlatova, Y., and V. Kotel'nikov. *Across Moldavia*. Moscow: Foreign Languages Publishing House, 1959.

Zuckerman, F. S. "Self-imagery and the Art of Propaganda: V. K. von Plehve as Propagandist." *Australian Journal of Politics and History* 28, no. 1 (1982): 68–81.

Index

Printed in the United States
By Bookmasters